Reference Guides to Rhetoric and Composition

Series Editor, Charles Bazerman

REFERENCE GUIDES TO RHETORIC AND COMPOSITION
Series Editors: Charles Bazerman, Mary Jo Reiff, and Anis Bawarshi

The Series provides compact, comprehensive and convenient surveys of what has been learned through research and practice as composition has emerged as an academic discipline over the last half century. Each volume is devoted to a single topic that has been of interest in rhetoric and composition in recent years, to synthesize and make available the sum and parts of what has been learned on that topic. These reference guides are designed to help deepen classroom practice by making available the collective wisdom of the field and will provide the basis for new research. The Series is intended o be of use to teachers at all levels of education, researchers and scholars of writing, graduate students learning about the field, and all, nationally and internationally, who have interest in or responsibility for writing programs and the teaching of writing.

Parlor Press and The WAC Clearinghouse are collaborating so that these books will be widely available through low cost print editions and free electronic distribution. The publishers and the series editors are all teachers and researchers of writing, committed to the principle that knowledge should freely circulate. We see the opportunities that new technologies have for further democratizing knowledge. And we see that to share the power of writing is to share the means for all to articulate their needs, interest, and learning into the great experiment of literacy.

EXISTING BOOKS IN THE SERIES
Invention in Rhetoric and Composition (2004, Lauer)
Reference Guide to Writing across the Curriculum (2005, Bazerman, et al.)
Revision: History, Theory, and Practice (2006, Horning and Becker)
Writing Program Administration (2007, McLeod)
Community Literacy and the Rhetoric of Local Publics (2008, Long)
Argument in Composition (2009, Ramage, et al.)
Basic Writing (2010, Otte and Mlynarczyk)
Genre: An Introduction to History, Theory, Research, and Pedagogy (2010, Bawarshi and Reiff)
Reconnecting Reading and Writing (2013, Horning and Kraemer)

Reconnecting Reading and Writing

Edited by Alice S. Horning and Elizabeth W. Kraemer

Parlor Press
Anderson, South Carolina
www.parlorpress.com

The WAC Clearinghouse
Fort Collins, Colorado
http://wac.colostate.edu/

Parlor Press LLC, Anderson, South Carolina, USA
The WAC Clearinghouse, Fort Collins, Colorado 80523-1052

Printed in the United States of America

S A N: 2 5 4 - 8 8 7 9

Library of Congress Cataloging-in-Publication Data

Reconnecting reading and writing / edited by Alice S. Horning and Elizabeth
W. Kraemer.
    pages cm -- (Reference guides to rhetoric and composition)
  Includes bibliographical references and index.
   ISBN 978-1-60235-459-3 (pbk. : alk. paper) -- ISBN 978-1-60235-460-9
(hardcover : alk. paper) -- ISBN 978-1-60235-461-6 (adobe ebook) -- ISBN
978-1-60235-462-3 (epub) -- ISBN 978-1-60235-463-0 (kindle)
  1. Language arts. 2. Reading. I. Horning, Alice S. II. Kraemer, Elizabeth
W., 1974-
  LB1575.8.R398 2013
  372.6--dc23
                              2013030688

Series logo designed by Karl Stolley. Copyediting by Jeff Ludwig.
This book is printed on acid-free paper.

Parlor Press, LLC is an independent publisher of scholarly and trade titles
in print and multimedia formats. This book is available in paper, cloth and
eBook formats from Parlor Press on the World Wide Web at http://www.
parlorpress.com or through online and brick-and-mortar bookstores. For
submission information or to find out about Parlor Press publications, write
to Parlor Press, 3015 Brackenberry Drive, Anderson, South Carolina, 29621,
or email editor@parlorpress.com.

The WAC Clearinghouse supports teachers of writing across the disciplines.
Hosted by Colorado State University's Composition Program, it brings together four journals, three book series, and resources for teachers who use
writing in their courses. This book will also be available free on the Internet
at The WAC Clearinghouse (http://wac.colostate.edu/).

Contents

Series Editors' Preface

Charles Bazerman, Mary Jo Reiff, and Anis Bawarshi

Reading and writing are indivisible. If nothing were written, what would we read? If no one read, why would we write? When we enter the world of literacy, we receive written words from others and respond with our own. Literacy is a reciprocal, two-sided game. At literacy's birth, the scribes who recorded were the scribes that read. Yet, we divide reading and writing in school, in instruction, in assessment, in the professions of scholars, and in research. Even in identities, some think of themselves as readers, others as writers.

Nonetheless, as teachers of writing we cannot keep reading out of the picture. Students write about what they read. To revise they must read their own texts and adopt the positions of their readers. In peer collaboration and peer review, students read each other's work, and in the process of giving and receiving feedback, experience the effects their writing has on others. An ability to read critically one's own and others' writing helps cultivate metacognitive reflection and rhetorical awareness that facilitates writing development and the transfer of writing knowledge. We sense that the best writers have wide experiences as readers.

The assumption that reading is a fundamental skill learned once and for all errs in the same ways as the assumption that writing is a fundamental skill learned once and for all. Our reading schemas develop in tandem with our writing schemas. As reading scholar Frank Smith (2004) described, experienced readers read in relation to specifications informed by genre knowledge. Knowledge of these specifications, among other things, allows us to anticipate textual moves and to predict rhetorical cues that enable our constructions (and critiques) of meaning. As writers, we use our knowledge of these genre specifications to guide readers or, in some cases, to surprise them.

By dividing reading and writing, however, we minimize the interactive roles of readers and writers in the composing process and in their co-construction of meaning. We deny students the opportunity to read as writers—that is, to pay attention to rhetorical choices and effects and to consider the texts they read (print or digital) as having *been written* under certain conditions within certain constraints to achieve certain purposes. Such a division between reading and writing contributes to distinctions between production and interpretation that have defined English studies and that have created hierarchies between literature/cultural studies and composition/rhetoric.

The need to connect reading and writing is greater than ever as students negotiate new information technologies and a multi-mediated world. Visual culture and the proliferation of multimedia texts have transformed literacy practices, as students learn to critically "read" visual texts and images and to participate in fluid, continuous online spaces that blur boundaries between reading and writing roles and redefine reading/writing interactions—rhetorically, spatially, and temporally. Through social networking sites, wikis, websites, blogs, bulletin boards, and digital video compositions, students are taking up new, multiple identities as readers and writers, making it even more important for teachers to understand the dynamic relationship between reading and writing.

This volume draws together many resources to encourage us to consider the need to reconnect reading and writing, moving from an historical and theoretical overview of reading-writing approaches in rhetoric and composition to more global, international perspectives on reading and writing instruction. Recognizing that reading and writing are social practices that are embedded in particular educational contexts, the book provides wide-ranging coverage of reading and writing in multiple instructional settings, from writing across the curriculum, to basic writing, to second language writing, to K–12 classrooms, and to libraries.

The book not only explores reading-writing connections within various contexts, but also from the varied perspectives of "new literacies" or multiliteracies, paying attention to both the influence of traditional print texts in literacy instruction (e.g., composition textbooks' treatment of reading) and the role of information and digital literacies in research-based writing (e.g., shifts in accessing, analyzing, synthesizing, and evaluating sources). Importantly, the book reminds us of the need to collaborate with our colleagues in libraries, in secondary schools, across the disciplines, and beyond the U.S. as we continue to explore and cultivate connections between reading and writing. With its coverage of multiple sites for reading-writing instruction, overviews of various theoretical and practical approaches, and inclusion of diverse perspectives on reading-writing (from professional policy statements to standardized tests to research studies on reading-writing relationships), this volume encourages greater understanding of the synergies that link reading and writing, making a compelling case for shaping curricular approaches that reconnect reading and writing, recognizing them as indivisible, reciprocal, meaning-making activities.

This volume marks a landmark in the Reference Guides to Rhetoric and Composition as Anis Bawarshi and Mary Jo Reiff join me as co-editors of the series. Their deft work on this volume confirms what great additions they are. The series looks forward to a long and bright future.

—*Charles Bazerman*

Reconnecting Reading and Writing

Part I: Overview

1 Reconnecting Reading and Writing: Introduction and Overview

Alice S. Horning and Elizabeth W. Kraemer

The co-editors of this book come to reading and writing from different directions.* One of us is a professional faculty librarian, while the other is a faculty member with a joint appointment in a writing program and a linguistics department. Our diverse perspectives find common ground in the view that reading and writing have been too much and too long separated in theory and in practice. This introduction begins with some key definitions and distinctions that provide the basis for the whole book, and includes a brief discussion of the ways reading has been separated from writing. The need to reconnect them emerges from this discussion, from a review of the impact of new technologies on all aspects of students' reading and writing, and even more clearly from an array of findings on the status of undergraduate reading abilities. Leading professional organizations in these disciplines also see the separation and need for reconnection, and their perspective appears in policy statements from various organizations working on literacy that are discussed here and referred to throughout this book.

In addition, we provide a brief overview of the chapters that look deeper at issues surrounding the need to reconnect reading and writing. The chapters in Part I review literature in this area and work done throughout the world on reconnecting reading. These chapters provide two different perspectives on the need to reconnect reading and writing: The former is an historical review of studies addressed this

---

* We are grateful to Amy Horning for collating sources from all the authors and correcting all of the formatting for the Reference list.

topic. The latter looks at how other countries and educational systems see the relationship of reading and writing. Part II focuses on classrooms and students, presenting "Monday morning" approaches to connecting reading and writing in first year writing and writing across the curriculum, and presents successful practices with basic writers and students who are non-native speakers of English. It also explores the impact of the new Common Core Standards in K–12 education that will shape the experiences of incoming college students in the foreseeable future. Part III explores contexts and resources for reconnecting reading and writing, such as textbooks, libraries, and digital environments. We are confident that reconnecting reading and writing helps us all improve students' performance, success in college, and their personal and professional lives.

READING ABILITIES AT ENTRY AND GRADUATION

Studies at both the beginning and end of students' work in college support the need for more attention to reading, not only in conjunction with writing but also across all disciplines. There have been various approaches to measuring students' reading abilities, including standardized multiple choice timed tests, un-timed tests, open-ended instruments, surveys and other quantitative and qualitative strategies. The picture of college students' reading performance using standardized measures at entry to higher education and at graduation is not encouraging.

Reading at Entry: The ACT Reading Test

The ACT Reading test is a direct timed test of reading of four passages of prose, followed by multiple choice questions, measuring RSVP elements of text (relationships, richness, structure, style, vocabulary, and purpose). A 2006 ACT study followed 563,000 students who took the exam over three years to measure their college success (defined as a 2.0 GPA and retention to the second year, in addition to other factors). Findings show that about 51% of this large cohort of students hit ACT's benchmark score of 21 on the test and were successful in college by its minimal definition (American, 2006). While there are some reasons to be cautious in drawing conclusions about the research, the ACT findings suggest that many students beginning post-secondary education do not have the reading skills needed to be successful in college or in their lives, in their work, or as citizens. Because first year writing is a common, shared experience, and because it is meant to help students develop key abilities they will need to succeed in other courses, it is surely a good place to work on reading in conjunction with writing. Writing teachers can help students become better writers and better readers through reconnecting reading and writing.

Reading at Graduation: Pew National Survey of America's College Students

Most college faculty members like to think that college improves students' reading ability, so that when they graduate, they are all expert readers, or at least stronger readers than they were at admission. However, another 2006 study done by the Pew Charitable Trusts organization shows that many students do not achieve this desirable outcome. The Pew study entailed a direct test of "Prose and Document" literacy, using an approach like that of the Adult Literacy and Life Skills study (discussed later in this book). The Pew study sampled "1827 graduating students at 80 randomly selected 2-year and 4-year colleges and universities (68 public and 12 private) from across the United States" (Pew, 2006, p. 4). The survey was conducted by stratified random sample in two stages—first to choose institutions and the second to choose students (Pew, 2006, p. 66). The findings show that fewer than half of college students studied in this random sample attain scores at the "proficient" level on "Prose and Document" literacy (Pew, 2006, p. 19).

Taken together, the ACT and Pew studies give us a picture of student literacy skills and the impact of college on their literacy development in the United States. The levels of literacy measured are based on readings of brief passages of mostly non-fiction prose on paper, revealing nothing of deeper reading ability with extended passages, with fiction and other types of writing, or with digital texts and documents of various kinds. Common sense suggests that students performing poorly on these rather reductionist tests of reading ability are likely to do even worse on more in-depth assessments of their understanding of more complex reading. However, the consistency between these studies shows a pattern of surprisingly poor results. Moreover, the work of the Citation Project—an on-going, multi-university study of students' use of sources in research writing—provides just this kind of evidence, showing that students have difficulty reading critically in order to use source materials appropriately, and will benefit from reconnecting reading and writing (Howard, Rodrigue, & Serviss, 2010).

DEFINITIONS

Before exploring the need to reconnect reading and writing, it is important to establish definitions of these abilities (and some others) to which they are often related in both theory and in practice. Reading, writing, "new" literacies, multiliteracies, and information literacy are sometimes used distinctly and sometimes interchangeably, so distinguishing among them with clear definitions is an essential first step.

Reading

Reading has been held under the magnifying glasses of many scholars. Some researchers have argued that reading is a solitary act; in fact, psychologist Philip Gough (1995) described reading as "one of the most unsocial things which people do," going so far as to insist that calling reading a social act "distorts our ordinary language" (p. 81). Others oppose this stance, contending that reading is a socio-cognitive act that is inextricably linked to listening, speaking, and interacting with others, and that it cannot be separated from "using language to think about and act on the world" (Gee, 2001, p. 714). Still other scholars confirm these intellectual connections from a psycholinguistic standpoint. Snow, Burns, and Griffin (1998) report that "many basic cognitive processes are shared during reading and listening. Syntactic and inferential processes . . . play a role in both" (p. 64). Research on first year reading and writing practices demonstrates an overlap in the cognitive processes involved in reading and listening, but also in reading and writing (Jolliffe, 2007).

Many researchers maintain that reading—critical reading—involves an understanding and interpretation of texts, and cannot be divorced from societal input. Freire and Shor (1987) stress that it is not enough to simply repeat words on a page; for "true reading" to take place, the reader must try to place the meaning in "some form of social context" (as cited in Roberts, 2005, p. 35). In this volume, we explore reading conducted primarily in post-secondary academic environments that particularly rely on *critical reading* skills, including writing and writing across the curriculum classes.

When considering the reading practices of all individuals, it is important to distinguish reading-to-write/learn from general reading, as the former mandates a more critical approach. Flower (1990) notes that the process of reading-to-write guides the way readers interact with a text, forcing them to "manipulate . . . and transform" the information for their own needs (p. 6). Kintsch (1998) elaborates, stating, "When reading to learn or to integrate, reader/writers construct elaborate models of the text structure and situation, enabling them to select information from the source text, evaluate it, and use it for writing purposes" (as cited in Delaney, 2008, p. 141).

There is an assumption in education that "if we just provide adequate basic skills, from that point forward kids with adequate background knowledge will be able to read anything successfully" (Shanahan & Shanahan, 2008, p. 41). Therefore, for many students, reading instruction that focuses specifically on such issues as vocabulary development, recognizing main ideas and details, drawing inferences, and so on, ends in elementary school. However, a number of studies point to a decrease in reading competence among adolescents in the United States. For example, the National Assessment of Educational Progress (2009) shows that high school seniors perform lower in reading than seniors in 1998; similarly, anecdotal reports by professors tell a similar tale as direct measures of entering college students being unprepared to meet reading expectations. Study results and tales of faculty woe indicate clearly the need for continued reading instruction in high school, in the first year of college, and across the curriculum.

The foregoing discussion makes clear the fundamental reasons why many students lack the reading skills they need to be successful in school and in their personal and professional lives. Their reading difficulty arises in part from a lack of instruction and motivation. It also arises from the idea that reading is a fundamental skill taught early in school, usually in first grade, and that little or no instruction is needed once the basic idea is mastered,. Their difficulty also arises from the view that there is less need for reading now that everything is on the computer. Their difficulty also arises because, while they increasingly engage with texts and visual displays (in games, blogs, IMs, and text messages on cell phones), they are less aware of the ways their attention and responses are shaped by the media. Their difficulty also arises in part because the tacit goals of critical literacy—including the integration of ideas in a larger context and applying reading material to the writer's own rhetorical purpose—are neither stated explicitly nor taught in a reading and writing context. It is this final manifestation of students' reading problems that is most important, and may be the one area in which writing teachers can help the most.

For the purposes of this book, then, reading refers to getting meaning from print, whether the print is viewed on paper or on a screen. In college courses in writing and elsewhere, however, reading must go beyond just getting meaning: Readers must be able to analyze texts to see how parts fit together. They must also be able to synthesize different readings on the same topic or issue so they can see a range of perspectives and/or research on the topic or issue. In addition, students must be able to evaluate the materials they read. (Librarians have done a particularly good job of setting standards for resource evaluation in the context of information literacy.) Finally, critical reading entails students' ability to make use of what they read for their own purposes. These aspects of reading are the ones that can be usefully reconnected to writing and writing instruction.

Writing

The value in reconnecting reading and writing is clear from similar definitions of key concepts. In a longitudinal study of college writers, Nancy Sommers and Laura Saltz (2004) tracked the progress of more than four hundred Harvard students from matriculation through graduation to chart their development as writers. After their freshman year, many participants reported relief that they had survived the press of writing assignments, but more importantly, they were proud of the input they had in the scholarly discourse of their classes. A number of student comments revealed, too, an understanding of the value of writing tasks: "If I hadn't written, I would have felt as if I was just being fed a lot of information. My papers are my opportunity to think and say something for myself, a chance to disagree" (Sommers & Saltz, 2004, p. 129). The study points to the importance of defining writing as a form of self-exploration and reflection—practices that are vital as transitioning students develop into independent thinkers.

It is no secret that in addition to the great *amount* of writing they do, college students are confronted with a wide *variety* of writing tasks. Fishman, Lunsford, McGregor, and Otuteye (2005) examined early college writing as part of the Stanford Study of Writing, considering both the in-class work (analytic essays, persuasive papers, lab reports, etc.) and non-academic writing (journal entries, email, blogs, etc.) of nearly two hundred students. In the study, researchers explored how considering one's audience positively influenced the focus and quality of his or her writing (both academic and extracurricular). The findings illustrate the same message as the Harvard study, that "writing is both a powerful mode of direct, often personal communication and a form of highly mediated expression" (p. 245), regardless of the writing product.

As with reading, our focus in this book is on writing in post-secondary academic contexts. Writing entails putting meaning into printed words, and like reading, it has a similar essential nature, whether the words appear on paper or on a screen. When students write, they are, as noted above, not only presenting the by-products of self-exploration and reflection and of research, inquiry and study, but also of their own experiences as writers. Writing in an academic context now includes traditional research reports and papers and a myriad of other kinds of work, both print and digital. It might be fair to say that a linchpin in the array of academic writing is the ability to call on and engage with source materials to enter on-going conversations on issues and topics. Because academic writing so often entails the use of what students have read, the need to reconnect reading and writing is clear.

New Literacies

Definitions of reading and writing show that they must go hand-in-hand; other studies and organizational policy statements (discussed below) validate the need to incorporate new technologies, seeing them as basic to reading and writing in all venues. University of Connecticut reading scholar Donald Leu and his colleagues propose a definition of these new literacies:

> The new literacies of the Internet and other ICTs [information and communication technologies] include the skills, strategies, and dispositions necessary to successfully use and adapt to the rapidly changing information and communication technologies and contexts that continuously emerge in our world and influence all areas of our personal and professional lives. These new literacies allow us to use the Internet

> and other ICTs to identify important questions, locate infor-
> mation, critically evaluate the usefulness of that information,
> synthesize information to answer those questions, and then
> communicate the answers to others. (Leu, Kinzer, Coiro, &
> Cammack, 2004, p. 1572)

Notice that this definition addresses both reading and writing in the
context of printed displays and various digital forms.

Leu, O'Byrne, Zawilinski, McVerry, and Everett-Cacopardo (2009)
further explain, "New literacies theory works on two levels: uppercase
(New Literacies) and lowercase (new literacies). *New Literacies,* as the
broader, more inclusive concept, benefits from the work taking place
in the multiple lowercase dimensions of *new literacies*" (p. 265). As
such, New Literacies theory is an ever-deepening area of research for
scholars across disciplines.

Why "literacies" instead of "literacy"? Consider the rapidly maturing technologies available through desktop computers, laptop computers, and mobile devices: McKenna and Conradi (2010) explain that
because of these advances, the Internet is so "well suited to more complex literacy activity that takes such a variety of forms that reference to
it is now in the plural" (p. 46). Lowercase "new literacies," then, is an
umbrella category for the buzzword "literacies" of the day, including:
digital literacy, computer literacy, technological literacy, and more.
While each of these knowledge sets contributes to an individual's overall aptitude, they all fall into a larger group of abilities that informs
research done on New Literacies. What new literacies all have in common—and what is so vital to understand in today's technology-rich
world—is that these skills do not supersede traditional literacy. Educators must emphasize this distinction, communicating to our students
that new literacies "almost always build on foundational literacies
rather than replace them" (Leu, Kinzer, Coiro, & Cammack, 2004,
p. 1590). It should be clear that students need both "foundational literacies" (i.e., skills in getting meaning from and putting meaning into
print) and skill in using these abilities in digital environments. Digital
"new" literacies require us of reading and writing together, along with
links, images, sound, and movement, to present ideas and get new
information.

Multiliteracies

The electronic aspects of reading and writing can also be approached from the vantage point of semiotic theory that offers research on multiliteracies. The term "multiliteracies" was coined in the mid-1990s by an international group of educators who convened to explore and discuss literacy pedagogy of the day; called the New London Group, this group of ten scholars included notable voices in the field, such as Mary Kalantzis, Bill Cope, and James Gee (New London Group, 1996). In their 2010 book chapter on the subject of multiliteracies, Kalantzis and Cope, along with co-author Anne Cloonan, explain that communication in the twenty-first century has bled well beyond the printed page, and that in order to operate effectively in this multimodal environment, young people today must become "capable and competent users of both print and other forms of meaning enabled by new technologies" (pp. 61–62). It was with this mission in mind, in fact, that the New London Group developed its initial set of criteria to define an individual as being multiliterate. Not surprisingly, in the subsequent decade, the criteria have been modified tow encompass the following multimodal proficiencies: written language, oral language, visual representation, audio representation, tactile representation, gestural representation, and spatial representation (p. 66).

Literacy is truly a marriage of many skills, applied to countless functions; as such, literacy is resistant to being pinned down simply. Indisputably, literacy is a prism through which one sees the world; however, when seeking to define the term, notes Ntiri (2009), we are prone to ask, "Which Literacy? What level? And for what purpose?" (p. 99). As Roberts (2005) noted in his article investigating definitions of literacy, "one can at best hope to specify 'the' definition of literacy for particular purposes" (p. 524). For our purposes, then, let us align our definition of literacy with that of Flower's (1990) *critical literacy*, whereby students call on critical thinking skills to navigate, understand, transform, and apply information for their use. To do so, they must learn to rely on critical reading and writing, reconnected for the purposes of analysis, synthesis, evaluation, and application.

Information Literacy

If critical reading and writing, as defined above, are the targets we hope to hit with all students, faculty should also take into account

the defining characteristics of information literacy (IL) offered by
the Association of College and Research Libraries (ACRL), a division
of the American Library Association. ACRL's *Information Literacy
Competency Standards for Higher Education* (2000) explicitly specify particular kinds of reading abilities that students should have to
complete research and writing tasks in college courses. (See especially
the Appendix A for a condensed version of the Standards and an ac-
companying list of ways to assess student abilities, called Performance
Indicators). The ACRL Standards include being able to formulate a
search strategy and find materials efficiently; Beyond these abilities,
the standards require—notably in Standard Three—that students be
able to analyze, synthesize, and evaluate source materials for their own
purposes and use them as needed to complete any research task. In
this light, information literacy can be seen as a crossroads where reading (evaluation and analysis) and writing (synthesis and incorporation)
converge. The need for these abilities is also pointed out by academic
librarian Patricia Breivik and college president Gordon Gee (2006) in
their report on the impact of the Internet on education.

It is vital to understand that information literacy is *not* synonymous with computer and/or technology literacy. Numerous studies
show that students entering college spend a significant amount of time
interacting with technology. Because of this constant use, young people have a great amount of confidence in their computer literacy. For
example, the 2009 *ECAR Study of Undergraduate Students and Information Technology* found that a majority of respondents rated themselves as being between fairly skilled and very skilled with tools such
as presentation software, course management systems, spreadsheets,
and websites (Smith, Salaway, & Caruso, 2009, p. 54). Nonetheless,
college students report significant difficulties when confronted with a
project that calls upon IL competencies: The 2010 report from Project
Information Literacy indicates that 84% of their respondents are "sty-
mied" by getting started in the course-related research process, 66%
find it difficult to define a topic, 62% have trouble narrowing down a
topic, and that evaluating results for relevancy is an obstacle for 61%
of respondents (Head & Eisenberg, 2010, p. 26).

Faculty librarians John Buschman and Dorothy Warner (2006) of
Rider University, a mid-sized private liberal arts institution in New
Jersey, note that, in fact, the concept of information literacy relies on
and requires print literacy as its starting point. They claim that there is

a fundamental need within information literacy for the kind of "critical reflexivity" that derives from literacy in a print environment. They draw on the work of literacy scholars such as Brian Street, Jack Goody, and Ian Watt, as well as the ACRL Standards, to show that in order for students or library users to develop information literacy skills, they must also have essential literacy skills that develop through sustained reading of printed texts.

Another definition of information literacy was developed by Christine Bruce, Associate Professor of Information Technology at Queensland University of Technology in Australia, wherein an information literate person "has a sound knowledge of the world of information, approaches information critically, and has a personal information style that facilitates his or her interaction with the world of information" (as cited in Bawden & Robinson, 2009, p. 187). This description of IL is particularly apt the real-world environments of constant informational stimulus, such as what students confront each day on the Internet and on social networking platforms.

Despite their constant use of computers and mobile devices of various kinds, students are not as adept at finding, reading, and using information as they could be and should be. Two measures of information literacy reveal students' weaknesses. As noted by Shanahan and Shanahan (2008) call for a set of skills that are "widely adaptable and applicable to all kinds of reading situations" (p. 40). That basic reading skills are translatable across reading situations grows ever more important as platforms for text delivery continue to increase and evolve. Data on information literacy comes from two different studies, both measuring students' ICT (information and communication technology) skills. The first comes from an early version of the Educational Testing Service direct test of ICT skills, called the iSkills test. Irwin Katz (2007a, 2007b), one of the lead researchers, reports in two papers the results of studies done in 2006 on the information literacy skills of college students: defining, accessing, managing, evaluating, integrating, creating, and communicating information. The test was designed to measure the skills articulated by ACRL, as described in their standards (see Appendix A). The data is not representative of any particular group, but the findings show that only 50% of students who participated have the skills that ACRL deems essential for appropriate use of ICT tools.

Further data on technologically-based reading comes from a different instrument, one designed collaboratively by librarians and faculty at Kent State University in Ohio, where they developed the SAILS (Standardized Assessment of Information Literacy Skills) test. This instrument measures students' abilities to develop a search strategy, and to find, evaluate, and document their sources. Because it specifically examines students' use of sources in writing projects, SAILS is particularly pertinent as a measure of online reading connected specifically to writing. The SAILS results also show that only half of the students have the skills described by the ACRL Standards. The results from both iSkills and SAILS clearly indicate that many students need help with reading and other critical thinking skills online and on paper, and that they could benefit from work combining reading and writing.

Undoubtedly, information literacy skills must be cultivated for students to become effective consumers of information, be that information for academic, professional, or personal use. These areas are increasingly coming together, as the National Council of Teachers of English and the International Reading Association point out in a policy statement discussed in more detail below. They write:

> For example, living with cell phones leads to texting, which changes how people view writing and how they write, and frequenting Web 2.0 sites, such as the video-sharing service YouTube, privileges a visual mode and shapes both attention to and facility with other modes of meaning making. (National Council of Teachers of English [NCTE], 2009)

To help students develop these skills electronically and on paper, academic libraries traditionally collaborate with faculty in first year writing programs to integrate information literacy into the writing classroom. In addition, many academic libraries expand their information literacy programs to support writing across the curriculum initiatives, team-teaching research methods courses with classroom faculty, and credit-bearing information literacy courses that wholly integrate reading and writing into the research process. Melissa Bowles-Terry and her colleagues (2010) describe how librarians and writing instructors at Utah State University collaborated on a problem-based instructional approach for basic writing classes, aligning student learning outcomes in IL and in writing. In an assessment of the project, students reported that they appreciated the real-world approach to research, but they nevertheless "struggled with integrating and synthesizing the information they found and wanted to see a stronger relationship between reading, research, and writing" (p. 227). The librarians and compositionists involved in the course learned that in addition to a unified instructional approach, it is vital to provide students with ample time for reflection, discussion of their research, and writing; it is through these practices that students begin to understand the processes of summary and synthesis. This study shows that research and writing can and should be successfully connected through the application of strong critical reading and thinking skills to writing in a context of information literacy. Aspects of digital and information literacy are discussed later in the book.

MORE REASONS TO RECONNECT READING AND WRITING

National Commission on Writing; DEEP Study of College Success

Some recent measures make clear students' difficulties with reading when writing; these reports provide additional evidence reconnecting reading and writing in both print and in digital environments. For example, in 2002, the College Board launched the National Commission on Writing to examine writing in American schools and colleges, with an eye toward adding a writing component to the SAT and toward a fuller understanding of the teaching and learning of writing around the country (College Board, 2003, p. 7). The Commission issued three reports: the first in 2003, called The Neglected "R": The Need for a Writing Revolution; a second report called Writing: A Ticket to Work . . . or a Ticket Out, issued in 2004; and, a third report in 2005 called Writing: A Powerful Message from State Government. These reports examine the status of the teaching and learning of writing and the need for writing skills among workers in both public and private sectors. Based on survey data and consultations with an advisory panel of leaders in education and the teaching of writing at the secondary and higher education levels, the reports note the need for skills in analysis, synthesis, and the proper documentation of sources read and used in various kinds of reports (College Board, 2005, p. 4). The Commission's initial findings point out that "Analyzing arguments and synthesizing information are also beyond the scope of most first-year [college] students" (College Board, 2003, p. 14). These studies provide yet another perspective on the need for reading-writing connections as students develop literacy skills for success in college and in the workplace.

An additional angle on the reading-writing connection derives from work on student success. By examining college success through drawing on careful study of graduation rates and student engagement at twenty colleges and universities around the country, George Kuh et al. (2005) reports on the Documenting Effective Educational Practice (DEEP) project. DEEP draws on data collected by the National Survey of Student Engagement (NSSE), a study taken by several million students at colleges and universities across the country (Kuh et al., 2005). In particular, Kuh and his colleagues report that an emphasis on reading and writing, particularly for beginning students, is a common characteristic of institutions that achieve high levels of graduation and engagement. Reading involves a range of different kinds of activities, including summer reading programs, common book approaches, extensive reading across disciplines, and including challenging material in first year seminar programs (Kuh et al., 2005, p. 187–188). Primary source materials, novels, and scholarly articles, as well as on-line materials, are among the kinds of reading assigned to students (p. 194). At some schools, students are asked to read a common book and related materials, write in response to that reading, share their writing with others, and read and respond to faculty writing about the book and related matters (p. 180). All of these activities are features of "effective educational practice," according to this very thorough study. This broadly based research supports the usefulness of reconnecting reading and writing.

Qualitative Research Supporting Reconnection: George Mason University and University of Arkansas Students' Reading and Writing

A different method of studying the need for reconnection appears in two qualitative studies that reveal the importance of a reading-writing connection. In Engaged Writers and Dynamic Disciplines, Chris Thaiss and Terry Zawacki (2006) report on their study of academic writing completed at George Mason University, a Carnegie High Research University public institution with about twenty thousand undergraduates in Fairfax, Virginia. In their study, Thaiss and Zawacki conducted interviews with a small group of faculty across fourteen disciplines, surveyed 183 students in upper level writing courses, and discussed writing with thirty-six students in focus groups. They also collected assessment data from departmental or college faculty assessments of student writing and examined samples of a timed writing exercise completed by forty students seeking exemption from the required, upper-level writing course.

In their results, Thaiss and Zawacki report on students' perceptions of the role of reading in their development as writers. George Mason students in this study pointed often to the importance of reading in their understanding of writing in their disciplines: "Reading widely and deeply, many students said, helped them understand not only the subject matter of the discipline but also the ways in which it can be/should be presented" (Thaiss & Zawacki, 2006, p. 128). In addition to reading experience and the use of models for the kind of writing they were expected to do, though, GMU students also "infer style from reading professional writing" (p. 128). Moreover, not only did reading within their disciplines help these writers, but reading from other areas was also useful. Thaiss and Zawacki say that

> Reading outside of their disciplines has also helped many of the students . . . appreciate the rhetorical differences that distinguish one discipline from another as well as the comfort level they've achieved as readers and writers in their chosen field. (p. 128)

One chief piece of advice more advanced students said they would give to new students in their major seeking success as writers and in college overall is to read (p. 129). It's clear from this study, drawing on careful self-report data, that at least some students see a useful connection between reading and writing.

A recent study by University of Arkansas literacy scholar David Jolliffe and doctoral student Allison Harl (2008) draws on a different kind of self-report data to show that student readers do in fact complete a lot of reading, but not of the kind investigated here; i.e., not the kind they must master to be successful in college coursework. Jolliffe and Harl paid a small group of students at the University of Arkansas, a Carnegie Very High Research University public school of about fourteen thousand students in Fayetteville, Arkansas, to complete a background questionnaire, keep a reading journal for two weeks logging their reading activities, and write a detailed exploration of one item they read each day, responding to a prescribed series of questions (Jolliffe & Harl, 2008, pp. 602–03).

From careful analysis of the data, Jolliffe and Harl conclude that their students do not read critically, and to help them do so, faculty need to work in three different areas. First, students should develop "text-to-world and text-to-text connections" (p. 613). In addition, students need to have opportunities to make broader connections between reading, coursework, and other kinds of educational opportunities. Finally, because of students' interest in, use of, and comfort with technology, faculty should encourage students to develop their "literacies in electronic contexts that instructors overlook or ignore" in ways that lead to deeper engagement with reading materials (p. 614). That deeper engagement helps students in writing tasks and in overall success in college. Further discussion of this study, in Harl's literature review, is included in the next chapter of this volume.

Quantitative and qualitative evidence, then, shows that students do not read as well as they could and should to be successful in writing classes and elsewhere in college. Critical reading to analyze, synthesize, evaluate, and apply ideas and information, and writing to make use of what students learn from reading in various print and digital forms, can be productively reconnected.

Organizational Policy Statements

All major professional organizations concerned with literacy have issued statements of various kinds reflecting a widespread view of the need to integrate reading and writing. The rationale for reconnecting reading and writing comes, in part, from an assortment of documents presented by professional organizations concerned with the teaching and learning of reading, writing, and literacy on paper and on screens. Every major organization has attempted to address issues focused on here, particularly those in conjunction with or in relation to changes in literacy activities in increasingly technological environments. The impact of new technologies informs our discussion at all points. Organizations that have offered major policy statements include: the National Council of Teachers of English, the International Reading Association, the Association of College and Research Libraries, the Conference on College Composition and Communication, and the Council of Writing Program Administrators. All these groups have reading and writing as their central focus, and are in a position to offer authoritative statements pertinent to reconnecting reading and writing.

NCTE and IRA: Redefining the Reading/Writing Connection?

In 2009, the National Council of Teachers of English (NCTE) and the International Reading Association (IRA) created a joint task force on assessing reading and writing, a collaboration itself that speaks to the need to reconnect reading and writing. This professional group drew up a set of standards for assessment based on their collective view of literacy and of changes within it, addressing the interwoven nature of reading and writing on pages and screens. Acknowledging ongoing changes in literacy practices, these organizations reflect the need for reading and writing to be linked in theory, in practice, in instruction, and in assessment. These two leading professional organizations see the essential connection between reading and writing, and believe it is important to appropriately assess these skills for such a connection. However, it is important to keep in mind that digital literacies build on foundational print literacies—those students must have to be successful in traditional and electronic venues.

Earlier, NCTE (2007) issued a research policy brief on twenty-first century literacies that addressed reading-writing connections. This policy brief provides the following "research-based recommendations for teachers":

> Research shows that effective instruction in 21st-century literacies takes an integrated approach, helping students understand how to access, evaluate, synthesize, and contribute to information. Furthermore, as Web 2.0 demonstrates, participation is key, and effective teachers will find ways to encourage interaction with and among students. (p. 5)

(The recommendations in the policy brief are quoted more fully in Appendix B of this book.) Underlying all new technology is essential skill in reading and writing for analysis, synthesis, evaluation, and application.

College English: CCCC and CWPA

Like NCTE (in collaboration with IRA) and ACRL, the Conference on College Composition and Communication (a sub-group of NCTE) has also issued a position statement on reading/writing relationships, instructional practices, and goals. In 2004, the CCCC adopted a position statement on Teaching, Learning, and Assessing Writing in

Digital Environments (NCTE, 2004). In assumptions preliminary to this position statement—those similar to the NCTE's 21st Century Literacies policy brief issued more recently—the CCCC makes clear the need to "engage students in the critical evaluation of information" (NCTE, 2004), consistent with the ACRL information literacy standards. Thus, like NCTE and ACRL, the CCCC has also addressed the essential skill of evaluation in reading and writing. (See Appendix C for excerpted text.)

The reading-writing connection is of particular interest and concern to the Council of Writing Program Administrators, the national organization for those who direct college and university writing programs. The CWPA has put out a widely-respected core document called the *WPA Outcomes Statement for First-Year Composition* (Council of Writing Program Administrators [CWPA], 2000). This statement consists of a series of planks—what sections of the Outcomes Statement are called—in various areas of writing, that describe the competencies students should have when they complete first year composition courses. (See Appendix D of this book for the full text of the *Outcomes Statement.*) The statement is intended to be a broad outline, and individual programs have adopted and modified to it describe their local courses and goals. The statement supports the role of reading in the teaching of writing as a key outcome of first year writing instruction, specifically mentioning analysis, synthesis, and evaluating materials students use in their writing.

From the findings of various studies mentioned here, from the perspective of major professional organizations in the teaching of reading and writing, and from the key terms in this volume used as the basis of our discussion, the importance of reconnecting reading and writing is clear. While some argue that new technologies make critical reading and writing less important because students can access and use online materials, research suggests that the foundational skills of reading and writing are, in fact, more important now than ever in the face of constantly changing technologies and literacies. Therefore, our goal in this book is to explore the various ways in which reading can be reconnected with writing, from a broad array of perspectives. The following overview of the book reveals the myriad directions we explore through which reading and writing can be connected to help students build skills for use on paper and screens, and for personal and professional purposes.

An Overview of the Book

Part I: Overview

Chatpter 1. Introduction.

Chapter 2. History/Theory—Allison Harl's historical review of literature on reading-writing connections provides an overview of the findings, theories, programs, and practices that have emerged in the field. The important publications that presented these developments are explored with a detailed focus on how theory, research, practice, and programs informed each other. The section starts in the 1800s and moves through key theoretical approaches to the reading-writing connection. More recent research and practical applications arising from this connection are also presented in Harl's chapter, giving a strong sense of the work of scholars on the need to connect reading to writing.

Chapter 3. International Perspectives—In this chapter, Jennifer Coon looks at the ways in which other countries connect reading and writing. This section examines how international, college level instruction understand the juncture between reading and creating texts. Historical perspectives and innovations are investigated. The insights of colleagues in the Far East, Latin America, and Europe comprise the focus of this chapter.

Part II: Classrooms and Students

Chapter 4. Best Practices in the Writing Classroom—Horning's chapter on "Writing and Reading Across the Curriculum: Best Practices and Practical Guidelines" looks at "Monday morning" approaches in writing classes and in courses across the disciplines. The chapter argues that there are specific strategies teachers can use to build more and better direct instruction in reading into their courses, leading to a happy outcome in students' writing and overall success.

Chapter 5. Basic Writers—A related thread supporting the reconnection of reading and writing comes from work with basic writers, reviewed by Kathy Skomski, in "First Year Writers: Forward Movement, Backward Progress." Basic writers have a special set of needs with respect to the reading-writing connection, as they are often very weak readers needing as much help with reading as they do with writing. This chapter examines the ways basic writers need to learn critical thinking skills and build upon those skills in both reading and writing. Additionally, the chapter considers students' personal beliefs about writing, evaluation, re-evaluation, writing/reading environments, as they are related to the reading-writing connection.

Chapter 6. L2—An additional illustration of the need to reconnect reading and writing comes from work with L2 writers—especially English for Academic Purposes (EAP) writers in pre-university and university contexts—who must learn to work with multiple text sources and carry out the same read-to-write tasks expected of any university student. Some of distinctive challenges facing these students include: issues of cross-cultural academic expectations, use of multiple (and sometimes conflicting) source texts, more limited experiences with read-to-write tasks and associated curricular genres, limited experiences with summary and synthesis writing, and limitations on language resources (i.e., vocabulary, grammar, and discourse structure knowledge) that L2 students encounter. Grabe and Zhang take up these issues in "Second Language Reading-Writing Relations."

Chapter 7. Common Core—David Jolliffe's chapter on the Common Core State Standards Initiative of the National Governors Association and the council of Chief State School Officers shows how K–12 and educators are beginning to use the reconnection of reading and writing to improve students' critical literacy skills. The implications of the coming changes for college and university teachers are explored in this chapter.

Part III: Contexts and Resources

Chapter 8. Textbooks—The fabric of reading and writing instruction can be tested by examining college textbooks that attempt, with varying degrees of success, to make use of the whole cloth. In the chapter, "Reading and Writing Connections in College Composition Textbooks," Jimmy Fleming examines ways that the most popular rhetoric texts that include readings and instructional apparatuses deal with reading/writing connections. While some books help students read effectively through vocabulary, comprehension questions, and strategies for rhetorical analysis, most do not help students see the reading-writing connection. The chapter highlights texts that offer the strongest connections.

Chapter 9. Libraries—Cynthia Haller's chapter, "Reuniting Reading and Writing: Revisiting the Role of the Library," traces conceptual connections among information literacy, reading, research, and writing, and reviews best practices in teaching research-based writing. Haller argues that the library serves as an important intersection of reading and writing in academic settings. By collaborating on information literacy instruction, librarians and disciplinary faculty can engage students to evaluate their research methods and their information sources in each phase of their writing. This chapter offers recommendations for how the academic library contributes to the development of reading and writing skills throughout a student's academic career, and suggests that compositionists pay closer attention to information literacy instruction.

Chapter 10. Digital—In this chapter, Drake considers how the digital delivery of traditional publications, such as journal articles, and new media resources has moved a significant portion of reading for research to digital environments. This trend has changed multiple aspects of the undergraduate research experience—from habits of annotating while reading to habits of selecting passages for referencing in assignments. Digital access to resources makes them immediate and easily available for consumption, exposing students to a wide variety of publications for any research project they confront. These efficiencies bring reading and writing ever closer temporally, while also posing urgent pressure for the critical judgment and assimilation of new ideas. Information literacy skills are paramount in such environments due to high demands for evaluating materials and incorporating them cogently and ethically in one's work. This chapter analyzes the research process in a digital context, discusses the importance of information literacy skills in it, and highlights the role of libraries in supporting and developing those skills.

2 A Historical and Theoretical Review of the Literature: Reading and Writing Connections

Allison L. Harl

Literature concerning reading-writing relations centers around a history of debates about what English Studies should be and what the teaching of first year college composition courses should look like. This review works to inform several underlying questions: In what directions have the theory and praxis of reading-writing relations evolved over the past few centuries? What new understandings of reading-writing relations have emerged over the past decade in an era contextualized by information literacy practices and technology in general? As Jackson (2009) has noted,

> How scholars have gone about researching the connections between reading and writing is based on whether they view reading and writing as consumption versus production, as constructing meaning from a text and constructing a text to convey meaning, or both as creating a conversation. (p. 154)

While many scholars of reading and writing relationships do not align themselves with one exclusive perspective, these three broad models of inquiry are useful in defining current theoretical approaches to reading and writing practices.

The first model of inquiry, consumption versus production, assumes that reading is a practice exclusively defined by the passive absorption of meaning from a text. On the other hand, writing is a practice specifically defined as a creative process where meaning is actively produced. The consumption versus production model perceives reading and writing connections extrinsically and dualistically through an either/or paradigm. The second model of inquiry assumes that both reading and writing have the potential to produce: either by constructing meaning from a text or by constructing a text to convey meaning. Through this perspective, reading and writing connections are examined in the context of their shared generative characteristics. Finally, the third model of inquiry views reading and writing as both consumption and production. This conversational model emphasizes the inherent reciprocal relationships between the two practices, in which meaning-making is defined through both reflexive and active processes.

Using these three broad models of inquiry, this chapter begins with eighteenth and nineteenth century mimetic approaches to reading and writing. In the era of *belles lettres*, English Studies limited connections between reading and writing to the first model of inquiry: consumption versus production. The second and third models of inquiry are demonstrated in a review of the literature and theory in subsequent sections. In a section titled, "Twentieth Century: Literacy Studies and New Criticism," the writing process and cognitive and expressivist approaches are detailed concerning debates about how reading and writing relate to one another. Next, the literature and theory at the turn of the century examines the social turn in English Studies, exploring new perspectives about reading and writing connections by examining socio-cultural contexts. The final section, devoted to the literature of the twenty-first century, considers how technology and new media in the past decade have created new contexts for examining how reading and writing practices interrelate. The chapter concludes with the prevailing argument that reading and writing need to be reconnected in first year college composition. However, lingering questions remain in the literature and theory of what these connections are exactly and how they should inform the way composition should be taught. Whether reading and writing are defined as based on consumption and/or production will continue to have broad implications for English programs in the twenty-first century.

ENGLISH STUDIES IN THE EIGHTEENTH AND NINETEENTH CENTURIES: BELLES LETTRES

Nelson and Calfee's (1998) exhaustive study of the history of English Studies in the United States shows us that when, historically, connections between reading and writing were made, they centered around mimetic approaches. This history could be traced back centuries to fourth century Greece and the practice of progymnasmata, or oratory exercises developed by Aphthonius. Students read the Great Works and wrote to imitate their forms. In Roman rhetoric, however, reading and writing practices were conflated with the oratory skills of listening and speaking (Jackson, 2009, p. 146).

British and Scottish new rhetoricians Joseph Priestley, Adam Smith, Hugh Blair, and George Campbell, among others, reconceived Classical principles in light of new developments in science and psychology in the eighteenth century enlightenment era. These principles were ultimately referred to as the new belletristic rhetoric, a study of the common ground shared by classical rhetoric and *belles letters*, emphasizing taste, style, criticism, and forms of discourse, typically studied through works of literature. George (1998) explains that Priestley revolutionized rhetoric with his famous *A Course of Lectures on Oratory and Criticism* in 1762. Priestly was hailed as an innovator of a new rhetorical theory of structure that ultimately influenced the form of the Declaration of Independence. Carter (1988) argues that the combination of *belles letters* and rhetoric, initiated by Smith and popularized later by his student, Blair, has profoundly influenced what is taught in English departments today.

By the mid-nineteenth century, rhetoric had more or less come to mean composition. This re-conception largely affected the ways reading and writing was understood. When Blair published *Lectures on Rhetoric and Belles Lettres* (1783), it served as a guide in composition and language theory, combining, for the first time, classical modes of oration with modern modes of written discourse. This text served as one of the first whole language guides (as it is referred to even today), focusing on making meaning in reading and expressing that meaning in writing. Blair, like his contemporaries, viewed the relationship between reading and writing through the model of consumption versus production. Meaning was found through reading texts, and created by producing them.

Though not as popular at the time, George Campbell's *The Philosophy of Rhetoric* addressed comprehensive principles of eloquence in speech and literary topics. William Riley Parker's (1967) and Ronald F. Reid's (1990) historical studies of English instruction suggest that the influence of Smith and Blair culminated in an emphasis on literary criticism and literary history in popular English program curricula. Such classical traditions of imitation were valued as "consumption" of valuable knowledge. Generating meaning through composing was not as central to the *belles lettres* tradition. Overall, Smith and Priestley hold a broader view of the relevance of reading—one reduced to the literary by Blair and Campbell.

In addition, belletristic rhetoric provided the roots of current-traditional rhetoric, defined by an emphasis on imitation through formal correctness and style. The current-traditionalist approach emerged from belletristic rhetoric primarily because it emphasized style in the form of the modes of discourse. Belletristic rhetoric overlooked the role of invention as a generative process that characterized the then new current-traditionalist approach. Smith transformed a focus on the matter of a topic to its arrangement:

> Thus, we see in [Smith's] lectures evidence of a shift from a rhetorical concept of arrangement as dispositio to a belletristic concept of arrangement as mode of organization, a shift which later turned into the methods of exposition found in many contemporary composition textbooks and handbooks, including definition, classification and division, contrast, comparison, and cause and effect, which are still taught as a means of structuring whole texts. (Carter, 1988, p. 10)

The current-traditionalist approach emerged in the late nineteenth century and remained popular through the 1960s.

Many scholars blame this approach for limiting composition studies to a reading-and-writing-to-imitate model focused on rhetorical patterns. This mimetic approach views reading and writing connections through the first model of inquiry—through the lens of consumption versus production. With such a reading-to-imitate model, reading connects to writing only in terms of a passive imitative process that emphasizes consumption. Reading does not function as a generative process linked to the invention of writing. Much attention has been given to the debate over the use of the "reading-to-imitate-development" function in the classroom. Prose (2006) argues that "not only does reducing writing into prose structures oversimplify the complexity of writing, as writers often employ multiple genres in their writing, but it assumes transfer between reading and writing will occur by 'osmosis'" (p. 3).

However, Christianson (2003) argues that teachers have largely misunderstood the uses of imitation in classical declamation. Imitation, she argues, is a highly effective form of instruction, providing models and precepts for beginning readers and writers. She says:

> Leaving students to describe their own analytical processes without introducing them to already known features of text and context asks them to continually rediscover the wheel, a slow and chancy endeavor, when by showing them the wheel, we can then enable them to invent the turbine. (p. 81)

In this view, reading-to-imitate, while initially ignoring more generative connections between reading and writing, eventually leads to stronger interplay between reading and writing practices.

How have these eighteenth and nineteenth century traditions continued to impact reading and writing relationships in modern and contemporary English Studies programs? As Janna M. Jackson (2009) explains, despite the early university's focus on oratory skills—or perhaps because of this emphasis—eighteenth and nineteenth century rhetorics held some promise in connecting reading and writing in that it studied the "relation between producing and understanding texts" (as cited in Nelson & Calfee, 1998, p. 5) However, over the course of the eighteenth century, a divorce between reading and writing occurred that has been central to pedagogical tensions ever since. In 1884, Thomas Hunt advocated for the inclusion of literary studies at the college level, with the caveat that "the writing one does about literary studies is different from literature"; thus, "the segregation between literature and writing . . . [was] born" (as cited in Yood, 2003, p. 527). As speech-making fell out of practice, and a focus on writing instruction took its place, literature and writing were divorced. Any relationships between reading and writing continued to be seen as an extrinsic connection, reflecting a consumption (reading) versus production (writing) model of inquiry.

The Twentieth Century

Literacy Studies and New Criticism. Nelson and Calfee (1998) explain that by the close of the nineteenth century, and as rhetoric shifted from a focus on oral expression to an emphasis on written expression, according to Scholes (1998), rhetoric transformed into literacy studies in English departments:

> With reading, writing, and speaking orations no longer the center of study when, at the end of the century, rhetoric met its demise as a formal course of study, the reading of literature and writing of criticism that Hunt advocated took its place, resulting in "transform[ing] the students from producers of work comparable to what they studied into passive consumers of texts they could never hope to emulate. (as cited in Jackson, 2009, p. 147)

New Criticism became the dominant literary approach, replacing earlier mimetic ideas about the relationship between reader and text. Nelson and Calfee (1998) explain: "New Criticism did bring together reading and writing at the college level, as professors used writing as a means to assess the readers' ability to derive the meaning of a literary work" (as cited in Jackson, 2009, p. 172). New Critics adopted the close reading practices that emerged from religious studies of sacred texts during the late eighteenth century. In the close reading practices of the New Critics, careful, sustained interpretation of a brief passage of text emphasized the particular over the general. The relationship between reading and writing was studied as a process of consumption. Readers paid close attention to individual words, syntax, and the order in which ideas unfolded as they were read. The role and intention of the writer was highly under-played, as the reading process was brought to the foreground. What ties remained between composition (writing) and literature (reading) further dissolved as progressives attacked New Criticism, arguing that students should value their own interpretations above those of experts.

The Writing Process

In the 1960s, as scholars began focusing once again on rhetoric, a new approach centering on the writing process emerged. Through writing process approaches, researchers focused on how writers draft, revise, and edit texts. Irwin and Doyle (1992) comment on the shift in research conducted by educators to that conducted by psychologists, as the cognitive approach became the popular mode of inquiry in the early 1970s and into the 1990s.

Scholars such as Janet Emig (1971), Maxine Hairston (1982), Linda Flower, and John Hayes (1981/2003) investigated the recursive process of reading and writing, suggesting that these practices are largely non-linear. Flower (1990) argues that "the process of reading-to-write guides the way readers interact with a text, forcing them to 'manipulate . . . and transform' the information for their own needs" (p. 6). Just as thinking and writing processes involve jumping around with stops and starts, so does the reading process (Jackson, 2009, p. 149).

Tierney and Leys (1986) acknowledge research that addresses the theoretical links between reading and writing processes, particularly how reading influences revision, how readers use writing during studying, and how writers use reading in preparing a critical essay. They question the benefits of learning outcomes that arise from connecting reading and writing in the classroom.

The authors cite a strategy study by Spivey (1983), in which college students read three articles on the same topic and then wrote an essay: "She found that the essays written by the more able comprehenders were better organized, more connected, and of higher content quality than those written by the less able comprehender" (p. 18). However, Tierney and Leys (1986) declare that do not suggest that reading and writing are largely linear operations that follow from one to the other: "On the contrary, we hold that writers use reading in a more integrated fashion. For as writers write, they are constantly involved in reading their own writing, reading other material, and using understandings they have acquired from past readings" (p. 19).

Considering studies that observe elementary grade school students, Tierney and Leys (1986) explore whether gains in overall reading performance contribute to gains in overall writing performance, and vice versa. They also ask how reading and writing influence one another. Their study revealed that while some students maintain a high or a low value for both reading and writing, others vary in their performances in reading and writing. They suggest that before we conclude that there is a weak relationship of reading and writing for some students, we should consider a more detailed examination of when and how reading and writing interact. They find that reading does influence writing, as students use their reading as a rich resource for considering possible topics, ideas, and stylistic options. In addition, readers also learned about the author's craft and developed vocabulary. Tierney and Leys conclude their study with four findings:

1. Depending upon the measures employed to assess overall reading and writing achievement and attitude, the general correlation between reading and writing is moderate and fluctuates with age, schooling, and other factors.

2. Selected reading experiences definitely contribute to writing performance; likewise, selected writing experiences contribute to reading performance.

3. Writers acquire certain values and behaviors from reading, and vice versa.

4. Successful writers integrate reading into their writing experience, and successful readers integrate writing into their reading experience. (p. 23)

These studies found that reading and writing work together in myriad ways as tools for information storage and retrieval, discovery and logical thought, communication, and self-indulgence.

In another study published the same year, Birnbaum (1986) concludes that reflective thinking is central to proficiency in written language, and explains why so many researchers find that subjects tend to be at comparable levels in reading and writing. She proposes to understand the components of the reflective thinking process, how it manifests in observed reading and writing behaviors, and most importantly, how we can foster its growth. In her study of college-level basic and experienced readers and writers, she found that the more reflection, the better the reader and writer. In addition, the more reflective students often demonstrated a deeper level of planning for different rhetorical purposes and audiences. Birnbaum suggests that instructors rejoin the teaching of reading and writing, viewing one as the mechanism for developing the other. In addition, she argues, educators need to emphasize higher-level reasoning and predicting strategies over recall strategies.

Finally, in their study on how pre-writing affects writing performance, Rohman and Wlecke (1964) argue the importance of the discovery process in pre-writing techniques, such as journal writing, brainstorming, and freewriting. They conclude that thinking is a separate function than writing, that thinking processes precede writing processes. Therefore, to improve writing, instructors should encourage stronger thinking skills in early pre-writing stages. In addition, they argue that writers may learn to form concepts as young readers;

however, they can and should be instructed to focus instead on "concept transference" that includes a preliminary stage of thinking before writing begins. Emig (1971) questioned Rohman and Wlecke's linear approach, suggesting instead that thinking, reading, and writing occurs more naturally in a recursive process.

Cognitive Approach

Psychologist L.S. Vygotsky (1934/1978, 1962/1986) conducted early studies on thought and language that were of primary interest to literacy scholars who explored the connections between reading and writing in the latter part of the century. His theories proposed that thought and language are highly interrelated, and that once learned, language transforms thought. His theory of cultural mediation suggests that a child's knowledge is defined by, and limited to, his or her inherited cultural language practices. In his book, Thought and Language, Vygotsky establishes a clear connection between speech, mental concepts, and cognitive awareness. These studies provided the foundation for twentieth-century scholars interested in language in the form of literacy acquisition and practices. They asked the questions: How does language function in the mental acts of reading and writing? What, if any, are the connections between reading and writing? This model of inquiry shifted from a consumption versus production method to a more conversational approach.

While Vygotsky understood cognition as arising within social interaction using cultural tools, those who studied cognitive information processing tended to look at closed box computer models, attempting to model fixed processing programs. The cognitive-development approach shifts the emphasis from the *what* of composing (the product) to the *how* of composing (the process). Jackson (2009) explains that

> scholars operating from the cognitive information processing arena use the metaphor of the computer as their lens for analyzing reading and writing. As such, they see reading and writing as processes composed of subprocesses, or to use computer lingo, routines and subroutines . . . . (p. 155)

Subprocesses include activities such as planning, comprehension, and metacognition (p. 155). McCarthey and Raphael (1992) explain three underlying assumptions of what they call "cognitive information processing theories":

> (1) reading and writing consist of a number of subprocesses used to perform specialized tasks, (2) readers and writers have limited capacity for attention so that trade-offs occur across the subprocesses, and (3) competence in reading and writing is determined by the degree of attention needed to operate subprocesses; thus, the less memory needed, the more efficient the operation. (p. 4)

Popular cognitive studies connecting reading and writing began with correlational studies originating in the 1960s. The cognitive approach became well-known through theorists such as Flower and Hayes (1981), who applied think-aloud protocols to study the thinking patterns of writers. They argued that composition studies should be more focused on the creative process of the writer. In relation to this creative process of the writer is the notion of audience awareness. Rubin (1984) argues that under all circumstances, writers are "actively engaged in constructing representations of their readers" (p. 238). Analyzing the transcripts of four proficient and four less-proficient writers as they composed aloud, Flower and Hayes concluded that proficient writers generated new ideas in response to the rhetorical problem of communicating with others, while less proficient writers focused on just ideas. Considering audience awareness, Tierney and Shanahan (1991) conclude that

> undoubtedly, readers read with a view to authorship, no matter what their own role as authors. Likewise, writers write with a view to readership in which they are their own audience, at least initially. In other words, successful writers not only consider the transactions their readers are likely to be engaged in, but they are also their own readers. (p. 265)

Similarly, Barritt and Kroll (1978) asked the question, "What guides the decisions writers make as they write?" (p. 365). The relationships between the kinds of thinking processes occurring during the act of composing were compared to those in the act of reading as well. Glenn (2007) cites an early study by Tierney, Soter, O'Flahavan, and McGinley (1984), concluding that "when taught together, reading and writing engage students in a greater use and variety of cognitive

strategies than when taught separately" (p. 10). Fitzgerald and Shanahan (2000) report that many subsequent studies (Aydelott, 1998;
Birnbaum, 1986; Kennedy, 1985; Spivey & King, 1989) also revealed
correlations between reading and writing scores at the college level.
Overall, most studies found that strong writers are also strong readers,
and poor readers are also poor writers. However, some meta-analy-
ses of these correlational studies are criticized for, among other concerns, using inconsistent types of measures to test reading and writing,
having small sample groups, and not considering outside variables
(Stotsky, 1983).

Tierney and Shanahan's (1991) comprehensive review of research
on the reading-writing relationship is organized by three main questions: What do reading and writing share? How do readers and writers
transact with one another? And what do readers and writers learn when
reading and writing are connected? Tierney and Shanahan examine
the degree to which reading and writing share "overlapping linguistic, cognitive, or social resources" (p. 247). They cite performance-
based correlational studies that examine writing for specific reading
outcomes (such as comprehension of a series of passages) as "external
manifestations of literacy knowledge or process" (p. 247). They refer
to Loban (1963, 1964), who completed one of the most notable studies
to date of the reading-writing relationship in an extensive longitudinal
study of the reading and writing abilities of 220 students progressing
through twelve grade levels. Loban argues that the reading-writing
relationship was "so striking to be beyond question" (p. 212). Specifically, the research suggested that superior writers read above their
reading age, while writers performing at an illiterate level read below
their reading age (p. 208).

Shanahan (1984) and Shanahan and Lomax (1986, 1988) conducted correlational studies following Loban, attempting to be more
detailed with examining the *types* of knowledge associated with reading-writing relations. They looked more closely at variances of proficiency based on grade level. The researchers studied 256 second
and fifth graders, measuring lexical, phonemic, syntactic, and orga-
nizational-structural information. The study found that correlations
between reading and writing measures accounted for 43% of the differences in these literacy skills.

Unlike performance-based correlational studies, process-based correlational studies do not typically examine reading or writing based on

the *products* of reading and writing assessments. Instead, process-based studies consider the parallels of the cognitive *processes* underlying reading and writing. These studies typically use think-aloud protocols, interviews, and observations to gather data. Tierney and Shanahan (1991) reviewed several process-based studies in the mid-1980s. For example, Wittrock (1984) found that reading and writing are generative cognitive processes in which readers and writers "create meanings by building relations between the text and what they know, believe, and experience" (p. 77). Similarly, Squire (1984) argues "both comprehending and composing are basic reflections of the same cognitive processes" (p. 24). Likewise, in a proposed composing model of reading, Tierney and Pearson (1983) suggest reading and writing are acts of composing that share similar underlying processes: goal setting, knowledge mobilization, projection perspective-taking, refinement, review, self-correction, and self-assessment. Taking a somewhat different approach, Kucer (1985) developed a model of "text world" production, a conception emanating from his suggestion that readers and writers participate in various strategies of "generating and integrating propositions through which the internal structure of meaning known as the text world is built" (p. 331).

Theorists advocating process-based correlational studies generally define reading and writing in terms of cognitive processes such as gathering ideas, questioning, and hypothesizing. In relation to these studies, Tierney and Shanahan (1991) observe

> Where reading and writing appear to differ is in the extent to which these strategies are enlisted by students, or by what features of the reading or writing act lead them to instantiate a particular strategy. It should be noted that different students enlist different strategies in accordance with the idiosyncratic approach and overall abilities as readers or writers. (pp. 252–53)

Finally, experimental, or instructional, studies investigate whether information and/or processes are shared across reading and writing. Generally, this research is founded on writing instruction and then examines potential reading outcomes, or vice versa. In one such study, Raphael, Kirschner, and Englert (1988) compared the processes of fifteen students who made substantial improvements in understanding and writing expository text to fifteen students who made little improvement, if any. Specifically, Raphael et al. explored the degree of

success associated with attempts to use writing as a means of enhancing students' understanding of the strategies used by authors of expository texts. The scholars concluded that students who made little or no
improvement demonstrated that they were unable to relate new elements to an overall goal or framework in reading or writing. However,
those who did show improvement did so because they were able to tie
ideas together. Tierney and Shanahan (1991) suggested that there was
a need at the turn of the century for more experimental studies like
those of Raphael et al.: "Studies have shown that instruction can have
joint benefits for reading and writing achievement, but studies have
generally lacked the detailed description necessary to allow such findings to be applied to instructional practice" (p. 258).

In the past decade, cognitive approaches continue inform research on reading and writing connections. Valeri-Gold and Deming
(2000) explain that higher-order thinking processes are characteristic
of strong college readers and writers who integrate reasoning, recognizing patterns of organization, and synthesizing the author's ideas.
While some scholars found that proficient readers and writers use
the same cognitive skills for both reading and writing, other recent
psychological studies suggest limits to the brain's ability to juggle too
much information at once. One such study, conducted by James and
Gauthier (2009), investigated the effect of writing on the concurrent
visual perception of letters. Among other findings, their research suggests a strong connection between the perception of letters and the
neural substrates engaged during writing. While connections between
reading and writing may exist in a variety of ways, the brain does
not necessarily wholly process the functions of reading and writing in
similarly.

Psycholinguist Frank Smith (2004) is an essential contributor to
reading theory and to research on the nature of the reading process,
particularly in developing the whole language movement. Whole
language takes a constructivist approach to knowledge, focusing on
knowledge creation. As such, this approach reflects the second model
of inquiry, viewing both reading and writing as generative processes
of production—making meaning in reading and expressing meaning
in writing. Together, Smith and Kenneth S. Goodman developed the
single reading process that comprises an interaction between reader,
text, and language. On the other hand, French neuroscientist Dehaene
(2009) studied how the brain developed, biologically, the surprising

and unlikely ability to read. Based on his findings, he criticizes the Piagetian whole language approach to teaching reading, arguing that the brain is constructed to better comprehend how pairs or groups of letters correspond to speech sounds. Dehaene cites research suggesting that teaching methods incorporating multiple senses and motor gestures, such as tracing the outline of letters, helps students learn to read. Cognitive psychologists interested in brain function have found evidence suggesting exactly how reading and writing are connected. They continue to question whether these connections are correlational or causal.

What have cognitive theorists told us about the processes of reading and writing? Should we conclude that reading and writing development go hand in hand? Are the foundational abilities of reading and writing governed by the same underlying processes? Petrosky (1982) believes that a further examination of these processes will help us become more informed about human understanding:

> One of the most interesting results of connecting reading, literacy, and composition theory and pedagogy is that they yield similar explanations of human understanding as a process rooted in the individual's knowledge and feelings and characterized by the fundamental act of making meaning, whether it be through reading, responding, or writing. When we read, we comprehend by putting together impressions of the text with our personal, cultural, and contextual models of reality. When we write, we compose by making meaning from available information, our personal knowledge, and the cultural and contextual frames we happen to find ourselves in. Our theoretical understandings of these processes are convergent . . . around the central role of human understanding—be it of texts or the world—as a process of composing. (p. 34)

Petrosky's view of reading and writing connections suggests a conversational model where we construct meaning from a text while we construct a text to convey meaning.

Expressivist Approaches

Within expressivist approaches in composition studies, reading and writing connect by allowing students to take ownership of their ideas through self-expression. Instead of working to locate pre-existing meaning in prescribed texts written by others, readers actively participate in creating meaning, either in the language communities through which they define themselves (as progressivists argued), or by tapping into their own creative imaginations (as expressivists argued). Adler-Kassner (1998) explains that early progressive compositionists such as Fred Newton Scott, along with his students and colleagues like Gertrude Buck and Joseph Villiers Denney, "created the foundation for much contemporary composition pedagogy as they worked to move the field away from essays focused on literary texts and the repetition of elite knowledge" (p. 209). Later, notable scholars like Donald Murray, Peter Elbow, Donald Stewart, and others developed their own expressivist pedagogies from the 1960s to today: "Where progressivists like Scott argued that composition would bring students into the values of participatory democracy, expressivists implied that writing would help students unearth their genuine selves" (Adler-Kassner p. 218).

Also referred to as Piagetian/naturalist approaches, expressivist approaches primarily consider learners' innate cognitive structures. Unlike cognitive approaches, these theories emphasize the natural development of reading and writing through a whole language approach. Though Piaget's theory integrates cognitive approaches, it is, in theory and in practice, defined primarily as expressivist. Researchers taking this approach believe that learning to read and write is not a mastering of sub-skills, but an organic process of self-expression originating from oral language.

Reflexive writing is motivated by the writer's needs or desires, as opposed to a more school-based, teacher-controlled model (Emig, 1971). Because the Piagetian approach stresses the importance of self in finding meaning when reading and writing, students are free to imagine alternatives to their own and others' cultural hierarchies and status quo (Emig, 1983).

Adler-Kassner (1998) cites an expressivist description of the complex interaction of reading and writing:

> In "The Interior View," Murray described the process of making the transition from writer to reader as one where a writer ceases communicating with him- or herself and begins communicating with readers. This process was effective, he said, only if the writer owned the experience at the center of the

writing, "if the words on the writer's page reveal the writer's meaning to himself through language." If this ownership of voice and representation was achieved, the product would "reveal what he has discovered to others . . . He doesn't want the reader to read language, he wants the reader to pass through the writer's own experience of discovery." (as cited in Adler-Kassner, 1998, p. 223)

The reader-response critical approach emerges from an expressivist approach, treating the reader as creator. The primary focus falls on the reader and the process of reading rather than on the author or the text.

Kathleen McCormick (1994) classifies reader-response theorists as promoting an "expressive" model of reading, a model wherein reading is perceived "primarily as an activity in which readers create their own 'personal' or 'subjective' meanings from the texts they read" (p. 30). According to Elbow (1968), the roles of both the writer and reader are defined through an expressive process of ownership. Writing is connected to reading because the writer has to imagine the role of reader in the act of composing: "The student's best language skills are brought out and developed when writing is considered as words on paper designed to produce a specific effect in a specific reader" (p. 119). That "effect," he said, should be to have the reader share the writer's "quality of experience." When reading good writing, he argued, "meanings jump immediately and automatically into the reader's head." The reader should "[feel] the writer in the words . . . [and believe] that the writer believes it" (pp. 119–22).

One popular instructional tool deriving from the reader-response approach in first year composition is the writing workshop model where peer readers respond to peer writers. Favored within expressivist approaches, this model also embraces the important connections between reading and writing because both acts are perceived as knowledge-making. Although reader-response theory and the writing workshop model both concern themselves with reading and writing interactions, each emphasizes one over the other. Jackson (2009) notes "Based on Rosenblatt's 1938 idea of meaning occurring as a transaction between the reader and text, the reader-response method expanded on the cognitive perspective by bringing attention to what the reader brings to a text" (p. 149).

The writer, then, becomes much more decentralized in reader-response theories. On the other hand, while the workshop model acknowledges the role of the reader and of audience awareness in a collaborative writing process, the approach still emphasizes the role of the writer over the reader in a community context.

According to Tompkins (1980), reader-response theories provide "a way of conceiving texts and readers that reorganizes the distinctions between them" so that, basically, "[r]eading and writing join hands, change places, and finally become distinguishable only as two names for the same activity" (p. x). Nelson and Calfee (1998) suggest the reader-response approach resulted in more expressive forms of writing, such as journaling and response papers, instead of the more analytical critiques of texts. According to Harkin (2005) and Nelson and Calfee (1998), at the primary and secondary education levels, reader-response "still holds sway," but at the college level, it has been replaced by "newer models of critical theory such as feminism, queer theory, and cultural studies, which use identity as a lens for analysis" (as cited in Jackson, 2009, p. 149).

As the twentieth century came to a close, disagreements about the connections of reading and writing continued to hold sway. At the 1991 CCCC, Peter Elbow and David Bartholomae engaged in a famous public debate about the authority of the writer and the role of literature in writing courses. They presented alternate perspectives of first year composition goals in speeches that were later published in *College Composition and Communication* in 1995. The debate centered on personal versus academic writing, reflecting the historical clash between expressivism and constructivism. The former approach situates writing as a product of the mind, while the latter situates writing as an external discourse. Each reflects different conceptions about the ways in which reading and writing are connected.

Elbow (2000) privileges writing-to-read methods in which the text produced through the generative act of composing is then used as the central classroom text to be read. He argues that student writers should produce the texts they work with and that they should not rely on reading textbooks written by others as they learn to write. In short, Elbow challenges the assumption that the role of writing is to serve reading. He argues that the act of writing inherently requires greater levels of action and agency than reading. Adopting the first model of inquiry of consumption versus production, he contends that writing and studying literature are indeed two separate "territories." Interested in questioning the authority of literary writers, he insists on putting imaginative student writing first, before reading. He justifies this approach by claiming it is important to "dispel the myth that texts are magically produced" (p. 363).

In their groundbreaking textbook, *Ways of Reading*, David Bartholomae and Anthony Petrosky (2005) ask students to engage as "strong readers" by assimilating themselves into the conversation of texts. According to Jolliffe (2007), the authors send a clear message about what they believe is the definition and function of reading:

> Reading is an active, constructive process that calls for the reader to juggle nimbly the following tasks: accepting a text's emergent meaning, resisting any pat formulation of the central idea, and assimilating the text's ideas in one's own view of the world. (pp. 474–75)

Gleason (2001) reduces the Elbow-Bartholomae debate to one central question: "Should first year college writing courses immerse students in academic writing, or should these courses encourage students to become writers?" (p. 1).

In support of academic writing as the goal, Bartholomae (1995) contends that students are embedded in a "linguistic present" that they should know about and work within as writers. Bartholomae argues for classes that entail critical reading, writing, and "struggling with the problems of quotation, citation, and paraphrase" (p. 66). Taking issue with this initial emphasis on academic reading and writing, Elbow argues that becoming an academic is different from becoming a writer; i.e., many "academics" are not confident or effective writers, and many "writers" are not academics at all. Elbow (1995) explains, "I see specific conflicts in how to design and teach my first year writing course. And since I feel forced to choose—I choose the goal of writer over that of academic" (p. 73).

Bartholomae and other critics of the expressivist approach often point to the lack of attention to the influences of both cultural contexts and the role of the instructor on reading and writing practices. Those embracing a social-cultural approach, for instance, believe reading and writing connections can be explored best by considering social contexts. As readers write and writers read, scholars embracing this approach examine the social interactions of these language practices. In sum, as Bartholomae and Petrosky (1996) contend, "you make your mark on a book and it makes its mark on you" (p. 1).

Expressivist approaches to reading and writing connections eventually gave way to a socio-constructivist approach, embraced by scholars such as Bartholomae. Concerns of how the reader and the writer are situated in influential social and cultural language contexts now dominated discussions about the connections between reading and writing.

The Turn of the Century: The Social Turn

At the turn of the century, researchers continued their interest in writing and reading as distinct but interdependent acts, while an interest in literacy grew. New definitions of literacy emphasized socio-cultural and political approaches. Mulititeracy practices, critical pedagogy, and the discourse community movements have challenged many educators to re-examine, among other practices, the role of reading instruction in the writing classroom. Innovative definitions of the term "literacy" emerged in the 1990s, providing new dimensions for thinking about reading and writing connections. Literacy no longer simply meant the ability to read and write; a much broader cultural definitions of the term brought new political concerns to college English. In 1994, the New London Group, a group of ten scholars in the field of literacy studies, coined the term "multiliteracies" to capture both the expanding nature of literacy studies and the dynamic nature of language as it is shaped by culture (Cope & Kalantzis, 2000).

James Paul Gee (2010) explains that new literacy studies is different from the cognitive approach taken by psychologists, who typically examine reading and writing relationships exclusively in the realm of mental processes. Gee argues that literacy is instead an external process, not done inside people's heads but in society, that literacy is about "ways of participating in social and cultural groups" (p. 166). This distinction calls for the need to understand relationships between writing and reading in all their contexts: "not just cognitive, but also social, cultural, historical, and institutional" (p. 166).

Practices of critical literacy, also referred to as resistant readings or reading against texts, grew out of Marxist ideologies and the social justice pedagogy of Paulo Freire (1968/2007). Reading and writing connections made within a framework of Freirean critical literacy examine the ways in which literacy can be used to balance social inequities and address societal problems caused by abuse of power: "Critical literacy views readers as active participants in the reading process; it invites them to move beyond passively reading texts to question, examine and evaluate the relations between readers and authors. It promotes reflection, transformation and action" (Freire, 1970, p. 36). Freire advocated for agency in adult education programs in Brazil, teaching reading and writing as interdependent skills focusing on the examination, analysis, and deconstruction of texts (Hagood, 2002). Resistant readings like Freire's foreground issues of power, asking readers to consider the connections between self and text. This approach questions whose text and whose agency are being considered, along with what assumptions are being made about the reader's knowledge and experiences.

Falk-Ross (2001) examined reading and writing connections in a critical literacy study focused on improving critical reading at the college level. She followed four first-generation college students in a course entitled "College Reading," where they were taught reading comprehension through a reading-writing-research connection model that included independent and shared reading events. The data sources for this study included field notes of class activities, participant observations, taped discussions, and student journal entries. Falk-Ross says the findings of the study suggested that students struggled with writing about their reading, but she concludes that reading-writing connections did, in effect, produce better writing.

> In addition to difficulties with reading comprehension, several students in the class had problems with writing organization, quality, and quantity. As a result, they were still having trouble writing their thoughts about how they approached reading assignments as the semester ended. (p. 284)

However, she does "notice progress in their thinking about reading and in their critical stances" (p. 284).

Another direction of new literacy, the discourse community movement, turned the conversation of reading and writing transactions to the topic of public forums and to how language is used by certain groups—defined by geography, socioeconomics, professions, age, race, or any other number of social factors. Bizzell (1992) suggests that "discourse community" definitions need to be further expanded by "acknowledging that discourse community membership implicates people in *interpretative* activities" (p. 222). For Bizzell, relationships between reading and writing need to be examined in the context of the cultural politics of literacy. Bizzell refers to linguist John Swales, who believes discourse communities should accomplish work as a "public goal" in the social world to which they belong. To do so, members of a discourse community must establish a discursive "forum" available to all participants: "Oral, visual, and/or print media may be involved," and "the group must use its forum to work toward its goal by "providing information and feedback (as cited in Bizzell, 1992, p. 225). For Bizzell, since discourse communities "implicate people in interpretative activities," the relationship between reading and writing foregrounds as an awareness of how a text is read within a community, and how a writer then responds to that reading within a community. Swales (1987) explains: "The discourse community has developed and continues to develop discoursal expectations. These may involve appropriacy of topics, the form, function and positioning of discoursal elements, and the role texts play in the operation of the discourse community" (p. 5).

Brandt (1986) and Gee (1999) were among many scholars who turned their attention specifically toward the socio-cultural and political contexts of reading and writing practices. Their inquiries questioned earlier assumptions about reading and writing connections that failed to consider historical and cultural contexts.

Brandt (2001) examines "sponsors of literacy," defined as "any agents, local or distant, concrete or abstracts, who enable, support, teach, and model, as well as recruit, regulate, suppress, or withhold literacy—and gain advantage by it in some way" (p. 19). Brandt (1986) suggests that "discourse communities enact the internal conversations" that take place "between the reader and the author and blur the distinctions between the writer as participant and the reader as spectator" (p. 2). Reading and writing connections, in Brandt's view of literacy, should be considered insofar as how they work as a "valuable—and volatile property" (p. 2) that can potentially help individuals gain "power or pleasure, [accrue] information, civil rights, education, spirituality, status, [and] money" (p. 7). Kathleen McCormick (2003) agrees that composition courses should teach reading practices that help students challenge dominant ideological discourses: "We need to think critically about some of the ways in which our students have been situated as reading subjects within our culture—well before we meet them in college" (p. 28).

Not to be confused with expressivist versions of reader-response discussed earlier, social constructivist versions of reader response consider an individual's social experience to inform his or her understanding of a text. For instance, Stanley Fish (1980) analyzed what he called "interpretive communities," examining how the interpretation of a text is determined by each reader's distinctive subjective experience within one or more communities defined by their own, unique epistemologies. While many social constructivists like Fish take a basic reader-response approach, examining what readers and writers bring to a text from the lens of their individual cultural backgrounds, Cope and Kalantzis (2000) examine the flip-side, exploring how reading and writing particular texts influences and shapes students. Popular in the 1970s and 1980s, reception theory subscribes to the tenets of reader-response theory. Reception theorists believe meaning in a text occurs when a group of readers who have a shared cultural background interpret the text in a similar way. The assumption is that the less shared heritage a reader has with the author, the less he or she will recognize the author's intended meaning. Moreover, if two readers have widely divergent cultural and personal experiences, their reading of a text varies to a large degree.

Reception theory investigates how reading and writing texts influences what Harkin (2005) calls "specific classes of readers" (p. 411). Specifically, Gee (2003) argues that reading and writing are often perceived simply as "mental achievements" going on in people's minds, but literary practices are social and cultural practices, and as such, should really be perceived more for their "economic, historical, and political implications" (p. 8). Wallace (2006) addresses the need to examine assumptions of commonality and shared experience and focus instead on the cultural differences between individual's reading and writing practices. Many courses that implement a service learning or community writing partnership component were born from this approach. For instance, Deans (2000) combines reading-to-write and writing-to-read instruction with community action in his service learning approach. Deans discusses how service learning is important not only to first year, upper-division, and technical writing courses, but also to critical pedagogy, writing across the curriculum, ethics, and literacy in general.

On the other hand, scholars such as Himley (2007) make the case that instructors should move beyond the idea that it is their responsibility to "invoke social justice" in the classrooms (p. 452). Critics of the social constructivist approach point out the difficulty of testing the complex relationships among individuals, contexts, and texts. Some claim the role of the learner is overlooked (McCarthy & Raphael, 1992, p. 20). Moreover, Elbow (2002) finds that this approach does not often easily achieve its purported goal of grounding students in cultural contexts:

> Teachers in the newer and powerful tradition of cultural studies usually *do* try to help students use texts for making sense of their lives (and often seek texts that students feel as part of their lives already—such as popular music or TV). But even here, I often sense the tradition of distancing. The goal in cultural studies tends to be to help students read with more critical detachment—to separate themselves from felt involvement in these texts. (p. 538)

Elbow argues that good critical readers and writers can make cultural connections, "but most students need help achieving this kind of personal entanglement with texts" (p. 538).

THE TWENTY-FIRST CENTURY: TECHNOLOGY AND NEW MEDIA

Because of the broad recognition that the connection of reading and writing plays an important role in student success, researchers in the twenty-first century have revisited a variety of theoretical approaches, re-examining the role of reading instruction in first year writing classrooms. Helmers (2003) suggests "researchers, teachers, and students should analyze . . . popular attitudes toward reading . . . to find out how they influence attitudes toward reading that appear later in the classroom" (p. 19). Making connections (and disconnections) between reading and writing needs to happen across disciplines and at all levels of education, including first year composition.

Near the turn of the twenty-first century, the technology revolution brought to the table discussions about how computers and other electronic media affect reading, writing, communication, and their interactions. Reading and writing research has focused increasingly on literacy practices that consider electronic contexts, such as the use of computers, the Internet, cell phones, and other popular, hand-held communication devices. A distinct definition of media literacy has proven to be a moving target, determined largely through multiple theoretical and interdisciplinary approaches. For instance, taking a cognitive approach, scholars explored brain function in relation to reading and writing on computers. Neuroscientists find that the ways our brains process language have profound implications for how we read and write. Expressivist theorists examined how readers and writers are more or less able to articulate ideas in the new electronic arena, and socio-cultural theorists considered how technological contexts affect the construction of cultural identities.

Hawisher, Selfe, Moraski, and Pearson (2004) argue for the importance of situating technology literacies within a defined "cultural ecology," or specific cultural, material, educational, and familial contexts that influence, and are influenced by, the acquisition, development, and interplay of reading and writing skills. Certainly, contexts have become a central concern as investigations into the connections of reading and writing in the new media age have expanded to include not just texts, but moving images and their multimodal interrelations. Similarly, Dewitt's (2001) cognitive study suggests that using hypertext on the Web creates more integrated active reading and writing practices, increasing students' metacognition. Electronic forums provide more agency for readers to write on blog walls or in comment forums. Conversely, writers are constantly being transformed as they read, with multiple "windows" influencing their composing process.

Fleckenstein (2004) defines the interaction of images and words as a "polymorphic literacy," or "reading and writing that draw on verbal and nonverbal ways of shaping meaning" (p. 613). This kind of literacy emphasizes the concept of place in learning environments. Fleckenstein suggests that instructors help their students attain a more polymorphic literacy by first increasing awareness of place by writing about their environments. Instructors can then invite critique through graphic design, analyzing the constraints of place on speaking, reading, and writing. Finally, she argues, through connecting graphic, verbal, and mental imagery with language, students can better understand visual-kinesthetic maps.

Hill (2003) stresses the importance of bridging the generational gap between instructors fluent in textual literacy versus students steeped in visual literacy. Teachers can bridge this gap, he suggests, through teaching writing in response to reading visual rhetoric. Definitions of "reading" have often been expanded to include not just printed texts, but also various images on digital screens.

However, Jackson (2009) points out problematic challenges hypertext presents. She says readers must sift through an enormous amount of hypertext documents on the Internet, forcing them "to reconcile contradictions, disconnects, and slippages they run across as they encounter multiple perspectives. Because there is no vetting process on the Internet, readers need to call into question the authority of texts and to examine bias" (pp. 164–65). Jackson questions whether readers really employ these active reading strategies, or if they simply passively accept what they read on the Internet, contradictions and all. Because of the lack of a focused reading strategy on the Web, she suggests students' writing performances typically also reflect weaker reading performances.

Ensslin (2007) also addresses the concern about how reading-writing relationships will be affected since he believes that students are not prepared for the critical task of sorting through reading material on the Web. He suggests helping readers navigate complex hypertexts, or "intelligent hyperdocuments," creating more meaningful literacy experiences. In addition, Pugh, Pawan, and Antomarchi (2000) conclude that "Maneuvering hypertext may well define what it means to be literate in the next century" (p. 36). Overall, exactly how reading and writing are connected in hypertextual contexts requires much more exploration.

New media has shifted what was once perceived as classroom distractions to the center of learning. Personal blogs, podcasts, and even text-messages are becoming topics for discussing reading and writing connections in the Information Age. One particular innovation, the study of massively multiplayer online role-playing games (MMORPGs), situates reading and writing processes within specific communities, claiming their own unique socio-cultural discourses. Real-time interactions with author and audience are created, and the act of reading and writing narratives results in a socialized production of texts. In these electronic contexts, the relationships between reading and writing processes become multi-layered and highly interdependent. Ramey (2004) uses the term "mediatext" to define the combination of image and text; however, Jackson (2009) argues Ramey's definition should also "describe the integration of the written word, pictures, graphics, video, and sound that mark the new literary products" (p. 166). Lewis and Fabos (2005) point out that even words themselves are shifting through their use in text messages and in IMs (instant messages), requiring of readers and writers a new variety of audience awareness and code-shifting.

Kress (2003) recognizes the connection between reading and writing, examining these literacy practices in the new media age. He asks how we might incorporate old and new teaching paradigms to best teach reading and writing in college composition courses. He asks also how we might incorporate new electronic modes of literacy to teach the critical thinking and active, imaginative responses that he, like many others, associates with reading longer, printed texts and with writing essays.

Gee (2003) suggests as well that new directions of literacy practices, such as computer gaming, can be used in the classroom to promote critical learning. Alexander (2009) explains that Gee's study identifies thirty-six different "learning principles" that computer gaming promotes, such as the "text principle," the "intertextual principle," and the "multimodal principle," in which participants learn how to read, understand, and manipulate a variety of texts in a variety of circumstances. According to Alexander,

> [Gee] believes that gamers/learners will learn all the more effectively and powerfully as they not only master the skills necessary to game but also experiment with the rules of the games they play, creating new skills and literacies in the process. (p. 39)

As a result, reading and writing in the first year college classroom has the potential for much more participation and agency than its print-bound counterpart.

Hawisher and Selfe (2007) collected life histories of computer gamers, asking participants to reflect on how they believe gaming influenced their literacy skills. The authors raise questions concerning the social dimensions of community building and how definitions of the cultural identities of race, gender, sex, and age are influenced. Hawisher and Selfe (2006) explain that both local and global communities are continually expanding and redefining their literacy practices as computers bring people together from all over the world. They argue that "the relationships among digital technologies, language, literacy, and an array of opportunities are complexly structured and articulated within a constellation of existing social, cultural, economic, historical, and ideological factors that constitute a cultural ecology of literacy" (p.

619). These new, dynamic relationships continue to be investigated by theorists interested in exploring how technologies might help or hinder students as they engage in reading and writing practices.

Theory and research across the disciplines in the past decade call into question the ways we traditionally defined and taught reading and writing. The revolutionary technological contexts in which students practice these skills create many new implications for how to examine the relationships between reading and writing. Current literacy practices suggest that the meaning-making processes in reading and writing can influence each other in more dynamic ways than ever before imagined. Many new questions about computer literacy, including composing with computers in a variety of contexts, and the acquisition of literacy through popular trends such as gaming devices, have challenged educators to re-evaluate their resources and strategies to help students become better readers and writers in ever-shifting electronic environments.

Conclusion

While most scholars focus on investigations related to the similarities and connections between reading and writing, some emphasize the importance of examining their differences. Two decades ago, Tierney (1992) announced that he felt cautiously optimistic about future research concerning reading/writing relationships, adding he had "a small word of warning to offer":

> I encourage researchers and practitioners to pull back from their enamorment with reading/writing connections to consider the drawbacks. Sometimes, writing and reading may stifle rather than empower. We should try to understand how and in what situations reading and writing contribute to didacticism versus dialogue, rigidity rather than flexibility, entrenchment rather than exploration, paraphrasing or plagiarism as opposed to new texts. (p. 258)

Many have answered this call for understanding differences, suggesting other variables that may be at play. Some conclude that certain correlations may have been too narrow or broad in their examinations. Others find that while, indeed, there are distinct similarities between reading and writing, the two are not the same, and should not be treated as such in composition classrooms.

For instance, while Emig (1983) defines both acts of reading and writing as generative, as acts of creation, she also differentiates between the two. The greatest difference, she argues, is "writing is originating," and reading is not (p. 124). Elbow (2000) makes a similar point that the act of writing inherently requires greater levels of action and agency than reading. Based on a review of several earlier studies, Langer and Flihan (2000) conclude that we cannot assume strong readers are strong writers, nor are advanced writers necessarily good readers.

Fitzgerald and Shanahan (2000) find similar disconnections in their research on reading-writing relations, arguing that they vary at different developmental stages. They argue that there are many elements of shared knowledge in reading and writing; however, "as connected as reading and writing are, they are also cognitively quite separate" (p. 42). As part of their investigation, Fitzgerald and Shanahan examined studies of various individuals who suffered a brain injury. Some patients were able to attain or to regain their reading skills only, while others could write, but not read. The fundamental difference between reading and writing, they say, is the ability to choose. Readers have less choice, limited by the writer's words; whereas, writers have many options—they choose the words they use to compose.

Miller (1997) is concerned that writing courses rely too heavily on cultural studies critiques. She argues that textual interpretation, or "reading," is *not* "writing" (p. 499). Her concern appears to stem from an assumption that current pedagogies drawn from a cultural studies ignore writing instruction by teaching students to interpret rather than to write.

While some research acknowledges differences between reading and writing, most scholarship, whether taking a cognitive, expressivist, or social constructivist approach, suggests a strong correlation between proficiency levels in reading and writing. In his presidential address at the 1982 MLA conference, Wayne Booth called for the coming together of composition and literature, providing one method for bridging the gap in the discipline by bringing together the divergent skills of reading and writing.

What is the importance of examining what we know and what we don't know about the connections of reading and writing? Petrosky (1982) argued that "reading, responding, and composing are aspects of understanding, and theories that attempt to account for them outside of their interactions with each other run the serious risk of building reductive modules of human understanding" (p. 20).

Traditionally, the theory, research, and praxis of reading and writing have been treated separately in higher education in the U.S. As a result, programs and curricula for each have evolved in separate disciplines without much dialogue. This divide continues to occur despite prevailing beliefs among educators that suggest an inherent relationship between reading and writing. Much literature has addressed the subject of reading and writing as psycholinguistic processes of reception and generation. However, due to the bifurcation of these topics, most scholars and educators have, historically, only indirectly addressed the deeper, inherent connections and relationships in their research and curricula. What Tierney and Leys (1986) argued in the 1980s still hold true today:

> In the past, what seems to have limited our appreciation of reading-writing relationships has been our perspective. In particular, a sentiment that there exists a general single correlational answer to the question of how reading and writing are related has pervaded much of our thinking. We are convinced that the study of reading-writing connections involves appreciating how reading and writing work together as tools for information storage and retrieval, discovery and logical thought, communication, and self-indulgence. Literacy is at a premium when an individual uses reading and writing in concert for such purposes. Indeed, having to justify the integration of reading and writing is tantamount to having to validate the nature and role of literacy in society. (pp. 23–24)

Whether scholars view reading and writing connections as consumption, production, or a conversational model that includes both, it is important for researchers to continue closely examining reading and writing relationships. One important implication of the recent literature and theory suggests that we are all—as college administrators, textbook authors, librarians, and faculty—responsible for creating collaborative programs and curricula designed for teaching reading and writing skills to our students, regardless of discipline. As reading and writing connections are further explored by us all, our students will have better opportunities to become more effective critical thinkers in a variety of contexts and environments.

3 How Other Nations Approach Reading and Writing

Jennifer Coon

In her work, "'Internationalization' and Composition Studies: Reorienting the Discourse," Christiane Donahue (2009) challenges us to look out from behind our own lenses to examine differing perspectives on the power of reading on the writing process. She suggests, "We might focus on internationalizing by opening up our understanding about what is happening elsewhere to adapt, resituate, perhaps decenter our contexts" (p. 215). To accomplish this, American educators may wonder how other countries regard reading as an influence on writing. Is it a bountiful relationship that marries literacy, job acquisition, use of technology, educational policies, etc.? Or, are they divorced acts, whose individual acquisition serves the purpose of functionality in an educational system that wishes for mastery of two separate skill sets? What influences student achievement in the international arena? Which countries are steering their students in the right direction? What can we learn?

It is the purpose of this chapter to aid in our understanding of international policies regarding the connections between reading and writing. We can merge this information with that of my fellow authors, who suggest that literacy is a combination of skills in both reading and writing—skills that should be applicable in any genre and context. How could data from Europe, Asia, South America, and Australia benefit us as writing and rhetoric instructors in the US? Through an international view, we can glean more understanding of how reading and writing are taught. A sample review of research studies and policies suggests that internationally, reading and writing tend to be treated and taught as separate skills.

GLOBALLY SPEAKING

In this chapter, I focus on three major studies that provide insight into how reading and writing are studied and taught internationally. The Programme for International Student Assessment (PISA) measures the accomplishments of fifteen-year-olds in several content areas. The Adult Literacy and Learning Survey (ALL) study by Statistics Canada and the Organization for Economic Co-operation and Development profiles literacy in multinationals from ages sixteen to sixty-five. The third study, International Reports on Literacy Research, by Mallozzi and Malloy (2007) from the *Reading Research Guide*, profiles foreign countries with data directly from the classroom.

PROGRAMME FOR INTERNATIONAL STUDENT ASSESSMENT

Several nations have been evaluated by the Organisation for Economic Co-operation and Development. This study, conducted every three years, is called the Programme for International Student Assessment (PISA), and involves fifteen-year-old boys and girls from thirty-four countries. The study measures and reports on young people's ability to use their knowledge and skills to meet real-life challenges (OECD, 2009).

The parameters of the study include the following:

- Policy orientation, which highlights differences in performance patterns and identifies features common to high performing students, schools and education systems . . . .
- Innovative concept of "literacy," which refers both to students' capacity to apply knowledge and skills in key subject areas and to their ability to analyze, reason and communicate effectively as they pose, interpret and solve problems in a variety of situations.
- Relevance to lifelong learning, which goes beyond assessing students' competencies in school subjects by asking them to report on their motivation[s] . . . .
- Regularity, which enables countries to monitor their progress in meeting key learning objectives.
- Breadth of geographical coverage and collaborative nature, which, in PISA 2009, encompasses the thirty-four OECD

member countries and forty-one partner countries and econo-
mies. (OECD, 2009, p. 3)

The latest version, from 2009, offers intriguing findings about the
reading and writing habits of a variety of international, multinational
students. Korea, Finland, and Canada are producing the most competent readers. Their students score well above a proficient level in
writing and several sub-categories of reading—levels ensuring the successful use of their socioeconomic status to lead productive lifestyles.
Some of the determining factors include: quality teachers with varied experience, rather than a high quantity of mediocre teachers; high
teacher salaries that affect student successes and achievement more
than small class sizes; student-teacher relations and a strong, positive
teacher attitude that ensures higher performing readers.

A student's gender can sharply affect his or her skills as a reader
and writer. The PISA found that "Girls outperform boys in reading
skills in every participating country"; in fact, girls scored almost four
times as high when measuring reading and literacy skills (2009, p.7).
In some countries, the research suggests, it was as if the girls had experienced one full year of additional instruction than the boys. In particular cases, the difference was as much as six years.

The PISA study found that students who talked with their parents
about life issues and current events had a better and wider knowledge
overall. Using one's parents as a sounding board for discussion seemed
to contribute to a well-rounded reader and writer;"The more discussion, such as in Turkey and Lithuania, the more literate the students
proved to be" (p. 10).

The PISA study also revealed a great deal about the importance of
transferring reading skills. Results showed that students who enjoyed
reading the most performed better than those who enjoyed reading
the least; reading a variety of materials, not just fiction, makes for
intelligent readers, and online reading and searching makes for better prepared readers than those who did not conduct these online activities. This study acknowledges the vital nature of reading readiness
and accepts it as a contributor to success in other realms, as countries
with students who do not read for pleasure at all scored lower on all
points of reading testing. Lastly, high-performing countries are also
those whose students generally know how to summarize information.

The PISA indicates that the highest functioning students are able
to utilize sophisticated skills that stem in reading and writing, but

flourish in research. Singapore, Shanghai, China, and New Zealand have a scant 1% of students who can access information in a new genre, understand secondary concepts not presented in material, gather data from multiple sources, manage new forms of text, synthesize several forms of data, and locate relevant text.

Adult Literacy and Life Skills Survey

The Adult Literacy and Life Skills Survey (ALL), conducted by the Organization for Economic Co-operation and Development (2003), is a report by thirty nations designed to investigate how one achieves skills in reading and writing and how those skills may be lost over time (p. 3). ALL is concerned with "assist[ing] individuals, educators, employers and other decision makers in four areas," including:

- Removing skill deficits that act as barriers to innovation, productivity and high rates of economic growth;
- Limiting and reversing social exclusion and income inequality;
- Reducing the unit cost of delivering public health care and education services;
- Improving quality in a broad range of contexts from public services to quality of life. (OECD)

ALL profiles several international learning environments, including those in Canada, Italy, Norway, and Mexico. They evaluated numeracy, information, and communication technology, and further describe four factors that may influence reading, writing, and researching skills:

- Prose literacy—the knowledge and skills needed to understand and use information from texts, including editorials, news stories, brochures, and instruction manuals.
- Document literacy—the knowledge and skills required to locate and use information contained in various formats, including job applications, payroll forms, transportation schedules, maps, tables, and charts.
- Numeracy—the knowledge and skills required to effectively manage the mathematical demands of diverse situations.
- Problem solving—Problem solving involves goal-directed thinking and action in situations for which no routine solu-

tion procedure is available. The problem solver has a more or less well-defined goal, but does not immediately know how to reach it. The incongruence of goals and admissible operators constitutes a problem. The understanding of the problem situation and its step-by-step transformation-based on planning and reasoning, constitute the process of problem solving (OECD).

The list above shows the necessity of having experience with text. Students must be made familiar with forms, maps, and brochures so they can, in turn, create their own when the time comes, either as an academic assignment or in the working world. In this way, reading and writing must be synonymous, and the reading must be varied and rich. These exposures will help build, in a budding writer, a foundation of knowledge from which to draw upon during intense problem-solving.

Overall, the results reflect an optimistic view of literacy and its practices in the marketplace:

> The footprint of good policy is evident in all countries surveyed. Bermuda is highly skilled and its population reports the highest level of health. Canada has succeeded in building equitably distributed [literacy] skills that have boosted productivity and growth. Italy has realized the most rapid improvement in skills benefiting the entire population. Norway has achieved uniformly high levels of skill, an inclusive society and is the closest to realizing lifelong learning for all. Nuevo Leon in Mexico has managed the most marked improvement in the quality of recent education output. Switzerland has lifted the performance of the least skilled the most. Proportionally to population size, the United States has built the largest pool of highly skilled adults in the world. (OECD, 2010, p. 4)

INTERNATIONAL REPORTS ON LITERACY RESEARCH

In 2007, Christine Mallozzi at the University of Kentucky, and Jacquelynn Malloy of George Mason University, surveyed foreign educational systems as part of the International Reports on Literacy Research to assess their use of a reading-writing relationship and subsequent successes and failures. While these results are not all-encompassing, they offer educators interested in global data a wide range of international perspectives. Global achievement in reading and writing serves as a framework for my discussion, and thus, several regions are profiled here: Italy, Hong Kong, Argentina, and Australia. These four countries provide a snapshot of varying regions of the globe.

Ten questions were used by Mallozzi and Malloy (2007) to gather data:

1. In your region, are reading and writing related in terms of literacy practice and research? If so, please describe how. If no, please explain why not.

2. How often are reading and writing given equal regard in terms of curriculum in your region?

3. How often is writing a focus of literacy instruction in your region of the world?

4. How often are reading and writing taught together in your region?

5. Do language differences influence writing instruction in your region?

6. Is writing instruction a major factor in assessment?

7. Are digital forms of writing included in the curriculum?

8. Do teachers in your region use digital technologies to teach writing?

9. In your region, does socioeconomic level influence students' purposes for writing?

10. What other comments might you wish to make about writing instruction in your region? (p. 161)

These questions were sent to international research correspondents (IRCs) in each region. The IRCs—all educators at the secondary or college levels—acted as reporters for their colleagues and institutions, compiling answers while crafting responses of their own classroom experiences.

Generally, these countries view reading and writing as disparate acts, a view that can be detrimental to shaping a skilled writer. Technology in the writing classroom is often lacking in these regions, and socioeconomic factors play a role in student success. Most notable here is the disparity with which the acts of reading and writing are viewed and practiced.

It helps to read and understand these countries' efforts to unite reading and writing skills with the following in mind. In 1997, Spivey proclaimed that

> in relation to the students' achievement levels, it is important to emphasize the fact that, not only in Chile, but also in several other Latin American countries as well as Spain and the United States, teaching practices currently in use do not seem to lead to the expected levels of language performance. (as cited in Parodi,2006, p. 240)

Such disheartening observations lead one to believe that instruction in reading and writing must go beyond the state-mandated guidelines. Countries that do not exceed these guidelines are failing their students. The discussion below indentifies the weak connections of reading and writing currently in practice around the globe.

International students need a place where literacy is a social practice, not just a technical skill to be practiced. It is about knowledge: The ways in which people address reading and writing are themselves rooted in conceptions of knowledge, identity, being (Street, 2001). We understand these to be fundamental in social culture.

READING AND WRITING INSTRUCTION IN ITALY

The report out of Italy states that reading and writing practices are two separate domains in both research and instructional practice. We discussed this concept earlier in Allison Harl's chapter on the historical practices of uniting reading and writing. Concurrent with the definitions put forth in this volume, Parodi (2006) claims that reading and writing are psycholinguistic processes. There is scant research, especially before 1970, but Parodi reports that significant correlations are found, and that the strongest links are detected at the levels of local cohesion and the micro structural. Parodi notes:

> Reading was essentially conceived as a receptive skill while writing was a productive one, so they were taught independently. Early testing focused on the wrong issues, thus it is important to point out that the concepts of discourse, comprehension, and production have evolved dramatically during the last few years. Modern concepts of written discourse

assign a central role to mental processes and the role of the reader/writer's previous knowledge. (p. 228)

Thus, according to Parodi, in Italy, the teaching of writing especially recognizes that texts inform one another. Spivey (1990) argues that if a written text is produced from particular sources, then the reader becomes a writer because the source text is transformed into a new text. The writer, while using other texts in the creation of a new one, employs constructive operations of organization, selection, and connection to elaborate meaning (Parodi, 2006). There is a complexity to the writing process we have not yet seen in other profiles. The layering of texts as information for future texts is a sophisticated skill for college writers.

Italy sees a movement toward reforming educational policy to include such nuanced and innovative concepts. Parodi (2006) notes that steps will be taken

> towards the consideration of discourse practices as the nucleus of the construction of meaning. Argumentation should be the focus of much investigation and the development of better teaching strategies. Also, the discourse approach in education should bring greater freedom in the access to knowledge and society. (p. 240)

Parodi must then agree that composition is best when preceded by discussion to flesh out topics and investigations. Yet, in the 1980s, Italian educators urged "text production rather than a writing process," giving way to writing as a discipline itself (Mallozzi, 2007, p. 165). Reading, as a central component, was not fully recognized as a substantial component of the learning to write process.

Grabe and Zhang write elsewhere in this volume that reading and writing are traditionally taught separately, and that reading is addressed more explicitly. The IRC in Italy reports that teachers see this relationship of reading to writing, yet make no strides to integrate them for struggling readers. Perhaps concurrent reading and composing could be a solution for Italy's student writers, as Belanger (1978) suggests. As early as the 1970s, he wrote,

> reading can provide a motive for writing. As one of many reasons for this to be a profitable relationship, students who are

readers are in fact writers. Thus, exposure and inspiration are ways reading is being used in the international classroom. (p. 73)

European teaching styles integrating reading/writing differ widely. For example, Isabel Sole (2001), an educator and researcher in Barcelona, Spain, experiences and reports on the relationship of reading and writing. They

> are procedures; to master them is to be able to read and write in a conventional form. To teach the procedures it is necessary to show, or demonstrate, their independent practice. In the same way teachers show how to mix paints to obtain a specific color, or how one should proceed to register the observations on the growth of a plant, they should be able to show that which they do when reading and writing. Some authors call this model demonstration. In essence, it is to offer the [student] the techniques, the secrets that the teacher uses when reading and writing, so he can gradually make them his own. (p. 54)

While acknowledging that mastery is the ultimate goal, Sole here advocates the appreciation of reading and writing as separate acts before they can be successfully combined by writing students. In accordance with the work of Boyarin (1993), Sole, along with her European counterparts, sees that writing skill develops with time and experience rather than with the more American-appreciated skills of exploration and attempt.

IRC reports that there is an effort in Italy to relate the instruction of reading and writing to literature studies. And while there is a conscious effort to give context to that type of instruction, writing and composition is conversely used as an "evaluation tool rather than outcome of a specific instruction" (Mallozzi & Malloy, 2007, p. 165). This design may still be at the forefront of international writing instruction, but it tends to differ from the ostensibly process-oriented writing instruction currently taught in American universities.

READING AND WRITING INSTRUCTION IN HONG KONG

In Hong Kong, students are expected to attend fourteen years of compulsory education, the final two of which bear resemblance to the first two years of U.S. college education. Instructors report that reading and writing are not often taught together during these final two years (Mallozzi & Malloy, 2007). Kucer (2009) identifies

> one of the most critical goals of the writer is to build internal coherence on a global level. As writers evolve their discourse, they attempt to work out the general semantic framework within which their more local meaning can be developed and attached. (p. 185)

In Hong Kong, integrated lessons are seen as complicated to teach and more demanding for many students; the effect is a failure to make a strong connection between reading and writing instruction (Mallozzi & Malloy, 2007). And while writing might show evidence of academic achievement, these scores and student knowledge could be increased by an integrative approach. This type of compartmentalized learning, instead of a holistic approach, may produce acceptable test scores, as national achievement scores are emphasized in this culture. One reason to maintain the high quality is that the allocation of funds at the local level is dependent on student achievement scores. Theoretical skills must be pragmatically applied so that today's writing students can, in the future, be adult writers. Hong Kong's students are also being prepared for a myriad of other writing tasks—especially those in the workplace.

READING AND WRITING INSTRUCTION IN ARGENTINA

Argentinean approaches to reading and writing also tend not to be integrated. According to the IRC, writing is not a part of literacy studies in Argentina, and reading and writing are not given equal treatment in the national educational plan (Mallozzi & Malloy, 2007, p. 164). If we use Horning and Kraemer's definition of reading (found earlier in this book), we can see that the focus of literacy is on perception and production, and that reading is the "same fundamental activity whether it is carried out with paper or digital texts." The Argentinean IRC reports that seldom are digital technologies used, and subsequently, students are unable to utilize their literacy skills in digital environments; thus, the blending of texts is difficult.

According to the IRC report, in Argentina, writing tends to be the completion of a written exercise; it is not the expression of content that allows students random, rather than processed, thoughts. Frequently, the creative aspect of writing—writing for answer, writing for pleasure, or writing for exploration—does not exist. Therefore, it is difficult to develop one's own voice, tone, and attitude toward a topic, issue, or problem. Developing writers do experience pressure, both in formulating their views and in writing about them, claims Badley (2009). Authenticity is then a matter of individuals of Argentina who are coming at things differently, taking hold of, owning, and using resources in their own ways.

We can also explore autonomous texts created by first year writing students and by individual experience to see how other countries function. Students in Argentina write with "decontextualized strategies." They organize their writing practice to produce autonomous texts. In contrast, Geisler (1994) reported on the perceptions and the transformations in British composition coursework. In the U.K., writing is assumed to lead to a deeper understanding, and reading and writing are measured by "competency, not . . . expertise" (p. 164). College writers are asked not for exploratory pieces, but to demonstrate their knowledge for a teacher or examiner. Geisler reports that 72% of student compositions rely on teacher prompts, and that 27% of student writing comes from personal experience.

Argentinean students are asked to complete written exercises as a form of writing. Mallozzi and Malloy (2007) report no elaborate envelopment in a traditional (by U.S. standards) writing process, and instead students are given less than one minute as prewriting for in-class assignments. Unfortunately, like so many other countries in the Mallozzi and Malloy survey, Argentinean students do not practice digital composition due to access. Literacy is an indicator of opportunity and status. Advantages clearly shape the path to literacy. In Argentina, literacy is a cultural practice (Mallozzi & Malloy, 2007).

By comparison, access to literacy opportunities in England is widely available. The British educational system does appreciate the movement to expand the writing process and its relationship to reading. Geisler (1994) reported evidence of skilled and practice-level writing, and that at the extreme, some students are "remarkably unengaged in the process of reproducing their knowledge in autonomous text" (p. 37). Britons understand that a developed text can lead to a deeper level of processing, but writing instructors are not seeing a deeper level of processing. They may be turning to modeling as a writing activity to direct students onto the right path of expression.

Reading and Writing Instruction in Australia

Australian reading and writing programs were evaluated at both the state and national levels; thus, the survey area included metropolitan and rural areas that observe variation in household incomes. Related to potential disparities at these two levels, Hall (2008) is concerned with achievement that might be measured in student learning when family income is low—rightly so, as accessing resources is a vital part of becoming a literate reader and writer. As Fleming points out elsewhere in this text, access to a variety of differing reading materials can sharpen reading strategies. Without exposure, students may suffer.

There are opportunities to write that appear only to the student who knows how to seek them out. Hall (2008) recognizes that students with more educational resources have more learning opportunities they can profit from, while wealthier students are already using these resources effectively. Students who understand how to gain access may be utilizing resources for writing activities that are based on higher-level thinking and collaborative work. Such access may make for better writers. So, can writers truly understand writing if they are not talking about it, planning it, compromising it, and constructing it—whether together or as peer writing tutors in what American classrooms have come to term the "writing workshop"? Hayes and Flower explore three components of writing in a workshop: planning, translating, and reviewing. Access to these "writing spaces" is dependent on quite a great deal of modification and discussion (as cited in Wengelin, Leitjten, & Van Wase, 2009). Workshop settings help readers in Australia to focus, sharpen, and then re-focus their audience and purpose, but only if they can find their way to it.

Astonishingly, in Australia, "writing" was reported from one instructor still as handwriting rather than composition; thus, many do not emphasize a relationship between reading and writing. Similarly, the national educational program describes literacy as reading alone. It is difficult to understand how these disconnects manifest in the classroom. Is the teacher caught between policy and theory? The IRC reporter for Australia writes that teacher knowledge is related to gaps in achievement, and the instructors who know audience and purpose stress the meta-language of writing (Mallozzi & Malloy, 2007). In "Critical Literacy in Australia: A Matter of Context and Standpoint," Allan Luke (2000) writes that

> Teaching pragmatic practices involves enabling students to read contexts of everyday use, assess how the technical features (e.g., genre, grammar, lexicon) of a text might be realized in these contexts and size up the variables, power relations and their options in that context. (p. 9)

Other tactics may be used, and as Wengelin, Leitjten, and Van Wase (2009) write, reflexive reading helps a writer understand their own writing. She suggests that reading while composing can accomplish clarity and develop inspiration. The college student writer is making constant decisions—constant connections—and needs to develop a terminology and ease that only some Australians writers are privileged to learn. So, as freshman writers are encouraged to participate with their own texts, they are reviewing their own work and reading to facilitate other parts of the writing process than revision. If a college writer, Australian or otherwise, reads their own emerging text as an approach to writing, they might look at their text to prompt content generation, to manage references, to maintain cohesion, and to engage in metacognitive strategies for revision (Wengelin et al., 2009). This connection, for simplicity's sake, could be labeled self-writing and self-reading. Yet, the Australian IRC reports that in classroom practice, gaps between ideal practices like self-reading and writing, and actual literacy practices, are wide and, at this moment, unmoving.

Australian students are subjected to assessment focused on writing. Fundamentally, the assessment is focused on the end product rather than any dynamic writing process (Mallozzi & Malloy, 2007). This equation, one that emphasizes the "functionality of writing of the quality of writing," seems askew to those of us who teach in American universities (Mallozzi & Malloy, 2007, p. 163).

CONCLUSION

By examining these four countries—Italy, China, Argentina, and Australia—we recognize the struggles of other countries as they work against educational policies, unequaled access, social and economic issues, and a pedagogy that divorces reading from writing. Evidence from Mallozzi and Malloy (2007) shows a strong push to develop academic writers, yet the above struggles—and most specifically, an unequal approach to instruction in reading and writing—leave students suffering as weak writers.

Factual data from the PISA study and the ALL survey prove that there are readers and writers with highly specialized skills in international countries, yet they must be supported and reinforced to maintain said skills. PISA data reiterates the need for autonomy when developing curricula that unites reading and writing to produce skilled communicators, and curriculum design that can be revisited, as we've learned that skill levels are not fixed for life.

A thoughtful way to close this examination might be to question what Americans are doing to strengthen the threads of the reading and writing bond and what can be learned from our international counterparts. We gain from an understanding of international writing, studies, and students; thus, we recognize their learning culture. Christiane Donahue (2009) suggests that "contrastive rhetorics have been primarily discussed from a U.S.-centric or at least Western Point of Departure," and hopefully, the emerging perspective will be slightly more global (p. 225).

Part II: Classrooms and Students

4 Writing and Reading Across the Curriculum: Best Practices and Practical Guidelines

Alice S. Horning

Although we built this book on the idea that reading and writing have been disconnected in theory and in practice and need to be rejoined, a fair amount of work has been done examining the relationship of reading and writing, offering practical suggestions for classroom work. The overall goal is to help students develop the strong reading skills that support and make good writing possible. This chapter offers a review of some of this work, particularly for classroom teachers looking for ways to work consistently on reading while helping students develop their writing. Reading is essential to success in all college courses, not only in writing courses. Because both reading and writing skills are essential to success in every discipline and in personal and professional realms, this chapter presents overall goals that warrant attention, and then focuses on specific approaches for both writing classes, such as first year composition and courses across the curriculum.

ISSUES AND PROBLEMS IN TEACHING READING WITH WRITING

In the United States, questions of how best to prepare teachers to teach reading and writing have been asked since the common school era of the 1830s. These same questions are asked today with much broader historical, social, and technological implications. There have been numerous proposals over the years about how to integrate reading and writing in the classroom. David Jolliffe (2007), a University of Arkansas scholar, leading researcher on college reading, and a contributor whose work appears in this book, argues that the problem for most instructors in teaching effective reading strategies in composition courses occurs because reading, as a topic, is typically delegated to other disciplines in most mainstream composition curriculums and pedagogical strategies. However, he believes writing program administrators and instructors can do several things to remedy this problem. One strategy entails incorporating several kinds of reading material, such as memoranda and reports, in addition to textbooks, that more realistically reflect the kinds of reading students do. Also, we need to determine our outcomes for reading in the writing class and work backward from them. After we have defined our outcomes for reading, we need to determine where exactly our students are as "critical, constructive, active readers" in relation to these goals. Diagnostic testing is one approach to finding clues. Finally, Jolliffe stresses we need to ask ourselves what techniques and strategies need to be taught as we help our students move from start to finish.

Some scholars find writing programs and pedagogies key in examining students' inability to fuse effective reading and writing practices. Many college instructors complain about how their students do not read the texts they are assigned, and even those who do are ill-equipped to fully comprehend the text or effectively integrate the material into a writing assignment. However, Jolliffe (2007) contends, "Students have to read in college composition, but rarely does anyone tell them how or why they should read" (p. 474). In fact, composition instructors often spend too much class time discussing the topic of a reading selection, effectively giving lessons on social issues like immigration or gender bias in popular music (culture issues about which they may be more or less informed). Too little time is devoted to explaining *how to* actively read an essay or *how to* transfer and assimilate the reading into effective composition. "The problem for these instructors," Jolliffe explains, "would be that most mainstream composition curriculums and pedagogical strategies aren't designed to achieve these goals" (p. 478). Since critical reading studies are often performed outside of college composition discourse, instructors do not have the required resources to implement more effective strategies.

Jolliffe (2007) argues that when the topic of reading as a curricular or pedagogical focus is actually taken up by instructors (and administrators and textbook authors), it is typically torn between two "diametrically opposed ends of a continuum of complexity" (p. 474).

On one end of the continuum, reading is reduced to lessons in study skills, or "search and capture" strategies of finding context clues and main and supporting ideas (p. 474). At the other end, reading assignments become overly complex for first year college students, requiring advanced analysis and interpretation skills. This kind of curriculum that promotes "strong reading" cannot represent the students' experiences in terms of how and what they actually read (pp. 475–76). Before looking at practical research in the categories set up by Jolliffe, there are some more general issues to consider, such as faculty skills and expertise with respect to reading, their ability to use what textbooks effectively provide, and the potential of developing collaborative relationships across disciplines and with library faculty.

Many instructors have a key problem in holding the skills and strategies to get students to complete an assigned reading. Good advice on how to achieve this end comes from Nilson (2010), director of Clemson's teaching and learning center, and author of *Teaching at Its Best*. In her chapter on reading, Nilson cautions faculty against lecturing on readings in class, and recommends "incentivizing" reading to encourage students. Using any one of a number of techniques (online responses, dialogue journals, quizzes, and the like), Nilson advocates making students' work with readings count no less than 20% of their course grade. The result of non-performance is significant if students do not complete reading-related tasks, so the likelihood of "reading compliance" is much greater (Nilson, 2010, pp. 21–22).

Doing the reading will not only help students use the reading in the ways enumerated by Jolliffe (2007), but can also provide them with an awareness of what formal and academic prose is supposed to sound like. Reading a substantial amount of non-fiction prose gives writers what language acquisition scholar Stephen Krashen (1983) calls the "din" of language—in this case, academic written language. Though Krashen wrote about second language learning and the need for exposure in order to have the sounds and syntactic patterns of the target language taken in by the learner, the concept also applies to learning to write. A number of years ago, I proposed that learning to write academic prose is, for an increasingly large number of students, like learning a foreign language (Horning, 1987). Whether in language learning or in learning to write, students need to have the sound patterns and sentence structures of the language they are trying to learn in their heads, through listening and especially through reading.

If teachers want students to produce solid academic prose, students must read such prose extensively and carefully for the "din" of that language to get into their heads. The absence of reading has a direct impact on students' writing, if their goal is to write in what might be called an academic voice. Moreover, better reading might help address the current plague of plagiarism in student writing in a range of courses and disciplines. I believe that true plagiarism is fundamentally a reading problem, not a writing problem or a problem of morals or ethics. I have argued elsewhere (Horning, 2011) that underlying true plagiarism (i.e., not simple theft or fraud) is an inability to read well enough to understand, analyze, synthesize, and evaluate sources and then use those sources in support of an argument. The problem appears not only in writing courses, but in courses in every discipline.

These issues require faculty to learn to teach and use reading in all courses. Callahan, Griffo, and Pearson (2009) emphasize the accountability teachers have in maintaining career and professional development. They dispel the myth that teaching reading is a simple process learned only through the experience of teaching, arguing instead that teachers are "made," not born, and current theory and research has a lot to teach teachers (p. 41). Likewise, Pearson (2007) argues that broad professional knowledge is a faculty responsibility, and teachers need to be willing to examine and change teaching practices to adapt to the changing needs of students.

Faculty must also consider carefully their book choices and uses in terms of how they address the reading-writing connection. Many researchers have found that textbooks used in the college composition course do not provide adequate approaches for helping students use their reading for writing, and vice versa. Harkin and Sosnoski (2003) accuse three popular argument textbooks of providing reading exercises that assume discovering authorial intention is the primary aim of reading. They argue students need to recognize that emotion and individualized readings create meaning in textbooks and other material. "We are not interested in some sort of return to 'pure' reader-response theory," they stress (p. 120–121). "On the contrary, we conclude by pleading for more respect for the intelligence students will bring to these texts. As teachers, should we not help our students see the unreasonableness of certain positions and the people who hold them?" (pp. 120–21). Fleming's discussion in a later chapter takes up this issue in detail.

Finally, the implications of recent studies suggest that educators from across disciplines and from the library need to recognize the importance of collaboration. Through the practical application of their various theoretical approaches, all faculty can strengthen both reading and writing practices by recognizing the connections between them. Haller and Drake discuss the possibilities elsewhere in this book.

In the past decade, anxiety over two reports from the National Endowment for the Arts have spurred much conversation and questioning about if, what, how, and why our students are reading. While findings from *Reading at Risk: A Survey of Literary Reading in America* (2004) and *To Read or Not to Read: A Question of National Consequence* (2007) indicate that Americans are losing interest in reading, particularly literature, more recent studies have fleshed out some issues about reading and writing connections more deeply. As John Schilb (2008), editor of *College English*, remarks, "To be sure, the findings can and have been challenged. Still, the reports serve to remind our discipline that teaching reading is a big thing we do so that we should continually ponder how to do it well" (p. 549). Jolliffe's critique provides a scheme for this pondering.

The Functions of Reading

In between the extremes of reading as a study skill and reading as a complex analysis of extended arguments, Jolliffe (2007) finds three functions of reading in the college composition course: (1) to promote critical thinking and writing (the "bounce off" function); (2) to model organizational patterns (the "reading-to-imitate development" function); and (3) to identify the general idea of a primary text for incorporation into the students' own arguments (the "digest-to-incorporate" function) (p. 477). Regardless of the chosen function, Jolliffe says, "no one is very clear about what reading is or does in such courses" (p. 477). These three functions set up an organizational structure in which to consider the research that has been done from a practical perspective.

The "Bounce off" Function

The first function of reading in writing courses discussed by Jolliffe is the "bounce off" function, where students are expected to read critically and use their reading as the basis for their writing. A number of studies support this kind of approach, showing that students who can engage in serious critical reading can effectively use sources in their writing. For example, Cynthia Haller (2010), another reading researcher whose contribution appears in this volume, has done three careful case studies to demonstrate that students' thorough, effective reading and engagement with sources produces a stronger, more rhetorically-based argument. In her study, Haller examined the ways in which three students incorporated source materials into their research writing. The students who went beyond simple reporting of data or summarizing evidence "established a new knowledge claim with a rhetorical argument" (p. 34), whereas the other students who simply used their sources for data or evidence were not able to do so. Students who learned to do careful critical reading produced much better writing.

Jolliffe and Harl (2008) come to a similar conclusion from their detailed study of a small group of University of Arkansas students, as discussed in the introduction to this book. After reviewing students' reading journals and other materials to see what first year students are reading and why, they suggest three program implications. First, they argue, faculty need to spend time teaching inter-textual connections. Second, faculty and administrators need to create curriculums, co-curriculums, and extra-curriculums that invite students to engage in their reading and connect texts to their lives, to the world they live in, and especially to other texts. (Learning communities and service learning opportunities are often useful for this purpose.) Finally, instructors should incorporate more technology into reading assignments to help students read critically in the electronic contexts they often prefer to textbooks.

Alexander (2009) agrees with this last implication especially, situating the idea of reading and writing in electronic contexts with more interactive, visual media. Based on research such as that of Hawisher & Selfe (2007), Alexander suggests that instructors can use massively multiplayer online role-playing games (MMORPGs) for guided reflections about literacy narratives of the present as they learn to play the game. Instructors might ask, "What kind of writing do you find yourself doing during game play?" or "What's the relationship between visuals and text (and writing) in game play?" Students could also become literacy researchers conducting field research about the reading and writing connections other gamers make. Alexander argues that students might even design their own MMORPG that would engage students as they practice multiple rhetorical activities, such as writing: proposals, literature reviews, audience analyses, position papers, and research proposals (p. 59). This approach builds on technology as the source of "bounce off" reading and writing.

Games are not the only source for "bounce off" work. A study by Peter Smagorinsky (1992), a literacy researcher at the University of Georgia, clearly shows that reading to improve student writing should take place in every discipline, and requires instructors' direction and supervision. Smagorinsky compared three groups of college students who either read models carefully; read them and received general instruction on composing procedures, like brainstorming and freewriting; or read them and received focused instruction on procedures needed to write like the model. Smagorinsky collected, transcribed, and analyzed think-aloud protocols from the composing work of six students in each group, where students spoke aloud about their work as they wrote. The findings showed that students who received instruction in combination with reading models showed significant improvement in the processes of critical thinking and composing. In every discipline, students needed to read more, but also needed instruction in how to use what they received from reading to improve their "bounce off" writing.

Recent research evidence supports this view. Bazerman et al. (2005) take up several studies in the writing across the curriculum (WAC) context that show the use of reading in the teaching and learning of writing. Drawing on the work of Risemberg (1996), Johns & Lenski (1997), and Haas (1993), Bazerman et al. (2005, pp. 54–56) explain that more extended reading of source materials has a direct, positive effect on the quality of writing produced. In addition, reading sources prior to writing also has a positive impact on writing produced. Furthermore, not only does the type of material read by students, such as reference works as opposed to trade books, but also the type of reading strategy used (i.e., careful reading rather than skimming) had a similarly positive impact on the quality of the writing students produced. Detailed studies of students' use of source materials in writing in the national research study called the Citation Project point clearly to students' weaknesses in reading. Papers analyzed in the project (174 drawn from a variety of institutions across the U.S.) show that students rarely use sources in ways that capture a full argument or that synthesize several sources in terms of their overall discussions (Howard, Rodrigue, & Serviss, 2010). If students are expected to "bounce off" the reading, faculty can use strategies discussed below to help them learn how to read well enough to do so.

READING TO IMITATE

Much attention has been given to the debate over using the "reading-to-imitate-development" function in the classroom, a second function for reading proposed by Jolliffe (2007). One example of this approach is teaching writing through rhetorical strategies such as comparison/contrast, definition, cause and effect, and so on, requiring students to read models that demonstrate these forms for the purpose of imitation. Prose (2006) argues that "not only does reducing writing into prose structures oversimplify the complexity of writing, as writers often employ multiple genres in their writing, but it assumes transfer between reading and writing will occur by 'osmosis'" (p. 3). Despite this critique, this approach is still widely used in composition textbooks and readers (see Fleming's chapter for illustrations of this point).

Foster (1997) also investigates the reading-to-imitate function, and his research surveys students' resistance to writing with such models. Foster's students mostly resisted modeling texts when they had the choice to write responses in the form of a personal essay instead. Foster was hesitant to conclude that reading/writing transferability does not generally work for students. Instead, his findings suggest that "students' willingness to enact this transferability is strongly affected by the pedagogical context of the task" (p. 537). Again, faculty approaches play a key role in reconnecting reading and writing in class.

READING TO DIGEST AND INCORPORATE

Students often write as they read by annotating, taking notes, and composing essays in response to assigned readings. Likewise, students read as they write and review their own drafts and those of their peers in collaborative workshops. While some scholars examine the processes of reading-to-write, others focus on writing-to-read. Bazerman (1980) suggests a "conversational model" for students to connect reading and writing through classroom practices by a process of first understanding reading content, then reacting to the reading, and finally evaluating the text to develop informed views on the issues.

Kathleen McCormick (2003) provides another practical approach, arguing that teachers start by meeting and validating students where they are, giving agency as they move toward becoming stronger critical, active readers. She suggests that after teachers acknowledge the specific personal experience and literacy practices individuals already bring to the classroom, they focus primarily on asking exactly how their students can acquire knowledge about what they *have not* lived. Students often have a difficult time with reading and writing connections because they do not share historical and cultural experiences with the texts they are assigned. They often struggle with producing and analyzing their ideas. Furthermore, McCormick says we can help students with symptomatic readings, as such readings help students understand cultural tensions and ideologies through an analysis of omissions, or what authors intentionally do not say. She suggests we help our students ask of themselves and write about three basic questions to bridge the gap from the street knowledge they already possess to the academic knowledge they strive to acquire: "What are their histories of reading?"; "How does the media encourage their reading?"; "What are their culture's dominant reading practices?"

Taking a different approach, Salvatori (2003) seeks to improve her students' reading through writing assignments situated in ambiguity and difficulty. She explains

> to name something as difficult is to demonstrate a form of knowledge, incipient perhaps, inchoate, not (yet) fully communicable, but knowledge nevertheless, and one that it is both profitable and responsible to tap into—whether to further develop or to "readjust" it. (p. 200)

Like Salvatori, Yancey (2004) stresses the importance of having students understand and actually chart their difficulties with reading surfaces. Most introductory literature or writing about literature courses end up teaching students about *readings* of texts rather than about *reading* texts (Jolliffe, 2007). However, Yancey (2004) provides a more effective approach as she examines three curriculums that students encounter in typical, introductory literature courses: the lived curriculum (i.e., students' own experiences with literature curriculum); the delivered curriculum (i.e., the syllabus); and the experienced curriculum (i.e., the course that is actually created rhetorically as students "read" the delivered curriculum and make it their own) (p. 17). Students map the way they read a text at the beginning and the end of the course. They generate their own questions and work collaboratively to answer them. Finally, the students use simple technology to create pop-up, multiple connections while reading.

Huffman's (2010) analysis of a handful of commonly-used composition textbooks supports the various approaches to the "digest and incorporate" function of reading. She analyzed the reading instruction and approaches of five different textbooks, in terms of six different functions of reading. Textbooks such as *Ways of Reading* and *Reading Culture* have all gone through multiple editions, indicative of their popularity and widespread use in the field. They represent both the "reader" approach (i.e., a compilation of readings with apparatus) and the "rhetoric" approach (i.e., using guidelines and processes) (Huffman, 2010, p. 164). The functions of reading include attentive, expressive, interpretive, evaluative, comparative, and projective (pp. 169–71). The interpretive function of reading entails understanding meaning and using it to answer questions or write analytically (p. 170). Close examination of five books shows that the most favored function is the interpretive, in terms of the books' approaches to pre- and post-reading (pp. 176–78).

Thus, it should be clear that plenty of research supports the "digest to incorporate" function of reading. Overall, the pragmatically-focused research offers a good array of support to connect reading and writing. Jolliffe's "bounce off," "reading to imitate," and "digest to incorporate" functions all find research backing. Teachers looking for Monday morning advice might find these various studies a little bewildering in terms of actual classroom use. Like a patient with a medical problem who hopes the doctor knows what the most current research findings are, teachers should be informed about the studies and findings that provide support for Monday morning approaches in class.

Monday Morning Goals

Reading and Writing in Writing Classes Monday Morning

The goal of helping students become efficient and effective critical readers who can analyze, synthesize, evaluate, and apply ideas and information can be achieved through specific strategies that can make faster, better reading possible for everyone. These strategies can be roughly divided into those useful in writing classes, such as first year composition, and those useful in classes across the curriculum. This division makes it easier to present the strategies in an organized fashion; in practice, some or all of them may be useful in either type of class.

Strategy One: Understanding Reading

As a first strategy, readers need to understand the nature of reading in both print and digital contexts. Effective reading is fast, not precise, and not strictly—or even mostly—a visual activity. These characteristics of reading are quite interesting and easily demonstrated with a few simple psycholinguistic exercises. Kenneth Goodman's (1996) work contains many examples of the right kinds of exercises, as does the work of Frank Smith (2004) and Steven Pinker (1994), such as the one from *The Language Instinct*, constructed long before text messaging became common. The example illustrates something of how redundancy works in language: "Thanks to the redundancy of language, yxx cxn xndxrstxnd whxt x xm wrxtxng xvxn xf x rxplxcx xll thx vxwxls wxth xn 'x' (t gts lttl hrdr f y dn't vn kn whr th vwls r)" (Pinker, 1994, p. 181). Psycholinguists can help teachers and students understand the nature of the reading process in ways that allow them to read faster and better. Goodman's (1996) *On Reading* includes exercises that show how readers rely on letter-sound relationships, sentence structures, and context to get meaning from print, rarely reading every word on a printed page. Understanding the nature of the reading process allows teachers to improve students' reading activities. Professional development of this kind is one approach mentioned in the NCTE Policy Research Brief (2011), and is an approach favored by Seattle University English professor and writing across the curriculum scholar, John Bean (2011).

Strategy Two: Overt Teaching of Critical Reading Skills

Readers must be taught specifically and overtly how to do critical reading so they can develop the key skills of critical literacy in all the reading they do. They must be able to analyze, including summarizing key points, the main ideas and the point of view of a writer. They must be able to synthesize, that is, draw ideas together from several sources to support their own views and ideas. In addition, readers should be able to evaluate what they read and judge authority, accuracy, relevance, timeliness, and bias. Finally, when readers can do all these things, they should then be able to apply information and ideas from their reading to their own writing, or for other purposes. There are a number of good guides to classroom activities that lead readers in this direction, including Bean's *Engaging Ideas* (2011, pp. 161–82), and Nilson's *Teaching at Its Best* (2010), along with Keene and Zimmermann's *Mosaic of Thought* (1997). Although the latter book is addressed to K–12 teachers, the strategies and approaches described, such as a reader's workshop that includes silent reading, a mini-lesson, workshop time for students to exchange responses and a whole-class exchange, can easily be used at the college level. Keene and Zimmermann advocate focused teaching of reading comprehension strategies to help move readers to critical literacy essential to successful reading in college and beyond. This approach can and should be expanded to include critical evaluation skills, speed, search capabilities, web page design, video conferencing skills, and other strategies that are essential for high levels of literacy in a digital age, according to Leu et al. (2004, p. 1589).

Strategy Three: Modeling by Reading Aloud

It's clear to most faculty that students do not read the way teachers think they should and the way teachers themselves read. One way to help students understand the kind of reading expected of them is to model it by reading aloud, showing students what they can and should be doing. This approach has shown by Coiro (2011) to be useful in working with online materials. In reading aloud, teachers can illustrate how to analyze, synthesize, evaluate, and apply ideas. They can also help students learn to deal with an array of "online cueing systems" now commonly used when texts are drawn from the Internet (Coiro, 2011, p. 109). These skills are crucial to careful reading of both print and Web-based sources; students definitely do not have them and definitely do need them.

Strategy Four: Intensive Reading Through the Use of Reading Guides

Teachers can also provide focused practice in reading in every assignment they give, building readers' skills over the course of every semester, through the use of a carefully constructed set of reading guides.

Examples are provided in Syracuse University education professor Harold Herber's *Teaching Reading in the Content Areas* (1978), an old but thoughtful approach to moving students from reading the lines of a text to reading between and beyond those lines (p. 56). Herber's procedures fit well with standard assessment techniques currently in widespread use: determining learning outcomes and creating reading guides to help students achieve those outcomes.

Herber advocates reading guides that first help students get literal meaning to develop basic comprehension and vocabulary. This is suitable, perhaps, for the introductory chapters of a textbook. He then suggests reading guides that move students to an interpretive level, where they must read to create, support, or respond to generalizations made by their texts. In this work, the kind of think-aloud approach suggested by Haswell et al. (1999) might be helpful. Finally, Herber recommends reading guides that help students apply concepts from the reading to broader issues and problems under discussion in the course, using material from the reading and other knowledge readers may have, from class discussion, from Internet sources, and from other materials. In my own experience using reading guides of this kind, I find that students become stronger readers over time, and that the reading guides serves as a basis of lively classroom discussion, small group work, and as a source of peer pressure to make sure students actually do the reading.

Strategy Five: Discourse Synthesis

The work of Carnegie Mellon reading scholar Nancy Spivey (1997) suggests additional types of reading and writing tasks that can support students' development as active readers and writers. Her studies of what she calls "discourse synthesis" offer opportunities for students to develop expert reading and writing abilities. Spivey defines discourse synthesis as

> the process in which writers are engaged when they read multiple texts and produce their own related texts" particularly for the purpose of the writing task and in which they use the texts they have read in some direct way. (p. 146)

Spivey conducted four studies of the discourse synthesis process, three of which involved undergraduates as participants, and one of which examined developing skills among younger students. These studies entailed having participants generate their own texts based on materials they were given to read. Participants were given a variety of rhetorical situations and audiences, such as preparing a research proposal or an informative article about a local event for newcomers to the area. Findings show that writers shape their meanings with organizational patterns, make selections on the basis of given criteria of relevance, and generate inferences that integrate material that might seem inconsistent or even contradictory (Spivey, 1997, p. 191). Discourse synthesis, a task common not only in college composition but also in disciplinary writing assignments, offers clear opportunities for students to practice reading more actively within their respective disciplines. This kind of task fits well with the NCTE Policy Research Brief (2011) that advocates the use of low stakes writing assignments to help students engage more fully with reading, as well as using a variety of texts at several of levels of difficulty (pp. 16–17).

Reading and Writing Across the Curriculum Monday Morning

All of the strategies discussed thus far are particularly well-suited to first year composition classes, regardless of individual teachers' preferred approaches or those required by a writing program. At many colleges and universities, students must complete additional coursework in writing at the upper level or within their chosen major. Whether these courses are officially labeled as "writing intensive" in the general education requirements, or whether they are required courses that incorporate writing in the discipline, these courses entail teaching writing, and can integrate and improve students' reading. In doing so, teachers can make use of the first five strategies discussed thus far. There are more strategies that can be especially helpful in discipline-based courses beyond first year writing.

Strategy Six: Scaffolding with Text Apparatus

Textbook writers and publishers spend fortunes providing supporting materials to help students read their texts efficiently and effectively. These materials are increasingly available online, as are a growing number of the texts themselves, thanks to the company called CourseSmart, a consortium of many of the major textbook publishers, including

Pearson, Cengage, McGraw-Hill, John Wiley, and Macmillan (Olsen, 2011; Eisenberg, 2011). While not all of these materials are useful and effective, some of them are. Their use of them can provide students with a kind of scaffolding, supporting stronger reading until students are able to read quickly and critically on their own. Teachers can review these materials and encourage or require students to use them if they are appropriate and helpful to the overall goal of improving reading. In a chapter of *Engaging Ideas* (2011) focused on reading issues called "Helping Students Read Difficult Texts," Bean supports this kind of approach, recommending an array of "low-stakes" writing tasks in conjunction with reading that moves students toward faster and more effective reading, such as: having students take notes that include writing "What It Says" and "What It Does" statements for each paragraph of an article (p. 170); summary-response notebooks (p. 178); interviews with the author (p. 179); and translations of complicated passages into ordinary language (pp. 179–80).

Strategy Seven: Scaffolding with Graphic Organizers

Research in second language learning suggests that students can improve their reading and learn about discourse structures useful to writing at the same time through the use of graphic organizers. Jiang and Grabe (2007), writing about teaching reading to ESL learners, discuss the usefulness of having students read to find text elements to put into visual diagrams that make clear their understanding of text structure. A series of boxes with arrows for a process text, or a t-shaped diagram for pros and cons of an argument, are two obvious examples. Graphic organizers allow students to see the organizational structure of a text as they work through the content. Bean (2011, p. 179) also points out the usefulness of this approach. For some students, a visual representation is more helpful than a traditional outline. In addition, having seen the visual layout of a particular discourse structure, students can use that same structure in their own writing.

Strategy Eight: Extensive Reading for Practice

Adults in the population at large, both students and others, are reading extended non-fiction prose less and less, as discussed in the studies presented in the introduction to this book. There is a clear need for more reading and more practice with focused critical reading. In my own teaching, I have created more reading practice, integrated with a writing task, in my outside reading assignment. My assignment requires that students read two books outside of class from a short list of choices of current books on topics related to those discussed in the course. They must also write about these books in reviews that summarize key ideas and tie them to concepts in the course, making cheating difficult. I grade these reviews, and they count in students' course grades for Nilson's (2010) recommended 20% of the course grade, so that they must do this work. The incentive is very important in getting students' compliance. The most interesting thing is that although I do not usually discuss the reading task in class beyond casual questions about their reading and their reactions to the books, this work has changed students' behavior, responsiveness, and level of engagement in every one of my classes, from developmental reading to graduate-level courses in psycholinguistics and sociolinguistics.

Strategy Nine: Learning to Read in Specific Disciplines

To be an expert reader in a particular subject area, students need to come to understand the genres and conventions of that discipline. In the natural and social sciences, for instance, understanding research reports that use typical APA form (Statement of Problem, Review of the Literature, Methodology, Results, Discussion, and Conclusion) is one way to facilitate reading in these areas. More detailed understanding of where an article fits in a body of work on a topic is also helpful to students and other readers. While teachers in any discipline already have an intuitive understanding of the discourse conventions of their discipline, several studies of reading practices within subject areas provide helpful background for discussion.

Literacy scholar Charles Bazerman's (1988) study of physicists' reading, for example, reports the reading approaches of seven practicing physicists in several different research fields within that discipline. In this study, Bazerman, who chairs the Department of Education at the University of California Santa Barbara, conducted detailed interviews with these scientists about their reading, and then observed them searching for and reading materials in their fields. Bazerman found a number of distinctive features of these scientists' reading: they have a clear purpose for their reading and rely on a schema, defined by Bazerman as "structured background knowledge" (p. 236). There is also useful research on the nature of communication patterns in different disciplines that is helpful to those teaching reading across the curriculum.

Bean (2011) takes up this point in his approach to helping students read difficult material, pointing out that students often lack an understanding of both the cultural and the rhetorical contexts for a text (pp. 172–73). Similarly, Sussex University professor Tony Becher's (1989) investigation of twelve different academic disciplines examines the nature of written and oral exchanges of ideas in the pure sciences, applied sciences, social sciences, humanities, and several other areas that do not fit into one of these recognized academic categories, including law, geography, and mathematics (p. 2). Across the disciplines, teachers can help students learn to recognize the discourse conventions of the texts produced in that field, and also learn to write them once they understand their conventions and expectations.

Strategy Ten: Learning to Read Critically on Screens

One kind of text that addresses students' need to deal with digital/visual as well as printed texts is Odell and Katz's *Writing in a Visual Age* (2004), a text and reader for college writing courses. In their presentation, Odell and Katz discuss the reading and analysis of web page elements: layout, including columns and spaces; page design, including tension and alignment; pictorial graphics, including photos and drawings; representational graphics, such as pie charts and bar graphs; and other features like color and font (p. 23). Their text provides multiple opportunities for students to read for writing using both print and digital materials. There is some discussion of other books that help students learn to read visuals (on screen or on paper), presented in Fleming's chapter on textbooks in this volume. Similarly, Kathleen Blake Yancey (2004a), a leader in college composition, pointed out in her Chair's address to the Conference on College Composition and Communication that students are increasingly working with texts of various kinds outside of school settings, and increasingly online. A full discussion of the implications of present and coming search strategies and other aspects of multimodal, online reading, and writing appears in the work of John Battelle (2005) and in Thomas Friedman's *The World is Flat* (2006).

Use of these strategies can help teachers improve students' reading in significant ways in writing courses and in courses across the disciplines. From the point of view of students, reading and writing has the potential to make all of their educational experience much more rewarding and successful. Reading is clearly the key to work in writing, and to courses and in every discipline. If students want to be successful in college and in their professional lives, more and better reading, together with writing, is essential. Thoughtful application of the strategies discussed here will provide the basis for student success across the curriculum. Teachers can make good use of practical research that has been done, and try the various strategies suggested here, to reconnect reading and writing in every class.

5 First Year Writers: Forward Movement, Backward Progress

Kathleen Skomski

Examining the connection between reading and writing for basic or developmental writers entering college as first year freshmen requires instructors to consider the reading, writing, and critical thinking skills they bring with them to the classroom, they need to move forward academically, and also the approaches teachers use in their classrooms to help students make the necessary connections.

UNDERSTANDING THE BASIC WRITER

Clearly, the transition for basic writers from high school to college is more problematic than it is for other first year students. Getting these students to reposition themselves in their freshman writing course by "switch[ing] allegiance from high school cliques to a more universal group of respected thinkers" (Haswell, 1991, p. 323) requires a deft approach by writing instructors who are wise to consider how these students perceive themselves and their own writing abilities. Shaughnessy (1977) explained, in *Errors and Expectations*, that "by the time he reaches college, the BW [basic writing] student both resents and resists his vulnerability as a writer" (p.7), and is so focused on the errors he knows he makes that concentrating on anything else is a challenge he can do nothing about. With that in mind, Sternglass (1977) maintained that we still must strive to understand the "whole" student to more fully assess existing reading and writing skills and the needs of beginning writers, or those considered "unprepared" or "underprepared." She proposed examining the external influences that impact learning and writing, such as home life and its connections to the learning environment, personal finances that influence students' abilities, and working hours that take up, in many instances, much of their free time, to get a clearer picture of these students and what they offer to and gain from the first year classroom. Likewise, Haswell (1991) noted that students are not "beginners, empty urns waiting to be filled, but already experienced, and their experience grows with each step of the course" (pp. 17–18). Flower (1994) refers to their literacy as "cultural capital" (p. 19) that can add to or detract from the learning experience.

Although writing theorists are optimistic about our ability to tap the potential of basic writers if we understand the contexts from which they come, recent research indicates there is much work to be done. The ACT's *Executive Summary* (2006) reports, that "based on 2005 ACT-tested high school graduates, it appears that only about half of our nation's ACT-tested high school students are ready for college-level reading" (p. 1). (For further information about the *Executive Summary*, see Horning and Kraemer's introductory chapter in this book.) Their reading deficiencies put students at an extreme disadvantage because they start out already behind many of their more advanced classmates. Additionally, a report from the Kaiser Family Foundation (2009) shows that with a plethora of media sources, students ages eight to eighteen favor spending their time playing video games, watching television, and instant and text messaging over reading. In 2004, the number of hours spent on media per day averaged 6.5 hours compared to the number of hours spent reading. Over the past ten years, "every type of media with the exception of reading has increased" and, in fact, "during this same period, time spent reading went from forty-three to thirty-eight minutes a day" (p. 2). Clearly, reading has declined to the point of impacting the basic reading/writing skills beginning students bring with them to the first year experience.

Composition instructors are wise to acknowledge both the pre-existing skills of basic writers and the challenges—particularly in reading and critical thinking—facing these students. By realizing this, instructors are able to construct course outlines, syllabi, and reading and writing assignments that prepare students to tackle the individual stages of cognitive thinking as outlined in the Revised Bloom's Taxonomy. Through a steady development of critical thinking that connects reading and writing, students will be prepared with cognitive skills ultimately transferable to the workforce.

THE READING/WRITING CONNECTION

The Revised Bloom's Taxonomy (RBT), attributed to Lorin Anderson, a former student of Bloom, and David Krathwohl (2001), emphasizes the importance of engaging students in higher level thinking and that cannot be accomplished by asking simple, knowledge-based questions about readings that require mere recitation of facts, descriptions, and interpretations. Anderson and Krathwohl's revision addresses three broad categories—terminology, structure, and emphasis—to create a taxonomy more reflective of and relevant to students and teachers in the twenty-first century. The RBT moves from the most basic level of thinking—remembering—to the most complex—creating. As students master each level, they progress toward more meaningful and critical thinking. These levels of thinking, and their direct application to basic writers, guide the structure and development of this chapter.

LEVEL I: REMEMBERING

The first, most basic level of the Revised Taxonomy is remembering, the act of retrieving "relevant knowledge from long-term memory" (Anderson & Krathwohl, 2001, p. 67). Many basic writers who arrive in their first college writing course often do so with limited reading skills, memories, and stored knowledge. Many admit to finding reading, especially academic reading, a chore and uninspiring. In fact, when we examine the "remembering" level of the RBT, we see that poor or inexperienced readers are challenged by the inability to recall or recognize factual material and terminology they can draw from, think about, and integrate into their own writing. Their writing is generally limited, weakly developed, and unsupported by prior knowledge. Composition instructors who create reading/writing assignments that ask students to recall relevant information from stored memory are likely to be dissatisfied by their responses. Those responses can, in part, be attributed to underdeveloped critical thinking skills. Sternglass (1971) notes this is a way for students "to remember facts and meanings, to analyze concepts, and to construct knowledge that [is] new to them" (p. 26). As is often the case, many of students are unaware of problems in their thinking. As a composition instructor, I have witnessed such frustration show itself in the papers of students who complain they have nothing to say, do not know where to begin, have not experienced anything worthwhile in their lives to write about, and though frustrated, seem content with those beliefs. However, students in Sternglass's study reported that writing actually helped them remember facts and information, and that writing assisted them in "seeing the relationships among the facts and ideas, thus facilitating the practice of analysis" (p. 30). Despite poor reading skills, basic writers find encouragement in writing when the process stimulates memories, facts, and ideas from past reading. Confidence can be gained, paving the way for further progress in both reading and writing.

Level II: Understanding

Basic writers who can master the next level of the RBT are capable of constructing "meaning from . . . oral, written, and graphic communication" through interpretation, exemplification, classification, summarization, inference, comparison, and explanation (Anderson & Krathwohl, 2001, p. 67). The mastery of these skills is crucial when it comes to writing and taking exams. Basic writers with limited reading skills are at a disadvantage when required to demonstrate any of the above competencies in their writing. As is often the case, basic writers with limited reading skills struggle to understand vocabulary, among other things, and use it correctly in sentence structure. Shaughnessy (1977) noted that teachers often assume students know words that they do not, and "this deficiency shows up most clearly in their writing, where words outside the basic vocabulary are usually either missing or erroneously used" (p. 216). As a reminder to basic writing instructors, she stresses that "words, for the most part, must be learned in contexts, not before contexts" (p. 217). Language recognition and its various usages are a challenge for basic writers as they struggle to compose text that demonstrates appropriate understanding and syntax.

Haswell (1991) notes "regression [in writing] continues as long as language competence continues to grow" (p. 197). What this suggests is that as new skills are acquired, or as students attempt to demonstrate in their writing new ways of thinking and using language, mistakes and errors occur. Thus, teachers would be wise to focus less on "surface" errors or non-standard usage and instead examine content, message, and organization as indicators of improving literacy. Further problems occur when students take written exams that require a demonstration of remembered facts or written responses to essay questions that ask them to clearly explain or summarize an idea or a concept.

From my own experience as a basic writing instructor, I have often been guilty of making assumptions about the skill sets basic writers bring with them to my classroom. When they arrive as deficient readers, vocabulary is limited and their writing shows a lack of understanding in how to situate language in its proper context. To move students toward improved reading skills that are vital to improved writing skills, instructors must become aware of several factors that occur while students read. Nelson (1998) explained that while reading, the student constructs meaning from the text and also for a possible "to-be-written text" (p. 279). In other words, meaning for what will be written is constructed while the act of reading itself takes place. The student is "in two roles concurrently—the reader building meaning *from* a text and a writer building meaning *for* a text" (emphasis added p. 279). Nancy Morrow (1997) pointed out:

> If we want our students to recognize that reading and writing are interconnected processes, it seems only logical that the goal of a composition course should also be to help students compose a theory of reading—or perhaps more specifically to compose *theories* of reading that will help them to understand their relationship to the act of reading in different contexts. (p. 464)

The ability of basic writers to apply any of the competencies Nelson and Morrow suggest requires writing instructors to make students aware of these two separate actions that occur concurrently while reading takes place. Focusing initially on meaning-building from the text itself by examining and discussing content, language, and idea development is one way composition instructors can help students become aware of one of the actions taking place during reading. The other—"building meaning for a text"—can be explained by encouraging students to make personal, community, and/or global connections between what they read and the kind of written text they will ultimately create. Explaining this separation allows students to focus on each process individually. When they can grasp each process, they are in a stronger position to understand how elements of reading can transfer to writing. Additionally, helping students understand this reading-writing connection positions them to have greater success with developing the

competencies required in this second level of the RBT, preparing them
to move forward.

Limited language and sub-par reading skills create additional problems. Horning (1978) explained:

> [O]ne must not only be able to read in the conventional sense,
> but also one must be able to develop the highly specialized
> reading skills needed to write successfully: the skills of proof-
> reading, of knowing where to look for information on the
> printed page, or sorting, storing, and analyzing the print for
> the total message. (p. 265)

These are certainly competencies that must be achieved if basic writers
are to experience any level of success in the first year writing classroom
and beyond. Once the reading skills of basic writers begin to advance,
these students show increased but limited proficiency in their writing,
as vocabulary expands and correct usage becomes more noticeable.
At this juncture, they may start drawing appropriate inferences from
readings and write in ways that show a slowly developing ability to
interpret and organize ideas in a genre-specific manner. As they add
information to their bank of knowledge, they begin stockpiling material from which to draw. Writing that shows this steady progression of
remembering and comprehending produces learning and influences
further and more critical thinking—the goal basic writing instructors
work hard to have their students achieve.

Improved reading comprehension from a basic writers means that
they are beginning to understand a piece of writing and all its component elements as part of, or a as response to, ongoing conversations.
Salvatori (1996) noted that a reader's responsibility is to give voice to
the text's argument, but writers have a responsibility as well: They
must write text that "asks (rather than answers) questions, that proposes (rather than imposes) arguments, and that therefore makes a
conversation possible" (p. 441). The writer's contribution to this existing conversation, therefore, means they understand that "conversation
requires absorption of what prior speakers have said, consideration of
how earlier comments relate to the responder's thoughts, and a response framed to the situation and the responder's purposes" (Bazerman, 1980, p. 657). Understanding those connections, being able to
summarize the words and ideas of others, drawing inferences from
written, oral, or graphic messages, and explaining, classifying, or inter-

preting what others have said or written is the challenge faced by basic writers. Gaining these competencies can be an empowering feeling for basic writers who are now becoming "participants in an ever changing and ever widening conversation" (Morrow, 1997, p. 462).

LEVEL III: APPLYING

The RBT describes the third level of cognition, applying, as carrying out or using "a procedure in a given situation" through execution or implementation (Anderson & Krathwohl, 2001, p.67). This level also includes constructing theories about ideas and issues raised in readings and discussions. At this level, students are expected to apply prior knowledge to existing knowledge for to create new knowledge. Sternglass (1977) noted that when students are able "to translate textbook and lecture jargon into their own language, they develop the ability to use writing as a means to critique existing materials and to develop their own insights" (p. xiv). Certainly this ability does not come easily to basic writers with deficient reading skills. At this level, writing instructors can have significant impact on the critical thinking and writing development of their students.

By assigning more complex readings, writing instructors challenge their students to apply what they have read and already know toward constructing new theories, explanations, and original thoughts about the ideas presented. When I ask my students, for example, to transfer their ideas just read to another genre (e.g., "How would the author's view on this issue play out on, say, a reality television show?" or "What other person do you know of who might think this way, and why?"), new ideas and connections are likely to emerge, making the process of applying critical thinking strategies less daunting and clearly something within basic writers' capabilities.

Getting students to actually apply knowledge and create their own theories inevitably leads composition teachers to allocating class time instructing students on how to "read" text. For writing instructors who feel that teaching reading strategies is out of their realm of expertise, Bosley (2008) noted that many scholars (Bartholomae & Petrosky, 1986; Elbow, 1993; Flower et al., 1990; Fulkerson, 2005; Lindemann 1993, 1995; Morrow, 1997; Tate, 2000) have researched and written on the "effectiveness of integrating reading and writing instruction in freshman composition courses" (p. 286). Additionally, "numerous studies (Downs, 2000; El-Hindi, 1997; McCormick, 2003; Quinn, 2003; Reither, 2000; Salvatori, 1996; Shanahan, 1993; Tierney & Pearson, 1993) have demonstrated that reading and writing are taught most effectively as integrated processes" (as cited in Bosley, 2008, p. 286). Accepting the idea that reading and writing are vitally connected, composition instructors cannot expect basic writers to improve their reading skills by avoiding spending classroom time in providing critical reading instruction. Asking basic writers to construct theories from what they read, and apply those theories to their writing, is a challenge that often pushes the limits of their abilities.

In fact, Bosley (2008) concluded from her research and from personal experience as an English professor that "many college freshmen have little experience with critical reading and need to be taught explicit strategies for this type of engagement with text" (p. 298). Their early experiences with written text, as Neilson (1993) concluded from her study with school teachers, "is often associated with maternity, nurturing, and sensuality" yet reading at the academic level—the kind of reading expected of our students "requires linear thinking coupled with a knowledge of rituals, rules, and conventions" (p.101). These are conventions that have, in most instances, eluded basic writers. As we now try moving our students forward with text that demands their engagement, we are met with further responsibilities in the composition classroom. Knowing this does not suggest we must exhaust ourselves with reading instruction, but that limited, focused reading strategies can efficiently and effectively be demonstrated to students, where text is presented on an overhead and suggestions offered on ways to approach reading it. Student-instructor interaction with sample text by way of questioning ideas presented, discussing organization, making personal connections, and explaining writing strategies used by an author builds confidence in students who often feel at a loss when confronted with a challenging reading. When I spend this time with my own students, I am able to see attempts at transferring the thinking and reading strategies learned in class to better, more reflective, and more thoughtful writing. Although not always successful, these basic writers are at least beginning to apply these newly-discovered strategies.

LEVEL IV: ANALYZING

Higher levels of thinking, beginning with analyzing, move basic writers toward even deeper, more meaningful thinking and writing. Analyzing—the fourth level of cognition in the RBT—is defined as breaking "material into its constituent parts" and determining "how the parts relate to one another and to an overall structure or purpose" through differentiation, organization, and attribution" (Anderson & Krathwohl, 2001, p. 68). In addition to these skills, students writing research papers assigned in basic writing courses that demand analysis and synthesis of material from various sources are expected to showcase these competencies; yet, for basic writers who continue to struggle with this level of the RBT, this task is anything but a demonstration of these competencies.

At this part of the reading-thinking-writing connection, students are encouraged to make observations about readings to disassemble ideas, analyzing each idea as a separate entity, making connections between and among the ideas, and then reassemble those ideas into a new whole. Shaughnessey (1977) asks these questions of her students to help "guide their observations" (p. 251):

> What are the parts? What gets repeated from one part to the next? What is unexpected or contradictory or missing? If what you are analyzing is part of something larger, how does it connect with the larger unit? (p. 251)

These questions move basic writers from a superficial level of analysis, a level with which they are most familiar, to a more profound level of examination, a place often new and confusing. Here, again, is where reading proficiency becomes necessary when the goal of composition instruction is to guide students toward higher levels of thinking. When basic writers are deficient in reading, getting them to recognize ideas that can be analyzed and connected, and then written about in insightful ways, remains the challenge for both student and instructor. Furthermore, basic writers who have difficulty recognizing effective organizational patterns in reading struggle to prioritize their own ideas clearly and coherently when they write. They often are text-reliant in that they closely stick to the language of the text, and do not venture into creating or formulating their own language that demonstrates their analysis. Shaughnessey (1977) argued that understanding complexity in writing is something often mismanaged by basic writers. Not only do they mismanage complexity, but they generally fail to recognize it. When they realize a text is beyond their abilities, as is frequently the case in the basic writing classroom, they are often quick to give up. This "throwing in the towel" directly relates to poor reading skills: Basic writers have not observed and internalized language patterns and structures because they have neither studied nor processed those patterns often enough. Additionally, they likely have not analyzed or been effectively taught to analyze those patterns to see how they developed. Clearly, basic writers who learn how to engage with written text learn skills that help them throughout college and into their working lives.

Level V: Evaluating

Evaluating requires basic writers to remember what they have read, understand meaning within the text, construct theories from text, and analyze ideas and structure to make an informed, thoughtful opinion or judgment. The RBT specifically defines this fifth stage in the critical thinking process as making "judgments based on criteria and standards" through checking and critiquing (Anderson & Krathwohl, 2001, p. 68). When basic writers function at the evaluative level, the belief is that they have already mastered previous levels in the taxonomy, an indicator that critical thinking is improving. Salvatori (1996) explained the process she undertakes with her students to help them see the interconnectedness of reading and writing by providing assignments that require students to demonstrate several competencies, including evaluation. She asks students to first write a response to a text, then to "construct a reflective commentary on the moves they made as readers and the possible reasons for them" (p. 446). Last, she has them assess the text they produced from the reading they did. Salvatori explains that this process and practice makes students consciously aware of the "mental moves" they make, what those moves produce, and learn to "revise or to complicate those moves as they return to them in light of their newly constructed awareness of what those moved did or did not make possible" (p. 447).

This awareness challenges basic writers in several ways. First, as they scaffold through the levels of the RBT, their continued demonstration of advancing thinking skills is put to the test, and the expectations of writing instructors grow. Second, the texts basic writers are assigned to read and produce become more involved and complicated as students are challenged to continue advancing. Third, as they become more aware of the connection between reading and writing, their thinking often gets "messy." They have much to sort through and try and make sense of before they begin writing in ways that show the challenges they face and their developing command over reading, thinking, and writing. When students can examine readings to critique ideas, arguments, and use of evidence presented in the text, and when they begin producing their own cogent writing that shows advancing competencies, they are poised to move on to the next level of the RBT. (For further information on evaluation in an ever-increasing digital world, see Drake's chapter in this book. For information on the role libraries play in research writing, see Haller's chapter.)

Level VI: Creating

At this final level of the RBT, students should be putting "elements together to form a coherent or functional whole" and reorganizing "elements into a new pattern or structure" through generating, planning, or producing (Anderson & Krathwohl, 2001, p. 68). This level has wider implications for students, especially in its application to major-specific courses and future employment. It is here where mastery of the five previous levels has been achieved, and where basic writers should clearly recognize and move with greater fluency between and among reading, critical thinking, and writing. Students should now understand that writing offers flexibility, and stronger decision-making skills are likely more noticeable in the writing they produce. At this level of creating, they can now, more often than not, draw relevant material from text and repackage it in unique and appropriate ways. Basic writers can look at one idea presented through reading and see it through different lenses. They can, for example, see how a narrative can also be expressed as a song, a report, or even a cartoon. They begin not just recognizing but utilizing the movement between and among genres, producing new ways of looking at the same idea. Sternglass's study (1997) showed that when students "find themselves in more challenging intellectual settings . . . where risk-taking and exploration of new ideas are valued" (p. xv), they rise to the challenge of more "complex reasoning tasks" (p. xv). Of greater significance to students are the implications this recognition, utilization, and risk-taking have for other course work and future employment.

It helps to look, for example, at the findings of Richard Haswell (1991), who studied basic writers, "advanced" upper-level college writers, and post-college employees working in fields such as engineering, radiology, sales, architecture, nursing, and geology—careers many of our students are likely to work in. These were careers that required a fair amount of writing on the job, and Haswell identified commonalities (if any) and differences among these groups, leading to some surprising and not so surprising findings. Although his study focused on more advanced college writers, the connections between these advanced writers, our basic, first year writers, and post-college employees become clear when noting how Haswell examined specifics, such as identifying significance, structure, analysis, and evaluation in both reading and writing. Haswell studied these non-professional writers (the employees), having them write the same kinds of essays "under similar conditions" (p.73) typically assigned to first year writers. Several areas of writing competence were examined, including: organization, specificity, coherence, diction, syntax, and mechanics—the very same competencies first year writers work on and are expected to master in their composition courses.

These findings revealed that non-professional writers (the employees) seemed less bound by structured organizational patterns. This is not to say their writing was not organized in the traditional sense of chronology or comparison or division of parts, for example, but that it turned more to "incremental patterns always ready for the evolution of further logical points, patterns provided by inferential arguments" (p. 77). Writing competence increased in employees, advanced college writers, and basic writers when they were able to apply problem-solving strategies to organize their writing. The idea of "creating,"—the most advanced level of the RBT—of being experienced enough to generate, plan, or produce text comes from having sufficiently advanced (if not mastered) prior levels of the RBT. Having the writing skills necessary to understand, craft, and modify text is a testament to the competencies we as composition instructors strive to have our students successfully achieve.

With respect to specificity, Haswell (1991) found that advanced writers demonstrated maturity in composing lengthier essays, use "exact and idiomatic language," preferring first person "I," restricting the subjects of sentences, and "deal less in high-level abstractions and generalizations" (p.77) than did their basic writing counterparts, who were accustomed to padding their essays to achieve greater length. What can be observed from specificity in writing as it applies to basic writers is that with improved or improving reading skills, students begin recognizing over-worded sentences and shape their own sentences to reflect conciseness and clearer meaning. This is not to suggest that students are likely to entirely abandon the process of inflating language, but when they begin realizing that "less is more" and that specificity demonstrates to their teacher a greater command and use of language, they feel more capable—maybe even more eager—to continue writing.

Another competency examined in Haswell's subjects (1991) was coherence, a skill that basic writers often struggle to recognize, let alone utilize, in their own writing. In more advanced writers, Haswell found an ability to use a "more rapid writing style," a preference for using more nouns as pronouns, attentiveness to starting sentences with simple subjects, and expanding sentences with "logical connectors" like the conjunction "and" rather than using more complex connectors like "rather than" (p.79). The advanced writers' decision to rely less on "explicit devices of cohesion often recommended by textbooks" is an interesting discovery, showing that advanced writers take what they learn in their writing classes and modify the "rules" and recommended strategies to suit the writing situation (p. 78). This writing maturity allows them to reduce the use of "word repetitions, synonyms, and logical transitions," but in no way suggests their writing lacks coherence (p.78). Instead, they experimented with other methods of achieving coherence, such as linking the first sentence of a new paragraph to the previous paragraph by rephrasing an idea, or understanding that ideas expressed in a sentence stem from the ideas expressed in the sentence prior. For basic writers, recognizing the skilled strategies and techniques of accomplished writers through analyzing the way they unify their ideas, and then integrating those same strategies into their own writing, is yet another skill they can add to their growing composition toolbox.

Diction and syntax were other competencies evaluated in Haswell's (1991) study. Haswell noted that the vocabulary of advanced writers and non-professional employees was "broader and more advanced" than the vocabulary of basic writers (p.79). Certainly an expanded word choice can be directly linked to age and the jargon of the profession, but advancing skills, maturity, and attentiveness to language and usage are also factors worth considering. Advanced writers and post-college employees demonstrate syntactical competency well beyond that of basic writers. Haswell found in his study that employees were more inclined to "construct long series of three or more items," their sentences were more varied and emphatic, and the length of sentences "increase[ed] over that of [basic writers] by a third" (p.79).

Clearly, the three highest cognitive levels in the RBT—analyzing, evaluating, and creating—are present here. Analyzing and evaluating the ways language is used and structured to create meaning comes from reading, a competency many basic writers lack. Greater, more regular exposure to formal written text, whereby students begin recognizing and understanding that advanced diction and syntax can produce clearly expressed ideas, is one way composition instructors can move their students toward better writing. Basic writers who can evaluate the effectiveness of language, understand its usefulness in developing ideas, and synthesize those new skills into their own writing, are progressing toward elevated levels of thinking.

A final competency examined by Haswell (1991) was mechanics. It was found—not surprisingly—that advanced writers make mistakes (e.g., misplaced commas, sentence fragments, or run-on sentences), but that they are "not ignorant of the rules" (p. 80). They often see "correctness" in their writing as "less worthy of their time and attention than matters such as production and flow" (p.80). This awareness is a clear indicator of maturity in writing, something composition instructors hope their basic writing students will achieve. The focus and seeming confidence of more advanced writers appears to stem from the ability to see their writing from a more "global" perspective, whereby they are able to quickly hone in on the task at hand and make the necessary adjustments to their writing as they go along. Conversely, basic writers with deficient reading skills are often unable to see writing from this global perspective, let alone systematically recognize mechanical errors or make "necessary adjustments" in their own writing.

Haswell (1991) noted that the working world puts a high premium on being concise, fluency, and flexibility—all characteristics that serve advanced writers well but generally elude basic writers, who have yet to develop those competencies. Haswell questions whether a "perspective of maturing can convert the differences into teaching standards" (p.80).

If composition instructors, especially those working with basic writers, expect from their students more "mature competencies" as they set about the task of preparing course objectives and writing assignments, it is possible that more students might be attracted to and see the value in writing. Students need to know that writing instructors have confidence in their growing abilities, and therefore expect those students to "rise to the occasion." The objectives and assignments that demand students to demonstrate improving skills in sufficiency and relevancy of evidence, examples, description, and detail in writing (among other rhetorical elements), challenge and help advance those maturing competencies. Students are likely to view this approach established by their instructors as more "graspable, more in tune with [their] understanding of their culture, more a part of their vision of their own success in it. As competencies to train for, being productive and adaptable look better than being decorous or emphatic" (Haswell, 1991, p. 84). In viewing Haswell's findings, it is clear that for basic writers, successfully achieving this final level of the RBT—"creating"—puts into action all that has been accomplished before it, and lays the foundation for further success in college and in a career.

Now What?

Haswell's study (1991) sheds light on the ways mature, non-professional writers learn to adjust their skills to real work-world situations, despite what these former students may have learned in their composition classrooms. Therefore, it becomes important to examine actual classroom instruction and how composition teachers often lock themselves into a "lecture-recitation" format, often ignoring the necessity of dedicating some amount of course time to reading activities. As is the case, composition instructors often relegate class time to lecturing on an assigned reading and then ask students questions about the reading to see whether or not they actually did the reading. The questions often center on Level I (Remembering) of the RBT. The main point, specific factual data provided by the reading, and any readily identifiable information are among the types of the questions teachers use to measure their students' knowledge of that reading. Testing students' memories has little bearing on the substantive and quantifiable measurement of learning, processing, and analyzing material. Surely we have to wonder how learning occurs under these conditions, or how this teaching format fosters improvement in furthering critical thinking, reading, and writing. Creating a learning environment that produces more engaged, active learners, or students more willing to take risks in their writing and verbal responses, is an environment most composition instructors wish to establish. If we allow students more say in the classroom "by developing questions for discussion, providing examples from their own experiences to support theories and principles being presented, and working with their professor to understand difficult concepts and problems," we might more effectively assist these basic writers in becoming more confident and engaged contributors to their own learning process and progress (Sternglass, 1997, p. 165),.

Chiseri-Strater (1991) argued that "if learning is accepted as a process rather than a mere transmission of knowledge, students will be better prepared for the critical thinking they will use in writing for the discipline and presumably in all their courses" (as cited in Sternglass, 1997, p. 165). That argument can be further extended to employees like the ones in Haswell's study, who synthesized what they learned in the classroom to writing that may be expected of them in their jobs. Similarly, as basic writers become more proficient in reading, composition instructors can steer them away from passive learning and reading of text toward more meaningful thinking that demands greater analytic and evaluative writing, and/or writing that demonstrates increasing flexibility. If that means composition instructors must abandon "tried and true" methods of classroom instruction (e.g., reading quizzes and exercises; pointless questions; recitation and learning environments that do less to prepare students for the larger demands of writing in the working world), and instead move students toward deeper insight, comprehension, analysis, and response, we can then feel as though learning competencies are gaining strength and advancing students toward better, more cohesive, and thoughtful writing.

Classroom Practices and Suggestions

Haswell's study is one well worth remembering for basic writing instructors when constructing syllabi and assignments. Our goal should be to prepare basic writers for the more advanced writing they will be required to do during the remainder of college, and, more importantly, for the professional writing they may be required to do once they earn their degree and become a member of the post-college workforce. An assignment I find particularly useful in evaluating advancing competencies is an informational career project, assigned mid-semester. This assignment requires students to research their major (if undecided, they can pick any major the university offers), to utilize information provided by Career Services at our university, and to examine that major from multiple perspectives, including social, technological, financial, and environmental, to educate themselves more fully about the field and to inform their audience about this major. In addition to learning about their chosen field, they must divide the project into manageable sections that address the specific and detailed requirements of the assignment. Not only are students reading and processing a significant amount of information, but they then must also decide on what to include and where to position information, arrange and organize each section, and attend to the needs of an interested and sympathetic audience.

This assignment challenges students to read and think about the many aspects of a major. Beyond that, the assignment helps students organize material and write about a major in both an informative and in an engaging way. With an assignment like this, composition instructors can be of great service to students by challenging their critical thinking and pre-existing ideas have had about their major and by working collaboratively with basic writers to help them understand, apply, analyze, evaluate, and create meaningful text from their reading. Doing this requires composition instructors to design assignments aimed at improving how students examine text for future use in creating text. These writing assignments "can help students become more perceptive readers and can help break down the tendency toward vague inarticulateness resulting from purely private reading" (Bazerman, 1980, p. 658). Furthermore, Bazerman explained that when students are required to examine the "technique of writing" to better understand the writer's purpose, they begin to recognize that the effects of writing "go beyond the overt content" (p. 659).

Additionally, Jolliffe and Harl (2008) suggest ways composition instructors can "think differently about reading in their courses" (p. 611). One suggestion has the instructor read aloud a short passage of about 250 words, pausing at intervals to offer up thoughts or connections the instructor makes to his or her own personal life, work, the world at large, and "to other texts that he or she has read" (p. 613).

This strategy can serve as a model for students, demonstrating that this reading behavior is natural and typical of someone engaging with text. Furthermore, Jolliffe and Harl (2008) suggest that students "list and offer a one-sentence description on an index card of every other class that they are taking" and the purpose of this activity is so composition instructors can help students identify "themes, issues, and motifs being raised in the other classes" that students can then connect to readings and discussions in their writing classes (p. 614).

One final suggestion from Jolliffe and Harl (2008) is that composition instructors ought to consider the integration of more technology "into their reading assignments" (p. 614). Basic writers are technology "natives" who spend a fair amount of time each day reading and posting on Facebook and MySpace, texting, tweeting, and instant messaging. These sources allow students to engage with each other electronically. Incorporating hyperlinked texts into their reading and writing assignments that encourage interaction in more "public spheres" not only taps into the skills and abilities they already possess, but gives composition instructors better chance of engaging them in areas of literacy with which they are already comfortable (p. 614). I find great success designing assignments that require students to engage electronically with each other. Because of their high comfort level with this medium, they are usually more engaged and willing to participate. As an added bonus, I see a dramatic reduction in missing or late assignments.

The fact remains that "reading itself will not improve [a] student's writing abilities unless the connections between reading and writing are made explicit" (Morrow, 1997, p. 455). When we expect students to examine text more carefully because of the questions we ask and the reading/writing/thinking activities we engage them in, our responsibility becomes ensuring this connection is clear. Surface errors in writing will remain, but deeper, more thoughtfully expressed ideas are certain to develop. As we consider ways to incorporate reading instruction into the composition classroom, or help our students improve their reading comprehension skills, we must do so intending to further their academic development and prepare them to transfer these skills to the work force.

The six levels of the RBT provide composition instructors with valuable guidance and assessment tools to help move students forward in thinking, reading, and writing skills. Providing them with opportunities to remember material they have read, to interpret that material for its meaning, to mesh prior and existing knowledge to create something new, to break down or take apart ideas and find connections, to judge what they have read, and to reorganize or repackage material to create something unique, are beneficial ways to proceed. Helping students see themselves as weavers of language who can overlay and mesh ideas to create text that is meaningful invites them into the framework of composition that is personal, practical, and professional.

6 Second Language Reading-Writing Relations

William Grabe and Cui Zhang

> As Kroll (1993), among others, has pointed out, reading has traditionally been seen as a skill to be taught separately from writing, as well as something students are somehow expected to already know about when they reach the writing course. Teaching reading in a writing course may seem like an odd idea, if not an entirely unnecessary one. It may also be the case that L2 writing teachers feel ill prepared to teach reading, especially in connection with writing. How many have actually been taught to teach the two skills together? (Hirvela, 2004, pp. 2–3)

Hirvela highlights a very important difference between first language (L1) and second language (L2) writing instruction contexts. L2 student writers, as a group, have much more limited English language skills. These limitations lead to difficulties not only with writing in English, but also with reading (as well as speaking and listening). The implication for teachers in composition classes is that reading skills must be addressed more explicitly if combined reading and writing activities are to be an important part of writing course goals, and if we want our L2 students to be successful. In addition, English L2 students typically have a range of other limitations, such as less exposure to English texts, and much more limited vocabulary knowledge. For these reasons, among others, teaching writing skills to L2 students creates unique challenges for the composition instructor, especially when reading and writing skills are expected to be used together for academic tasks (see Horning in this volume).

Reading and writing are now often combined in both English L1 and English L2 writing courses. English L1 composition classes commonly assume reasonably fluent and critical reading skills, and explicit reading instruction is seldom addressed consistently. In fact, as the quote above notes, many writing instructors feel somewhat ill-at-ease incorporating explicit reading instruction in the composition classroom, even though explicit reading support may be a good idea in certain contexts, as with L1 students. In contrast, in L2 English for Academic Purposes (EAP) language learning programs (e.g., pre-university intensive language programs), combined reading and writing tasks are often assigned, and L2 students are typically provided with direct instructional support in both academic literacy skills, though usually at a much lower level of task demand. This issue of reading instruction needs in university writing courses is one good example of some of the difficulties facing L2 students in the English L1 composition classroom. Building on the points raised in this initial example, the chapter develops four major goals: (1) identifying sources of difficulty for L2 students in the composition classroom; (2) reviewing research on the challenges facing L2 students as they carry out assignments that combine reading and writing skills; (3) highlighting implications from research for ways in which L2 writers differs from L1 writers in carrying out reading-writing tasks; and (4) offering suggestions for writing instruction that provides more realistic support for L2 students.

To introduce this chapter, we describe L2 student groups and identify the ones address in the discussion that follows. We assume that the L2 students we discuss are primarily English-as-a-Second-Language (ESL) students in academic settings who have come to the U.S. to enter post-secondary institutions to earn an academic degree. Most commonly, these students are labeled as visa students or international students. Some of these students may also be immigrant students who have entered the U.S. within the past one to two years, and who have a green card, but whose control of academic English is much like international visa students (Ferris, 2009). These students have a wide range of English-language reading and writing abilities: Some ESL students have excellent reading and writing skills and have few difficulties in the composition classroom. However, most have English language difficulties that set them apart from English L1 students in the writing classroom (especially if a university admits international students with fairly low TOEFL or IELTS scores).

A second major group of L2 students are also enrolled in post-secondary composition classes. These students are often referred to as Generation 1.5 students, and include those who may have arrived as immigrants as children or who, as younger adolescents, worked their way through some part of secondary schooling in the U.S. and are now entering U.S. post-secondary institutions. The Generation 1.5 student designation is broad and somewhat controversial (Ferris, 2009; Harklau et al., 1999; Leki, 1992; Losey, 2009), and surprisingly little is known about these students as a group, or even if they can be defined as a group.

These two groups of L2 students have some commonalities but also a number of significant differences from each other. Individual students in either group may write as well as, if not better than, most English L1 student writers (it is important not to stereotype all English L2 students). Generally speaking, however, L2 students in post-secondary composition classes have overall language proficiency levels below most L1 students. Because little empirical research has been done on Generation 1.5 students apart from a few published case studies (Ferris, 2009), we restrict our review to ESL L2 students (primarily international visa students) in post-secondary contexts.

The L2 Student in the L1 English Composition Class

One of the most obvious issues for ESL student writers is the array of English language proficiency problems these students bring into the composition classroom. They have varying degrees of limitations with vocabulary knowledge (including spelling), grammar knowledge (including basic structures that L1 writers have no problems with), and discourse knowledge (including how to organize paragraphs and texts into expected patterns). They do not usually have the same amount of exposure to reading in English as do English L1 students, and they read slowly. As a result, they have difficulty with very long reading assignments, reading assignments that involve extensive inference "between the lines," and reading assignments involving complex conceptual content. They also have much less experience with academic writing tasks, and do not write fluently with easier writing tasks.

Most L2 students do not have background knowledge in American culture (including cultural topics, recent popular culture trends, U.S. historical information, university background knowledge) or university course expectations (including how to behave in class, how to analyze a writing task, how to meet writing task expectations, and how to talk with a teacher). They also have different attitudes toward, and motivations for, getting a degree at a U.S. post-secondary institution (e.g., they see their stay in the U.S. as temporary). These issues are discussed in some detail in Ferris (2009), Grabe and Stoller (2011), Leki (1992, 2007), Silva (1993), and Silva et al. (1997). These differences lead to implications for writing instruction with L2 students that we suggest in the final section.

Two brief examples of these language differences between L1 and L2 students illustrate the extent of the challenges facing L2 students in the composition classroom. With respect to vocabulary knowledge, the typical L1 student entering college knows about forty thousand different English words (Grabe, 2009; Perfetti, 2010; Stahl & Nagy, 2006). In contrast, most L2 student entering university courses may know about ten thousand English words (as a reasonable guesstimate), and sometimes, many fewer words. This large vocabulary gap includes less frequently used, but informationally more important words, and L2 students are often unable to find precise wordings for complex academic writing. With respect to grammar, L2 students struggle with many complex sentences with multiple embedded meanings, whether reading these sentences or producing them. Moreover, many aspects of grammar are never fully under the command of the L2 writer. Prepositions, phrasal verbs, articles, and subject-verb agreement all represent important grammatical systems in English that often do not have transparent rules for their use.

The combination of English difficulties for L2 students in the English writing classroom are captured in a number of overviews (Ferris & Hedgcock, 2005; Grabe, 2003; Hirvela, 2004; Paltridge & Starfield, 2007; Silva, Leki, & Carson, 1997). Most recently, Ferris (2009) categorized a wide range of differences between L1 and L2 writers, supporting many of the points made by Silva, Leki, and Carson (1997) and also adding other points. For reference, we developed an extended list of differences, drawing primarily on the discussion in Ferris (2009, pp. 13–41). (See Table 1.)

Table 1. L2 Student Differences in Reading, Writing, and Instructional Experiences in English University Writing Contexts

1.	Less writing practice with English academic writing tasks
2.	Less support for developing critical thinking skills for academic reading and writing tasks
3.	Weaker and widely varying reading skills in English
4.	Very limited experiences with extensive reading and/or application of information from reading for writing tasks
5.	Much less practice with specific tasks that involve reading and writing interactions
6.	Weak and varied speaking and listening skills in English
7.	Very limited vocabulary knowledge in comparison with L1 students
8.	Very limited grammatical accuracy skills compared with L1 writers
9.	Limited awareness of how to interact with other students and with the teacher, both in the class and outside of class
10.	Limited awareness of how to behave in English L1 writing classes
11.	Common feelings of isolation, intimidation, and frustration in English L1 writing classrooms
12.	Differing motivations for being in a writing classroom in a U.S. university
13.	A relative lack of *tacit knowledge* about how English texts are organized, and how they should be organized while writing (intuitive knowledge is largely missing)
14.	Limited fluency in English writing—composing takes longer and proceeds with more fits and starts, and they do not produce longer automatic phrasings while writing
15.	Less English L1 cultural and background knowledge to draw on

All of these differences can be overwhelming for the L2 student in the English composition classroom, and it is sometimes a marvel how so many L2 students manage to learn and develop useful skills writing in English. At the same time, L1 composition teachers can be unrealistic in their expectations: As Harklau, Losey, and Siegal (1999) state, "the widespread expectation that adult language learners can attain completely monolingual command of an L2 is unrealistic and only possible in a nation that is overwhelmingly monolingual" (p. 8). In addition, it is not always the case that L1 students are skilled readers even if they have basic literacy skills (Horning, 2010; Moje et al., 2010; Shanahan, 2009; Shanahan & Shanahan, 2008). In exploring these issues further, especially with respect to research on L2 students' abilities to integrate reading-writing tasks, the next section reviews studies that support many of the points identified in Ferris (2009) and also in earlier syntheses.

RESEARCH ON L2 READING-WRITING INTEGRATION IN THE WRITING CLASSROOM

As Coon points out in this volume, reading and writing are often treated as separate entities in schools, and this situation exists in many countries in the world (e.g., China and Argentina). When students from these countries study in U.S. universities, they need more explicit instruction in integrating reading and writing skills (Leki & Carson, 1997). In focusing specifically on the issue of integrating reading and writing skills in writing courses, there are a number of writing tasks that are common in the university context. In many cases, success in academic writing depends on reading input to a large extent—either directly from source texts, or indirectly from background knowledge—that results from experience with texts (Hale et al., 1996; Hirvela, 2004; Horowitz, 1986; Johns, 1997; Leki & Carson, 1997; Rosenfeld, Leung, & Oltman, 2001; Spack, 1997, 2004; Zhu, 2004). These tasks make a fairly straightforward set of activities to explore in research studies, activities that also provide students with practice in combining reading and writing skills. These reading-writing tasks include:

1. Summary writing (with related issues of plagiarism and paraphrasing)
2. Note taking
3. Reading guides as homework (in which students write down responses to questions)
4. Synthesis writing tasks (including in-class essay exams)

5. Critical response papers (often a brief summary followed by a critical analysis or a personal interpretation)

6. Essay questions in subject area courses (including take-home exams)

7. Research papers

We expect that these reading and writing tasks are equally common in L1 and L2 writing contexts across the university (including pre-university, L2-intensive English program curricula, and in various disciplines across the university). Some of these tasks have been a source of L1 writing research over the years, including research on summary writing, synthesis writing, and the research paper. With respect to the other tasks listed above, it is not clear that they have been sources of extensive writing research (that is, research that provides evidence that the task leads to improved writing and/or improved reading abilities). In many cases, sufficient research simply hasn't been done and deserves greater attention from the writing research community. Given the focus of this chapter on L2 contexts, L2 research on a number of these writing task types are examined in an effort to understand how to teach them more effectively in composition classes.

In this section, we focus on four specific themes in L2 writing research that address the reading-writing relationship: summary writing (and direct copying), synthesis writing, research paper writing, and contrastive rhetoric and the problem of plagiarism in reading-based writing tasks. Summary writing is the quintessential reading-writing task, involving general comprehension, attention to main ideas, frequent re-reading of the text, translation of ideas into one's own writing production, and a responsibility to have the written summary reflect information in the text. Synthesis writing makes the same reading-writing demands on students, and also requires students to select the information most appropriate for linking ideas and issues across texts. Oftentimes, synthesis writing forces the writer to generate a discourse framework for the information distinct from the texts being read. In this way, synthesis can become a much more difficult task, especially with challenging texts. The research paper, while often discussed as a very traditional task, is still commonly assigned in both composition classes and in disciplinary courses. While the research paper can vary considerably from context to context, its common feature is a strong demand on students to integrate reading and writing skills. The final area of research review examines the notion of contrastive rhetoric

(Kaplan, 2005) and the commonly associated problem of plagiarism in student writing. This problem certainly reflects key issues in the reading-writing interaction in the writing classroom.

SUMMARY WRITING

Summary writing, or the summarization of content, forms a large portion of university academic writing (Horowitz, 1986). Research on ESL students' summary writing reveals a typical characteristic: direct copying of source text language is pervasive, and this is even more so with students of lower English language proficiency. Keck (2006), for example, found that ESL students, when compared with native English speakers, used significantly more exact copying (direct replication) and near copying (changing only one or a few words in a string) in their summary writing.

Researchers have suggested two main causes for students' reliance on direct copying. The first is related to students' English language and writing proficiency. Johns and Mayes (1990) examined eighty university-level ESL students in the U.S. and found that summaries written by less-proficient ESL students tended to directly copy original text language to a much greater degree. In contrast, higher-proficiency students performed more text modification and paraphrasing in their summaries. Similarly, Kim (2009) studied summaries written by the ESL students in an intensive English program in a U.S. university. She found that higher-proficiency ESL students produced more occasions of moderate revision and near copying of original text language, while lower-proficiency students used more direct copying (see also Keck, 2006). These studies, though limited in number, indicate the influence of ESL students' language-proficiency levels on their language use in summary writing. ESL students, especially those with lower English proficiency, find it very difficult to rephrase original text language, or they think that the language used by the original author or authors is much better than their own. Thus, they are more prone to directly "borrow" language from source texts to use in their summaries.

In addition to the issue of language proficiency, ESL students' direct copying of text language may also be traced to differences between the writing practices in their home culture and in U.S. academic contexts. Many students, especially students from China, Japan, and Korea, have a different understanding of text ownership compared to Western countries (Pennycook, 1996). Students from certain cultural and educational backgrounds (and in the cases discussed in Pennycook, China) may think that texts do not belong to a particular author, but are documents for public use. Many teachers in Chinese educational contexts even encourage students to memorize "classic" sentences or entire texts to use in their essays. In these students' native cultural and educational context, the practice of taking someone's sentences and putting them in their own writing, without reference, is fairly common. Thus, students from these cultural backgrounds and educational contexts often do not have a clear understanding of plagiarism. Shi's (2006) study of university-level ESL students and their views of plagiarism support Pennycook's (1996) arguments. In her study, Shi (2006) interviewed forty-six students in a Canadian university from five L1 backgrounds: English, German, Chinese, Korean, and Japanese. In her interviews, the Chinese, Japanese, and Korean students said they did not extensively practice citation in their L1 writing. Even if they understood the term *plagiarism* in the abstract sense, they did not know when they needed to or how to cite.

It is also important to note the real difference, though not always recognized, between direct copying of smaller segments of text and plagiarizing as an act of handing in someone else's work as one's own (whether in whole or by the use of several significant segments of text). In many cases, copying reflects an inability on the part of students, most likely due to reading and vocabulary limitations, that leads them to use words showing comprehension of key ideas. Often, both teacher and students know the source text (because the source text is assigned), so there is no effort to hide the source of the words used, but rather an inability to read and write well (Horning, 2010; Valentine, 2006).

Apart from the issue of directly copying source text language, other studies of ESL/EFL students' summary writing found that students' abilities to write summaries were directly influenced by the level of difficulty of the source text, students' reading comprehension abilities, different instructional activities associated with the summary task, and students' relative unfamiliarity with the topic and task. All of these issues have been shown to affect the quality of students' written summaries. As an example of source text difficulty, Kim (2001) studied the written summaries produced by seventy Korean university English as a foreign language (EFL) students during their freshmen year. Students who summarized the shorter and easier text included significantly more idea units and more accurate information in their summaries; on the other hand, students who summarized the more difficult text experienced greater difficulty with language in their summaries.

With respect to the role of reading comprehension abilities, Yu (2008) studied 157 Chinese undergraduate EFL students' summaries of the same source text in English and Chinese. The students' summaries were given holistic ratings and were analyzed for the correctness of information presented. Results showed that the quality of English summaries was influenced by the students' English reading comprehension abilities (assessed by the TOEFL reading section). In a similar vein, Baba (2009) studied sixty-eight Japanese undergraduate EFL students, and showed that the quality of L2 students' summary writing was significantly influenced by their reading comprehension abilities. Baba also found that summary performance related to students' abilities to write appropriate definitions of key terms. This result suggests that differences in vocabulary proficiency and students' abilities to extract accurate information from texts are important factors in L2 summary writing.

Associated instructional activities and the topic of the text also influence summary writing. Allison, Berry, and Lewkowicz (1995) analyzed the written summaries of eighty U.S. university-level ESL students involving three instructional conditions following the reading, but before summarizing: oral discussions, reading questions, and no support. Analysis of idea units included in the students' summaries revealed an influence of reading questions on students' summary writing, but oral discussion was not shown to facilitate students' summary writing. They also found that time allotment influenced summary writing, with more writing time leading to better summaries. Finally, Yang and Shi (2003) studied six first-year MBA ESL students in a U.S. university, focusing on the processes and the quality of summary writing. Their study revealed a positive effect on students' previous, business-related writing experience and on familiarity with the topic.

Synthesizing the results of these studies, we see that L2 summary writing in English is influenced by L2 proficiency in reading and writing, L2 vocabulary knowledge, reading text difficulty, time on task, writing task experience, and topic familiarity. It is useful to point out, in light of the results from the Allison, Berry, and Lewkowicz (1995) study, that writing assignments in English L1 composition classes often rely on discussions of a text as a springboard for writing, but such discussions may not be very helpful for L2 students. In contrast, composition classes usually do not require reading comprehension activities prior to writing from text sources, but such activities would most likely be helpful for L2 students. Some common English L1 composition practices may run counter to effective L2 student support for summary writing tasks, as well as other writing tasks, in their classes.

Synthesis Writing

Synthesis writing involves integrating two or more source texts in a writing task. Like summaries, synthesis writing is a task that students are expected to perform in university classes (Hirvela, 2004). In some cases, synthesis writing might be assigned as a writing task in a writing course. In many contexts beyond the composition class, synthesis is a normally expected outcome of reporting on reading extensive amounts of content material for a course, for an essay exam, for a research project, or for a thesis. In this section, Plakans's (2008, 2009a, 2009b) studies on the process and products of ESL students' synthesis writing represent a useful starting point for examining L2 students' performance and the difficulties they encounter. In general, Plakans (2008, 2009a, 2009b) found that reading-to-write (synthesis) tasks elicited more interactive writing processes involving personal experiences, though this finding may have also been due to the specific task requirements presented to students in her studies. While synthesis writing is usually seen as analytic or objective writing in which writers select and rearrange source text content, students in her studies were asked to use examples both from their own experience and from source texts to support their opinions on a pre-determined topic.

Plakans (2009a) examined use of reading strategies from twelve ESL students in their synthesis writing process. Participants included graduate and undergraduate students majoring in different fields in a U.S. university. She specifically focused on these students' reading strategies used in their writing processes. Results showed that ESL students' reading strategies differed between proficient and less proficient writers. Among all reading strategies utilized by students, more advanced ESL writers purposefully used more mining and global strategies, whereas less proficient writers relied on a wide range of different reading strategies, varying from individual to individual. Mining in reading is the process of reading with the specific purpose of finding particular information. In this study, more proficient ESL writers more frequently used strategies such as scanning to find ideas to include in writing, and also re-reading the source text for information to use in writing (Plakans, 2009a). More proficient writers in the study also used more global reading strategies, including goal setting by checking the task, skimming for the gist, and asking themselves questions (Plakans, 2009a) All three of these reading strategies are empirically supported as effective academic reading strategies (Grabe, 2009; Grabe & Stoller, 2011).

In a further analysis of data gathered in the same study, Plakans (2009b) examined specific sub-processes in the synthesis writing of six ESL students (three graduate and three undergraduate students). According to her findings, when students wrote essays requiring them to synthesize information from two texts, they used the processes of organizing, selecting, and connecting in much the same ways as Spivey's (1991) English L1 students. Specifically, Spivey (1991, 1997) studied the composing processes of secondary school and university-level English L1 students while writing synthesis essays using two source texts. She identified three sub-processes in which reading and writing were integrated: organizing, selecting, and connecting. The finding that ESL students use similar sub-processes when writing synthesis essays indicates that synthesis writing promotes the integration of reading and writing strategies. However, since ESL students differ in English proficiency and in experience with this task type, the degree to which they can successfully integrate reading and writing strategies varies. In Plakans's (2009a, 2009b) studies, ESL students of different proficiency levels produced synthesis essays of different quality. However, because there were only twelve students in all, it was not clear if the differences between high- and low-proficiency learners' writing was generalizable.

Beyond studies by Plakans, Qin (2009) carried out a study of 242 Chinese EFL university students writing argument essays drawing on information from two source texts. She found that most students, who were English majors in upper-division undergraduate courses and graduate courses, were able to identify and shape the relationship between the two source texts and use argument claims from the texts in their own writing. However, students with higher levels of

English proficiency (graduate students) used more counter arguments and rebuttals, indicating more sophisticated reasoning and applications of source information. Her finding suggested that EFL students in certain advanced EFL contexts can write relatively effective argument papers in English (at least in terms of argument structuring) if they have enough writing experience and sufficient English language proficiency.

In addition to quantitative research on synthesis writing, a number of case studies have been carried out with L2 students. Spack (1997) reported on a longitudinal study of a Japanese ESL student learning while writing academic papers across three years of university study. The student's self-assessment of her synthesis essays indicated a belief that good writing in the U.S. is opinion-based. When she could not clearly express her opinion in English (her L2) and support her argument with background knowledge, but instead had to use information from the readings, she was dissatisfied with her writing even though she received good grades from her professors. She felt frustration because she did not use many of her "own words," but represented information and language primarily from source texts. This study suggests the need for teachers to be explicit about the requirements of a given writing task, and also to engage students in exploring how synthesis tasks can be carried out more generically.

Leki (2007) reported on four extensive longitudinal case studies of U.S. university ESL students' literacy development over four years. In her study, she followed L2 students in four different disciplines: engineering, nursing, business, and social work. Each of the four students had very different experiences with writing, reading, and their interaction. Most importantly, she found that most writing outside of English writing courses—even when there wasn't much—involved information that drew specifically on reading and listening skills. Leki also found that for many assignments, vocabulary limitations proved to be problematic for these students. Ongoing problems with vocabulary were most likely reflected by their approaches to reading tasks, as there were many times when assigned readings were not read if students were not to be assessed on that material, or were not using the readings for writing tasks. What was assessed for a grade mattered quite a bit for these university students across the curriculum. Also notable, in Leki's (2007) research, was how few explicit synthesis tasks were assigned over the course of these four students' undergraduate careers, especially in lower-division general education courses, where one might expect more of these types of writing tasks.

Research Papers

There is not extensive research on L2 students writing research papers, and existing research is largely in the form of case studies. These studies reveal common difficulties but distinct individual responses by ESL students while carrying out writing tasks. The studies reported here highlight a number of difficulties faced by ESL writers, including: (a) developing an effective organizing framework; (b) meeting the demands in mastering sub-technical academic vocabulary; (c) avoiding plagiarism and providing appropriate attributions; (d) building skills for selecting good topics for research; and (e) recognizing audience and developing authorial voice. In almost all cases, studies on research papers involve students in disciplinary rather than composition settings.

In one case study, Zhu (2005) reported on an MBA ESL student's process of writing research papers. In her study, she found that the student relied on an overview article as an organizing foundation, and then inserted additional information from other sources, resulting in the completed research paper following the structure of the overview article. This choice represented a logical strategy for a student who did not know how to collect, select, and integrate information using a framework generated by his or her own goals for writing. In the absence of explicit instruction in organizing a research paper (or a few relevant and useful models of related research papers), this student found a realistic solution to term paper writing. (See also Hirvela, 2004, and Johns, 1997, on the need for students to be taught relevant models and to interrogate those models as part of instruction.)

In a second case study investigation, Tardy (2005) reported on two ESL graduate students writing high-stakes academic papers at a U.S. university. One of the participants was a student in the Master's program in computer science writing his master's thesis; the other was an electrical engineering doctoral student writing several research papers. Over the course of the study, both participants gradually realized that they needed ways to persuade the reader more explicitly about the arguments they were making. Both were becoming more aware of the need to situate the importance of their study in their respective research literatures and to consider the audience as readers they needed to persuade. In this study, Tardy (2005) also highlighted the importance of mentoring in the students' development of rhetorical knowledge. Explicit support by mentors greatly helped them rethink and reshape their papers during the writing process. Additionally, she suggested that explicit instruction in audience, voice, and persuasive rhetoric should be taught regularly in advanced EAP classrooms. In an extension of her case-study research among L2 graduate students in the U.S., Tardy (2009) further highlighted the importance and usefulness of explicit instruction in genre knowledge—including the particular structures, move-stages, and linguistic features in different genres.

Angelova and Riazantseva (1999), in a study paralleling that of Tardy, followed four ESL graduate students from different L1 backgrounds, touching upon many of the themes noted above and in the discussion of synthesis writing. They found that L2 students struggled with topic decisions, discourse structure, and appropriate vocabulary in their writing processes with discipline-based academic research papers. L1 students are often expected to develop their own topics, but this may be quite difficult for L2 students who do not have intuitive knowledge of what might be acceptable, or even preferred, topics. For these four ESL students, deciding on a topic for their research papers was difficult because they were not accustomed to this practice and were relative novices in their fields. With respect to text organization and vocabulary in their writing, this study revealed that these students lacked knowledge of, and had difficulty in, using discipline-appropriate essay structures and vocabularies (see also Shanahan, 2009, and Shanahan & Shanahan, 2008), for discussions of disciplinary variation in reading-writing tasks in L1 secondary school contexts). Based on interviews with both students and professors, the authors suggested that more and earlier support should be given to ESL graduate students, and that more communication is needed between students and professors about academic expectations.

Research on L2 students writing longer research papers and Master's theses points to many reading-writing problems. Even at very advanced levels, ESL students continue having problems with more limited vocabulary knowledge, impacting both their reading and writing skills. They also need to learn explicit ways to structure and organize the information they want to present in their papers. Moreover, they need to go beyond reporting information to interpret information in ways that effectively address their primary audience and support a position or an argument. L2 students do not have experiences in writing sustained arguments or explanations, and thus need explicit instruction and support with such writing tasks. In response, a key for teachers lies in explaining and being more explicit in teaching discourse organization in texts, specific goals for writing, audience awareness, and persuasive development. To emphasize the seriousness of this problem, Leki (2007) reported that the four students she studied over four years, in general, did relatively little writing, did very few prototypical research papers, and received little instructional support for these assignments during their time as undergraduates. Much more research is needed on writing instruction and support for research papers, both in writing courses and in subject area courses—especially in upper-division courses.

CONTRASTIVE RHETORIC, SOCIALIZATION, AND PLAGIARISM

Most ESL students in U.S. university contexts are adult learners. Most have had received many years of literacy instruction in their L1 before entering U.S. universities to study English or receive a degree. The literacy instruction they received from their home countries may be quite different from U.S. educational settings. In some cultures, reading is largely defined as recitation of text, while the practices of finding main ideas and details and making inferences are never explicitly taught in their L1 reading instruction. Writing instruction in the students' L1 may also be different from practices in U.S. university settings, though not always (see, for example, Qin, 2009). In many countries in East Asian (China, Japan, Korea), for example, the argument has been made that the reader of the text is responsible for figuring out its meaning. The writer does not have to make everything clear and straightforward; in fact, a piece of writing that is too straightforward may be considered low-quality because there is no room for the reader to make inferences (Connor, 1996). When these students study in U.S. universities, they may experience difficulty in the expected/conventional reading and writing demands in U.S. university classes. At the same time, their own reading/writing behaviors may be considered inappropriate.

Literature on contrastive rhetoric has been discussed, argued over, and criticized for almost fifty years. Yet, the insight that students bring distinct socio-cultural preferences from their L1 educational socializations, and that these are reflected in their writing/rhetorical preferences, is a persuasive notion. It has been well-documented in many contexts that it needs careful consideration in any L2 writing instructional setting (Casanave, 2004; Connor, 1996, 2002, 2008; Kaplan, 2005). Since Kaplan (1966) first raised the notion of contrastive rhetoric based on his study of ESL students' paragraph structures, contrastive rhetoric has been criticized for essentializing whole groups of students and their writing abilities simply because of their L1 background. This is a legitimate concern; for example, simply because a student is Japanese does not mean he or she writes with odd or unusual patterns of text organization. At the same time, if the goal is to identify discernible patterns of variation associated with L1 socialization outcomes, and to note them as contributing factors to L2 writing performance, contrastive rhetoric represents a useful line of inquiry, one that does not essentialize as much as note socialization preferences as possible contributing factors to L2 student performance.

More recently, Connor (2004, 2008) has proposed that contrastive rhetoric be reconsidered as intercultural rhetoric, as a way to expand inquiry into rhetorical practices and written texts as they cross cultural contexts and social situations. Her goal is to integrate research that examines a wide range of written genres in a large number of contexts—both academic and professional, written by a range of writers, and achieving a number or purposes more or less effectively. These comparisons might include L1 writers in two different languages producing the same functional genres, for example: letters of recommendation, types of editorial arguments, research grant proposals, research articles in economics journals, academic book reviews, etc. Her approach, however, suggests that contrastive rhetoric, traditionally involving L1 cultural preferences and the effects of educational socialization practices on academic writing, offer useful insights for writing instruction with L2 students. Her views align with others who suggest a moderate position for the possible implications of contrastive rhetoric without having this perspective dominate other explanatory factors influencing L2 writing performance (see, for example, Casanave, 2004, and her "investigative pedagogical approach").

One current example of English L1 writing socialization practices that has gained currency in the past decade, and is often discussed in relation to contrastive rhetoric, is the matter of plagiarism and text borrowing. For students from other cultural backgrounds, especially some Asian and Middle Eastern countries, plagiarism is not treated as seriously as it is in North American universities. Students from multiple countries do not share the conceptual understanding of the intellectual ownership of ideas that is assumed in U.S. university settings, and this creates a cultural barrier for them.

For example, Shi (2004) investigated the influence of eighty-seven university students' L1s on their language usage from source texts and suggested significant differences in the language use and citation behaviors between English L1 and English L2 students. Participants of the study were forty-eight English L2 students in a Chinese university, and thirty-nine English L1 students in a U.S. university. They were asked to write a summary and an opinion essay based on two source texts, and their language use was compared to that of the original text. Results showed, first, that the Chinese students directly copied more source text language in longer word strings and provided few citations overall. This was even more true with their summaries because the students had to rely more so on source texts for information. Second, Chinese students did not realize they were plagiarizing by not citing the authors of the original articles.

In a second study (noted earlier), Shi (2006) interviewed twenty-five university-level ESL students who spoke Chinese, Japanese, and Korean as their L1s. She found that plagiarism was not seen as a serious issue, nor was it treated as such in their school systems. Students typically did not study citation conventions as they might apply in their L1 writing. The students' claims of not having been explicitly taught the practice of citation is also supported in Scollon's (1997) study. It showed that, in Chinese news writing, there is no standard practice for quotations, and the distinction between borrowed and original language is ambiguous.

In contrast to the above studies, Wheeler (2009) surveyed seventy-seven EFL students in a Japanese university on their judgments of two pieces of student writing on the same topic. The students gave low scores to both essays that plagiarized a (fictionally) published paragraph on the same topic, citing a lack of academic honesty to support their judgments. His results suggested that English learners with Japanese cultural backgrounds were aware of the issue of plagiarism, showing disapproval. Based on his result, Wheeler (2009) argued: (a) it oversimplifies to say that plagiarism is inherent in a particular culture, and (b) that Japanese university students are well aware of the issue of plagiarism. Nevertheless, despite a growing recognition of the issue of plagiarism in many cultures, including China (Bloch, 2008), having an abstract understanding of plagiarism does not prevent students from plagiarizing in their writing for a variety of reasons. Research has shown that many students, though having an abstract understanding of plagiarism and being aware that they should not do it, still unintentionally and intentionally plagiarize because they do not know when to cite, how to cite, and what to cite (Pecarori, 2003).

Bloch (2008) reviewed this debate on plagiarism from the perspective of contrastive rhetoric, situating occurrences of plagiarism in L2 student writing as a possible outcome of different historical, cultural, and social orientations to writing and authorial ownership. He reviewed the history of contrastive rhetoric, tying the review in with a history of plagiarism and textual ownership (see also Horning, 2010). He also examines the arguments of researchers who assert that plagiarism is primarily a reflection of educational socialization practices and their impact on L2 students (Fox, 1994). From a pedagogical perspective, Bloch (2008) argues that contested views about plagiarism in student writing create ideal opportunities to have discussions about what counts as plagiarism, for who, and why. In this way, student views on text borrowing are treated respectfully, but experiences with plagiarism create the opportunity to teach ESL students about U.S. academic expectations for writing, ownership of ideas, and providing appropriate attribution.

Similar to Bloch (2008), Valentine's (2006) case analysis of one Chinese graduate student's (Lin) plagiarism behavior revealed the complexity behind simple "academic dishonesty" charges. Lin was charged with plagiarism and had to go through an academic hearing because his professor realized, for the final research paper, that he had used direct quotations from his sources without marking them and that there were few of his own words expressing his opinion. Lin was initially shocked because he considered himself an honest student, spending a lot of time reading the sources, understanding them, and arranging information in his paper. He directly copied the information because he misunderstood the professor's intention (to provide a point of view instead of demonstrating knowledge of the field) and the differences in acceptable citation behaviors between America and China. Through the analysis of this case, Valentine (2006) cautioned educators not to simply view plagiarism as the dishonest practice of students, but to view it as a complicated literacy practice that involves social relationships, attitudes, and cultural values. Along the same lines, teachers should not simply punish students caught plagiarizing, but teach them appropriate literacy practices. In doing so, teachers should discuss choices that writers make while citing information in relation to different contexts and also ways to incorporate different types of knowledge into their own writing.

The four themes addressed in this section all identify ways in which reading, text input, and writing performance, in combination, introduce many complications when working with L2 students in composition classes. Summary writing is more difficult for the average L2 student (as compared with the typical L1 university student), who has certainly had much less experience summarizing in English. Both summary and synthesis writing highlight language proficiency limitations of many L2 students and the need to provide these students with more explicit reading instruction in support of text comprehension for writing. Research papers add the complexity of working with many resources for an extended length of time and the need to develop ways to use text resources effectively. All three types of reading-writing tasks highlight issues of direct copying and plagiarism. Finally, different L2 students use texts in line with varying historical, cultural, and social perspectives they bring to writing tasks in the composition classroom.

L2 LANGUAGE PROFICIENCY AND THE LIMITS ON ENGLISH L2 WRITING ABILITIES

An obvious inference running through most research on reading and writing relationships for English L2 students in university settings is that many (but not all) have limited English L2 language resources in comparison with English L1 students. It is a straightforward observation that L2 students who take the TOEFL exam, or the Cambridge-based IELTS exam, do not perform very well in writing tasks when their other language skills (e.g., grammar, vocabulary, reading, listening) are relatively weak. We would be quite surprised to find students performing well on L2 writing tasks while performing relatively poorly on all other L2 language skills (certainly in comparison with most university L1 students).

The association between L2 writing abilities and L2 language proficiency more generally suggests that L2 students can be quite different from English L1 students in composition courses. For example, Delaney (2008), through the examination of 139 English L1 and English L2 learners at several universities, found that both her ESL and EFL participants' reading-to-write task performance (timed summaries and response essays) were influenced by their English proficiency. Works by Ellis and Loewen (2005), Jarvis (2002), Jarvis, Grant, Bikowski, and Ferris (2003), and Grant and Ginther (2000) all suggest that L2 writing abilities are correlated with L2 vocabulary knowledge—a key aspect of language proficiency. Both Leki (2007) and Spack (1997) comment on their case-study students' lack of vocabulary knowledge to read relevant material, interact effectively, or follow lectures with ease.

In research specifically concerned with the impact of reading abilities on L2 writing, Baba (2009) and Plakans (2009a) showed that reading constituted an important ability for writing performance (see also Risemberg, 1996, and Spivey and King, 1989) for L1 studies showing that reading abilities contribute to writing performance). Lee (2005), in a study involving 270 Taiwanese university students, showed that the amount of free, voluntary reading by students was the most significant factor in explaining essay writing scores. Spack (1997), in her case-study research, showed that her student experienced significant difficulties with reading as a part of her writing difficulties in both composition classes and in a range of other undergraduate courses. The impact of reading on writing is also strongly supported by the large-scale educational research of Elley (1991; 2000), showing that extensive reading and extensive exposure to print significantly impacted L2 students' writing development (see also Ferris, 2009).

This association between L2 writing and a range of L2 language skills (including reading) indicates that expectations for academic writing success among L2 students must be tempered by students' L2 language abilities generally, and also more specifically by their reading comprehension abilities. In tasks that involve some integration of reading and writing skills, L2 students need to have adequate reading comprehension abilities if the task assigned requires them to be accountable for the content of the reading text. While it is not the task of the writing teacher to also become a teacher of overall language abilities in L2 English, it is, nonetheless, important for the writing teacher to find out if English language proficiency—especially in reading comprehension and vocabulary knowledge—is a major factor in an L2 student's performance on writing tasks. If this turns out to be the case (possibly through initial writing and diagnostic tasks), the question becomes what the writing teacher's responsibilities are and the extent to which the writing teacher can accommodate the L2 student's language needs.

IMPLICATIONS FROM L2 RESEARCH ON READING-WRITING RELATIONS FOR WRITING INSTRUCTION

As we noted in Research on L2 Reading-Writing Integration in the Writing Classroom, most writing tasks in academic contexts require some type of reading (Leki & Carson, 1994, 1997; Johns, 2002). Students who take ESL (pre-university) writing classes may receive useful instruction in both academic reading and writing before they take mainstream university classes; however, according to Leki and Carson (1994), many L2 students state that they wanted more instruction on reading-based writing, such as summary, synthesis, and research paper writing, when interviewed after having completed pre-university EAP instruction. This desire for more practice with academic reading and writing tasks suggests that L2 students receive as much attention to their reading comprehension needs as to their writing production needs when they move into the composition classroom.

L2 students certainly need more practice in identification, interpretation, and use of main ideas and themes in texts (i.e., reading skills). However, there is relatively little explicit discussion on how to address main idea identification and interpretation in writing classes; this ability is commonly assumed by writing teachers. Most L1 students do, in fact, have good skills in main idea identification and interpretation from texts, even if they are not aware of just how they implement these skills. Because of L1 students' reading abilities, there is usually little practice given to skills in reading comprehension. Moreover, most university writing courses engage in discussions of texts assuming that the texts are understood by students. This assumption can be a reason why "discussion in preparation for writing" may not be very useful for weaker L2 students.

An additional outcome of this review of L2 research on reading and writing relations is the recognition that a number of L2 students will have difficulties with the concept of plagiarism and with not appropriating too much material directly from source texts. With L2 students, instruction in dealing with plagiarism should focus more on proactive teaching to lead students towards correct use of source texts, rather than a focus on post-writing punishment (Horning, 2010; Pecorari, 2003; Valentine, 2006). In addition, efforts should be made to work explicitly on paraphrasing skills to help L2 students use text information more appropriately (Keck, 2006).

It is not possible to address every difference between L1 and L2 students in the composition classroom and still have time to carry out every writing goal of the course. However, there are a number of specific suggestions that can be considered if L2 students constitute a fair percentage of students in the class. We offer suggestions that involve reading-support activities, reading-writing support activities, awareness-raising activities, and pre-discussion activities.

With respect to support for reading tasks in the composition classroom, L2 students may need more explicit intervention in comprehension, particularly when asked to read more challenging material. Providing a reading guide for students can be very helpful, especially as a preparation resource for other reading and writing tasks. A reading guide might ask students for a brief list of key ideas, the perspective or bias of the author (and what signals exist in the text for these interpretations), one or two interpretation questions that force "between the lines" thinking, a question or two about intended audience, and a question or two about a controversial issue or problem that might also be a lead-in to class discussion. L2 students would also benefit from explicit attention to the organization of a text and the rhetorical patterns used to present major information. Teachers can begin this process by simply asking how a text is organized and why it is organized that way. Attention to key, thematic vocabulary and unusual words or to metaphoric use would be helpful as well, either as an activity filling in glosses or as a homework activity directed to L2 students.

There are a number of ways writing teachers can provide L2 students with support for vocabulary development: The teacher can identify eight to ten key terms, metaphoric uses, and culturally loaded terms and ask students to work in groups to check their understanding of these terms. (This could also be done as homework for L2 students). The teacher can hand out a set of glossaries to L2 students for key and additional terms that are likely to cause problems for L2 student comprehension and interpretation of the text. The teacher can provide a set of key thematic terms on the blackboard for a quick, in-class writing response to an assigned reading, allowing L2 students to recognize vocabulary they might use in their responses. The teacher can ask L2 students to underline and nominate eight to ten words and phrases that they can't figure out, bring them to class, and work in groups to sort them out while L1 students complete another short, in-class writing task. Teachers can also meet and share ideas about other possible ways to provide vocabulary support for L2 students who are struggling.

L2 students can also be encouraged to engage in extensive reading with texts they find interesting and are also related to course themes. Teachers can develop lists of book chapters, Internet sources, and magazine articles that allow L2 students to expand their background knowledge while also giving these students more exposure and practice with reading in English (Horning, 2010). Teachers can also give L2 students a small amount of extra credit for engaging in additional, extensive readings on a key topic. At the same time, teachers can develop a simple, section-by-section summary or outline of main points in a longer reading assignment to ensure better understanding and interpretations of texts. This support allows L2 students to read longer and more understand complex texts assigned to everyone.

More explicit attention to the purpose of reading-writing tasks would also raise L2 students' awareness of course expectations while allowing L2 students a safe way to ask questions about specific task expectations. Such attention to reading and writing goals can be developed overtly through close interrogation of the prompt, clear teacher expectations for the writing task, and critical analyses of model assignments. In preparing more generally for in-class discussions of a text, L2 students would be helped by first doing a quick-write on a key point in the text, by generating and sharing a main-idea list, or by skimming the text before discussing and reflecting on (and noting) some interesting aspect of the text. In addition, asking L2 students to generate a list of key ideas from a reading text and then write a summary is a very effective method of comprehension and writing support for L2 students (see also Shanahan & Shanahan, 2008).

It is also important to hold L2 students accountable for assigned text materials. This accountability can be created by: (1) assigning for quick response writing the next day in class; (2) generating a list of key issues or ideas from a text on the board before in-class discussions; or (3) having students respond to a key paragraph and/or statement in the text in class, and then collecting the responses. Alternatively, L2 students can be assigned to keep reading journals in which they write down ideas from the text, respond to key information, reflect on issues in the text, or comment on ways to use text material in their writing.

They can also write down four to six key words and phrases from each reading in the back of their journals that they would like to go back to and review. These journals can be collected every few weeks, checked very quickly, and given a grade.

With respect to reading-writing tasks themselves, explicit analysis of model writing assignments—especially in relation to teacher/task expectations—is very helpful for L2 students. Looking at model assignments, students can be asked to identify how issues and arguments from source texts are shaped to be persuasive for an audience. They can also examine how selected ideas from texts are attributed to the text's authors (Valentine, 2006). These awareness-raising activities should improve reading comprehension and writing performance. It is important also to ensure that writing assignments do not have tacit cultural or academic assumptions of which L2 students might not be aware. If such tacit assumptions are part of an assignment, they need to be explicitly discussed. Exploration of tacit assumptions can even be part of whole-class discussions in which students propose hidden assumptions embedded within the writing task.

Put simply, L2 students also need much more practice in writing. Reading-writing tasks need to be frequent enough so that L2 students build confidence and fluency and also receive consistent feedback on their writing. In providing feedback to L2 students, teachers or peers often need to address incorrect grammatical forms in L2 student texts. If L2 students are struggling, a goal is not to fix everything in a given assignment, but to address a few grammar problems progressively and move on with another task. It is also very helpful for L2 students to read their writing assignments aloud to others in a group so they become more aware of writing weaknesses. Reading aloud will improve phrasing, clause structuring, and sentence rhythm, and it will allow other students to give useful feedback. It also ensures accountability within the group work. Finally, peer feedback guidelines should be used to provide very explicit support to L2 students. The guidelines need to give explicit directions for what to attend to, how, and how much. Some very basic pointers could include: "Can you state what the main idea is in two sentences?"; "Does every part of the text address the main idea, or are other, non-central ideas introduced?"; "How is the text organized?"; "Is the organization clearly indicated?"; "Is there sentence variety?"; "What part of the text do you like the most, or is the most effective? Why?" (See Grabe & Kaplan (1996, pp. 382–92) for various format options.)

Of course, a brief list of possible ideas supporting L2 writers in the composition classroom does not begin to address all the issues likely to arise (see Table 1); nor does it handle many of the challenges faced by the writing teacher working with a complex mix of reading and writing abilities and L1 and L2 students. However, L2 students in the composition class are more likely to succeed with more complex reading-writing tasks if provided with concrete ways to attend to reading input and given ways to generate, organize, and revise ideas they use in their writing. L2 students are also more likely to succeed if the writing teacher finds ways to focus on key vocabulary from core texts, highlight vocabulary learning activities for L2 students (perhaps as part of more individualized classroom and homework activities), support text comprehension and interpretation, and give students more opportunities to engage in several short writing tasks (perhaps as part of the larger writing tasks in the curriculum).

Writing teachers might say that the complexities created by several L2 students in a writing course limit what she or he is able to do with all students in the class. One of the most useful ways to address this problem is for groups of teachers to get together to explore how to integrate L2 student needs with larger instructional goals. Teacher groups can begin with a set of teaching issues (such as those listed in Table 1) and prioritize those most important to address. They can make lists of suggestions and "ideas that work," sort through them, and discuss ways to successfully adopt or adapt ideas for their teaching contexts. They can experiment in small ways with teaching ideas and report back to their group on difficulties and successes. Over time, discussions with interested colleagues are likely to provide useful techniques and tasks that will make a difference for L2 student struggling with both reading and writing.

In closing, it is important to recognize that L2 student writers encounter more challenges with integrated reading-writing tasks than do L1 students. Most L2 students who get as far as university writing classes also manage to be successful in these writing courses. It takes a tremendous amount of will and desire for L2 students to completely undertake a university education in a second language, and a large majority of L2 students are strongly motivated to succeed in their writing courses. A composition teacher who is well-informed about the challenges facing the L2 student will make it that much more likely for that student to succeed.

7 The Common Core Standards and Preparation for Reading and Writing in College

David A. Jolliffe

When college faculty members, whether in English or other disciplines, teach entering first-year students, the instructors generally expect their charges to be competent, critical, analytical readers, and to write about what they read in an array of different genres. They usually presume that a student graduates from high school with the ability to comprehend the main and supporting ideas of a text, to understand how an author develops those ideas with evidence and reasoning, to appreciate how the form of a text supports its functions, and to demonstrate their knowledge of these things in their own compositions. These college faculty members are often surprised and disappointed.

Working to ensure that students graduate from U.S. high schools prepared to succeed in college or careers, a joint committee of the National Governors' Association and the Council of Chief State School Officers has worked since 2009 to develop a set of Common Core standards (2010) to guide the teaching of reading, writing, and mathematics in U.S. elementary and secondary schools. Adopted by forty-six states and the District of Columbia (and counting) as of March 1, 2013, these standards hold the potential to affect the ways reading, writing, and math are taught for decades to come and, as a result, influence the preparation of first-year college students to interact with texts in the ways, sketched out above, that their instructors expect them to.

Will the standards achieve this goal? Will students in the future come to college or enter careers better prepared to meet the reading and writing demands they encounter? Perhaps, but not unless educators take pains to teach students the connections between reading and writing inherent in college and career intellectual work—connections that are *not* evident in the Common Core document—and not unless educators substantially finesse the scope and specificity of the standards. In this chapter, I initially provide some back story related to the development of the Common Core standards, and I unpack why college and university faculty members should understand the implications of the standards for the preparedness of their students for college-level work. Then I focus on the standards related to the teaching and learning of reading and writing in grades six through twelve, explaining what the reading standards imply for the teaching of writing, and vice versa. Finally, I note some gaps in the standards germane to any consideration of reading in the high school-to-college transition, and offer a modest proposal about *what* students should read and write about in high school that could affect *how* they are made ready for success in college and in careers.

History and Goals of the Common Core Standards

The Common Core standards might be seen as the latest in a line of "let's-improve-education" products stretching back at least to Congress's 1965 passage of the Elementary and Secondary Education Act, moving through the famous *Nation at Risk* report in 1983, the failed national history standards project in 1994 and 1995 (about which, more below), and also the authorizing of *No Child Left Behind* in 2002. Indeed, the Common Core standards represent the latest attempt by educational policy makers to determine what students should know and be able to do at certain points in their progress from kindergarten through high school.

While the document provides focuses on only two content areas—English/language arts and mathematics—the standards for the secondary grades provide guidance for "literacy in history/social studies, science, and technical subjects" (Common Core State Standards, 2010, p. 1). Divided into two large chunks, for grades kindergarten through five and for grades six through twelve, the Common Core standards aim to guide what teachers teach their students about how to read, write, understand the English language, conduct research, and do mathematics throughout the curriculum and in several content areas. Of more exigence for the current educational culture, the Common

Core standards promise to undergird the construction of new standardized assessments to determine what students know and can do, and that schools are making adequate yearly progress toward the goals of proficiency in literacy and mathematics established by their states under the *No Child Left Behind Act*.

The potential conflict between the underlying philosophy of the Common Core standards—namely that young people everywhere in the United States should be held to the same expectations for academic performance at their grade levels—and the doctrine of states' rights is palpable in public discussions of the standards. Strict constitutionalists remind supporters of Common Core that providing and guiding public education is a responsibility of the states, and they look with suspicion on any initiative that might be construed as advocating a national curriculum. Proponents of the Common Core standards, however, make clear that the creation of the document was sponsored by two states' organizations, the National Governors' Association, and the Council of Chief State School Officers, and that adopting the standards is strictly voluntary. Encouraging states to adopt the document, though, evinces an interesting bit of hegemony at work: U.S. Secretary of Education Arne Duncan made it clear that states adopting the Common Core standards would have an inside track in "Race to the Top" funds authorized by Congress in 2010 (Lewin, 2010).

WHY SHOULD COLLEGE AND UNIVERSITY FACULTY MEMBERS BE CONCERNED?

As I have noted elsewhere (Jolliffe, 2003, 2007; Jolliffe & Harl, 2008), a substantial amount of "water-cooler conversation" and some research corroborate the skeptical attitude that my years of teaching have fostered, supporting the assertion that many college students do not read with the careful, critical acuity required for academic success, and embodied in the Common Core standards. Corroborating hallway discourse, for example, 83% of faculty in California's public two- and four-year colleges maintain that a "lack of analytic reading skills contributes to students' lack of success in a course" (Intersegmental Committee of the Academic Senates of the California Community Colleges, the California State University, and the University of California, 2002, p. 4). Horning and Kraemer's introductory chapter in this volume summarizes an array of research studies, all of which likewise suggest that contemporary college students' reading abilities constitute a problem for their academic viability and success. Clearly, any college or university faculty member who hopes his or her students succeed must have some stake in the Common Core standards' potential to influence those students' reading abilities.

The Reading Standards: In Isolation and in Relation to Writing

What are the standards? The Common Core document presents the reading standards first, before the standards for the teaching of writing, language, and speaking and listening. For English/language arts, the teaching and learning of reading in kindergarten through fifth grade, and sixth grade through twelfth grade, are based on the same ten "anchor standards":

Key Ideas and Details

1. Read closely to determine what the text says explicitly and to make logical inferences from it; cite specific textual evidence when writing or speaking to support conclusions drawn from the text.

2. Determine central ideas or themes of a text and analyze their development; summarize the key supporting details and ideas.

3. Analyze how and why individuals, events, and ideas develop and interact over the course of a text.

Craft and Structure

4. Interpret words and phrases as they are used in a text, including determining technical, connotative, and figurative meanings, and analyze how specific word choices shape meaning or tone.

5. Analyze the structure of texts, including how specific sentences, paragraphs, and larger portions of the text (e.g., a section, chapter, scene, or stanza) relate to each other and the whole.

6. Assess how point of view or purpose shapes the content and style of a text.

Integration of Knowledge and Ideas

7. Integrate and evaluate content presented in diverse formats and media, including visually and quantitatively, as well as in words. (This standard references a footnote about related material in the "Writing" and "Speaking and Listening" anchor standards.)

8. Delineate and evaluate the argument and specific claims in a text, including the validity of the reasoning as well as the relevance and sufficiency of the evidence.

9. Analyze how two or more texts address similar themes or topics in order to build knowledge or to compare the approaches the authors take.

Range of Reading and Level of Text Complexity

10. Read and comprehend complex literary and informational texts independently and proficiently. (Common Core State Standards Initiative, 2010, p. 35)

Following the tenth anchor standard, the document appends the following:

> *Note on range and content of student reading*
>
> To become college and career ready, students must grapple with works of exceptional craft and thought whose range extends across genres, cultures, and centuries. Such works offer profound insights into the human condition and serve as models for students' own thinking and writing. Along with high-quality contemporary works, these texts should be chosen from among seminal U.S. documents, the classics of American literature, and the timeless dramas of Shakespeare. Through wide and deep reading of literature and literary non-fiction of steadily increasing sophistication, students gain a reservoir of literary and cultural knowledge, references, and images; the ability to evaluate intricate arguments; and the

capacity to surmount the challenges posed by complex texts. (p. 35)

Throughout the document, this notion of "range and content of student reading" results in a classification of three types of texts: literary (fiction, poetry, drama), "informational" texts for English/language arts, and "informational" texts for history/social studies, science, mathematics, and technology.

To flesh out and expand the anchor standards, the document provides individual sets of ten student learning expectations (SLEs), using the same categories as the anchors, for reading literature and informational texts in grades six, seven, eight, nine/ten, and eleven/twelve. Here, for example, are the ten SLEs for the teaching and learning of informational texts in eleventh and twelfth grades:

Key Ideas and Details

1. Cite strong and thorough textual evidence to support analysis of what the text says explicitly as well as inferences drawn from the text, including determining where the text leaves matters uncertain.

2. Determine two or more central ideas of a text and analyze their development over the course of the text, including how they interact and build on one another to provide a complex analysis; provide an objective summary of the text.

3. Analyze a complex set of ideas or sequence of events and explain how specific individuals, ideas, or events interact and develop over the course of the text.

Craft and Structure

4. Determine the meaning of words and phrases as they are used in a text, including figurative, connotative, and technical meanings; analyze how an author uses and refines the meaning of a key term or terms over the course of a text (e.g., how Madison defines faction in Federalist No. 10).

5. Analyze and evaluate the effectiveness of the structure an author uses in his or her exposition or argument, including whether the structure makes points clear, convincing, and engaging.

6. Determine an author's point of view or purpose in a text in which the rhetoric is particularly effective, analyzing how style and content contribute to the power, persuasiveness or beauty of the text.

Integration of Knowledge and Ideas

7. Integrate and evaluate multiple sources of information presented in different media or formats (e.g., visually, quantitatively) as well as in words in order to address a question or solve a problem.

8. Delineate and evaluate the reasoning in seminal U.S. texts, including the application of constitutional principles and use of legal reasoning (e.g., in U.S. Supreme Court majority opinions and dissents) and the premises, purposes, and arguments in works of public advocacy (e.g., The Federalist, presidential addresses).

9. Analyze seventeenth-, eighteenth-, and nineteenth-century foundational U.S. documents of historical and literary significance (including The Declaration of Independence, the Preamble to the Constitution, the Bill of Rights, and Lincoln's Second Inaugural Address) for their themes, purposes, and rhetorical features.

Range of Reading and Level of Text Complexity

10. By the end of grade 11, read and comprehend literary nonfiction in the grades 11-College and Career Ready (CCR) text complexity band proficiently, with scaffolding as needed at the high end of the range.

11. By the end of grade 12, read and comprehend literary nonfiction at the high end of the grades 11-CCR text complexity band independently and proficiently. (pp. 39–40)

All told, the document provides eleven sets of standards and SLEs to guide the teaching and learning of reading in grades six through twelve.

What exactly are the standards asking teachers to teach and students to learn? For anyone teaching students to read critically and analytically, the standards are not rocket science, and their foci and emphases are perfectly adequate. In the anchor standards and SLEs, numbers one through three direct teachers to teach and students to learn how to determine the main point of a text, how to understand the main point's development with examples and reasoning, and how to draw inferences—ideas, conclusions, and extensions *not* on the page—based on what *is* in the text. Standards Four and Five guide teachers to teach and students to learn about analyzing the diction and structure of a text, while Standard Six directs their attention to the author's purpose, perspective, and to the point of view of a literary text. Standards Seven, Eight, and Nine are a grab bag: Standard Seven focuses on teaching and learning how to read and analyze multimodal texts; Standard Eight centers on teaching and learning argument structure—claims, evidence, and reasoning; Standard Nine points teachers and students in the direction of what reading specialists, following Ellin Oliver Keene and Susan Zimmermann (1997), call "making text-to-text connections" (p. 55).

The problem with the reading standards resides in the contradiction that emerges when one considers them in relation to the writing standards. As the following section shows, the writing standards hint (not too clearly, I might add) that students should learn to write in different genres to address various purposes for a range of audiences; yet, the reading standards and the sample performance tasks that grow out of them suggest that the most important type of writing students must do—perhaps the *only* type they must do—is straightforward, analytic writing about their reading.

THE COMMON CORE WRITING STANDARDS: A DISCONNECT?

As it did with the reading standards, the Common Core document presents ten "College and Career Readiness Anchor Standards for Writing," and then provides more specific versions for individual grades kindergarten through eight, and then paired grades nine and ten and eleven and twelve. The first three anchor standards for writing call on students to "write arguments to support claims in and analysis of substantive topics and tasks, using valid reasoning and relevant and effective evidence"; to "write informative and explanatory texts to examine and convey complex ideas and information clearly"; and "to write narratives to develop real or imagined experiences or events using effective technique, well-chosen details, and well-structured event sequences" (p. 36). The next three anchor standards take up issues of good writing in general, writing process, and technology. These standards guide students to "produce clear and coherent writing in which the development, organization, and style are appropriate to task, purpose, and audience"; to develop a fully-elaborated and effective writing process; and to "use technology, including the Internet, to produce and publish writing and to interact and collaborate with others" (p. 36). The last two anchor standards for writing require students to "conduct short as well as more sustained research projects"; to "gather relevant information from multiple print and digital sources, assess the credibility and accuracy of each source, and integrate the information while avoiding plagiarism"; "to draw evidence from literary or informational texts to support analysis, reflection, and research"; and to "write routinely over extended time frames . . . and sort time frames . . . for a range of tasks, purposes, and audiences" (p. 41).

Educators will need to do a bit of conceptual straightening out of the writing standards for them to be useful guidelines for preparing successful writers in high school, college, and the workplace. Moreover, educators will need to work hard to help their students see connections between learning to read and learning to write, as these are connections that are not transparent in the standards document.

First, the conceptual issue: The Common Core writing standards blatantly confuse the concepts of purpose and mode. Purpose, as all composition scholars know, refers to what action the rhetor wants his or her text to accomplish for the audience. Taxonomies of purpose range from Cicero's three "duties of an orator"—to teach, to delight, and to move—in *De Oratore* to James Kinneavy's (1981) broad "aims of discourse": to self-express, to persuade, to refer (i.e., to inform, explain, or demonstrate), and to create a pleasing artifact. In contrast, the traditional modes of discourse, as all compositionists know, were codified in Alexander Bain's 1866 text, *English Composition and Rhetoric*, and, as Robert Connors (1981) explained, gained a tenacious foothold in composition pedagogy. Bain's four modes, still alive in the "rhetorical table of contents" in many composition anthologies, are narration, description, exposition, and argumentation. The modes are not ends in themselves; they are tools a writer can use to develop his or her composition and to achieve a purpose for a reader.

The first of the anchor standards calls for students to write "arguments," a term that names a mode, not a purpose. I presume the framers of the standards document intended "writing arguments" to be synonymous with "writing to persuade." The second anchor standard guides students to write "informative and explanatory" texts—two terms that denote purposes (to inform and to explain) that fit under Kinneavy's general category of "referential discourse." The third anchor standard urges that students "write narratives"—again, a term used to denote a mode rather than a purpose. The authors of the document try, unwittingly I believe, to finesse the distinction between purpose and mode when they offer this advice about writing narratives: Eleventh- and twelfth-graders are guided in their narratives to "engage and orient the reader by setting out a problem, situation, or observation and its significance" and to "provide a conclusion that follows from and reflects on what is experienced, observed, or resolved over the course of the narrative" (p. 46). In other words, for high school students, narratives generally have an explanatory purpose. Had the authors of the Common Core standards simply explained, "Here is what we mean by purpose in writing and here are the types of purposes you should learn to accomplish," and "Here is what we mean by modes of writing and here's how you should learn to use the modes to develop your texts," then students could benefit from a conceptually unified curriculum that prepared them for the demands of college and career writing.

Second, the lack-of-connections issue: Even though the Common Core standards call on teachers to teach and students to learn how to write arguments, informative and explanatory essays, and narratives, the sample "performance tasks" in the document are solely explanatory—nothing is provided that hints at what kinds of reading students should do to prepare to write arguments and narratives, and nothing is offered to suggest what types of argumentative and narrative writing tasks students should be taught to complete. Indeed, an examination of Appendix B to the Common Core standards document that sets out text exemplars and sample performance tasks, reveals solely explanatory writing-about-reading assignments. For example, a sample task involving literary texts for this grades eleven and twelve calls on students to "analyze Miguel de Cervantes's *Don Quixote* and Jean-Baptiste Poquelin Moliere's *Tartuffe* for how *what is directly stated in the text differs from what is really meant*, comparing and contrasting the *point of view* adopted by the protagonist in each work" (Common Core State Standards Initiative, 2010, Appendix B, p. 163). A sample reading task involving informational texts for the same grade level requires students to "*delineate* and *evaluate* the *argument* that Thomas Paine makes in *Common Sense*" and to "*assess* the *reasoning* in (Paine's) analysis, including the *premises* and *purposes* of his essay" (p. 171). A sample reading task using informational texts in history/social studies, science, mathematics, and technical subjects at grades eleven and twelve requires students to "*analyze the hierarchical* relationships between phrase searches and searches that use basic Boolean operators in Tara Calishain and Rael Dornfest's *Google Hacks: Tips and Tools for Smarter Searching, 2nd edition*" (p. 183).

There is certainly nothing inherently wrong with these kinds of formalist, close-reading writing assignments. As I have suggested elsewhere (Jolliffe, 2003, 2007), close analytic reading is the baby that was thrown out with the bathwater when "the writing process" approach, with its strong initial emphasis on accessing students' affective responses to texts as a starting point for composing, came to dominate high school and college instruction in the 1970s and 1980s. I welcome any curriculum that puts close, rhetorical-analytic reading at its center. If the framers of the Common Core standards are serious about placing equal emphasis on persuasive and informative/explanatory writing in school curriculums, the document needs to attend more fully to how reading and writing tasks can work together to teach students how to write persuasive arguments.

Issues and Concerns about the Standards in General and about Reading in Particular

Educators who have been observing the evolution of the Common Core standards have expressed concerns both about the process of their formation and their content. About the former: The Common Core standards are distinct from earlier educational-improvement projects for the apparent lack of federal involvement in their creation, for the role that both private foundations and for-profit educational organizations played in their writing, and for the speed with which the whole initiative was brought to fruition. While the standards movement is generally lauded by the Obama administration and members of Congress, both the executive and the legislative branches know that the present political climate does not favor any effort that looks like a usurping of states' rights. The creation of the initiative by the National Governors' Association and the Council of Chief State School Officers, therefore, is not only a strategic move, but also a politically correct one.

While the initiative has been directed by two organizations for state officers, some observers are uncomfortable about the involvement of both not-for-profit organizations and for-profit education-product vendors in the standards' creation. The Charles Stewart Mott Foundation and the Bill and Melinda Gates Foundation have been generous in their support of the initiative, and the first-line panel of authors of the standards was heavily populated by vendors—not-for-profits that, despite their name, stand to make a great deal of money as the standards are adopted, put into play in state curriculums, and made the basis of assessments. Of the fourteen members of the work group that wrote the English standards, for example, there is only one actual educator: Sandy Murphy, professor emeritus from the University of California at Davis. The other thirteen members are from ACT (formerly American College Testing); the College Board; organizations called "Achieve," "America's Choice," and "Student Achievement Partners"; plus VockleyLang LLC, a public relations firm with some of the aforementioned entities as their clients. Educators were included on the "feedback" and "validation" panels that examined the standards after they were written. Given the deliberate pace at which educational standards are typically written, examined, and validated, the Common Core standards came into being at lightning speed: The initiative was announced on July 1, 2009, and by March 20, 2010, the standards were available for public inspection and comment. One wonders how much influence the educators on the "feedback" and "validation" panels were able to exert in such an accelerated development process.

These potentially troubling financial/logistical elements aside, other observers have scrutinized the potential educational effectiveness of the standards. How good are the Common Core reading standards? Will they really help elementary and secondary teachers teach, and their students learn, how to read carefully, critically, and analytically so the latter are prepared for college and careers? I admit that I share the misgivings that other educators have voiced about the standards, and I have some of my own. The most salient problem with the reading standards, I maintain, was clearly enunciated in a document from the Thomas Fordham Institute, an educational think tank directed by Chester E. Finn, Jr.: In its analysis of the Common Core reading standards, the Fordham Institute report, *The State of State Standards—and the Common Core—in 2010*, asserts baldly, "the standards do not ultimately provide sufficient clarity and detail to guide teachers and curriculum and assessment developers effectively" (Carmichael, Martino, Porter-Magee, & Wilson, 2010, p. 24). The Fordham Institute document unpacks six other troubling issues about the reading standards:

- Its organization is hard to follow. In particular, the division of the standards into four categories "creates a false sense of separation between inextricably linked characteristics" (p. 23).
- The standards emphasize texts from American literature only in the eleventh grade.
- The standards "fail to address the specific text types, genres, and sub-genres in a systematic intersection with the skills they target" (p. 25).
- The standards "don't properly scaffold skills from grade to grade" (p. 25).
- Several of the standards for reading literature "are also repeated verbatim in the informational text strand, thus making no distinction in applying this skill to literary or informational text" (p. 25).
- The treatment of both literary elements and principles of argumentation in spotty. For example, while students in grades eleven and twelve are expected to "analyze the impact of the author's choices regarding how to develop and relate elements of a story or drama," nowhere in the reading standards or SLEs are students led "to define plot" or "to identify the elements of a plot" (p. 25). Similarly, nowhere in any of the SLEs related to anchor Standard 8, about argument structure and argumentative reasoning, are students led to understand the definitions, uses, and limitations of inductive and deductive reasoning (pp. 25–26).

While the authors of the Fordham Institute document take the Common Core standards to task at a microscopic level, I am more concerned about the shortcomings of the reading standards at a macro level. I am at least marginally satisfied that the *how* of teaching and learning reading is approached adequately in the standards. That is, I think that mastering the reading skills and abilities inscribed in anchor standards One through Nine, if thoroughly understood and taught well by teachers (more on that below), can render graduating high school students better prepared for the reading demands of college and career than many are now. My concerns are about the ways the Common Core standards document handles the *what* of student reading. Let me unpack two of these concerns.

First, while I understand the distinction the standards document tries to make between "literature" and "informational" texts, I believe the differences between the two kinds of texts are naively treated in the standards, and I maintain that "informational" texts is a decidedly limited—and limiting—term. Anyone familiar with either formalist literary criticism, from its heyday in the early twentieth century onwards, or with reading theory, as it has developed in roughly the same time period, recognizes that the "literariness" or "ordinariness" of any text does not reside in the text itself, but instead in the mindset, the intellectual and cognitive schemata, that a reader brings to the text. As Louise Rosenblatt (1978) makes clear in explaining her distinction between "efferent" and "aesthetic" readings, a text *invites* a reader to encounter it at some location on a continuum between a single-minded "carrying away" of information (*effere* is the Latin verb, "to carry") and a pure experiencing of it as beauty, pleasure, and emotion, but the reader himself or herself makes the decision about where his or her reading lands on the continuum. By bifurcating "literature" and "informational texts," not only on the anchor standards but also throughout the sets of SLEs, the Common Core document obviates the fact that some pieces of literature can be read efferently—one can certainly garner lots of "information" about the Dust Bowl from *The Grapes of Wrath*, for example, a text that the document holds up as "illustrating the complexity, quality, and range" of literary works for grades nine and ten—and that some pieces of what the document calls "informational" text can be read aesthetically (Appendix E). I can't imagine reading Churchill's "Blood, Toil, Tears, and Sweat" (recommended for grades six through eight), King's "Letter from Birmingham Jail" (recommended for grades nine and ten), or Thoreau's *Walden* (recommended for grades eleven and twelve) solely for "information."

These are beautifully crafted texts that young readers can analyze for their rhetorical effectiveness and power and, quite simply, also enjoy for the beauty of their organization and prose. I certainly understand and concur with the framers of the standards' apparent goal of getting teachers to teach, and students to read, more excellent, non-fiction prose, but I fear that the adjective "informational" does not support the best practices of such teaching and learning.

Second, I am concerned about the great pains the authors of the document take to emphasize that nothing in the standards remotely resembles a common or required reading list. The opening paragraph of the document's Appendix B is the clearest statement of the framers' position on a "common core" of texts:

> The following text samples primarily serve to *exemplify* the level of complexity and quality that the Standards require all students in a given grade band to engage with. Additionally, they are *suggestive* of the breadth of texts that students should encounter in the text types required by the Standards. The choices should serve as *useful guideposts* in helping educators select texts of similar complexity, quality, and range for their classrooms. *They expressly do not represent a partial or complete reading list.* (Common Core State Standards Initiative, 2010, Appendix B, p. 2, emphases added)

The standards' authors, I imagine, have no desire to revive the dispute that came to the fore in late 1994 and early 1995, when scholars at the University of California at Los Angeles affiliated with the National Center for History in the Schools produced a set of "national voluntary standards" for the teaching of history. Former U.S. Undersecretary of Education Diane Ravitch relates this debacle eloquently in her recent book, *The Death and Life of the Great American School System: How Testing and Choice are Undermining Education* (2010). Though the center had been established with the support of the National Endowment for the Humanities, the NEH chair, Lynne Cheney,

> lambasted the standards as the epitome of left-wing political correctness, because they emphasized the nation's failings and paid scant attention to its great men. The standards document, (Cheney) said, mentioned Joseph McCarthy and McCarthyism nineteen times, the Ku Klux Klan 17 times, and Harriet Tubman six times, while mentioning Ulysses S. Grant

just once and Robert E. Lee not at all. Nor was there any reference to Paul Revere, Alexander Graham Bell, Thomas Edison, Jonas Salk, or the Wright Brothers. Cheney told an interviewer that the document was a "warped and distorted version of the American past in which it becomes a story of oppression and failure." (p. 17)

After being thoroughly castigated by editorialists and talk-show hosts—Rush Limbaugh claimed that the standards should be "flushed down the toilet" (p. 18)—but endorsed by a range of educational organizations, in January 1995, the standards were officially condemned in the United States Senate in a resolution that passed ninety-nine to one, with the lone dissenter a senator from Louisiana "who thought the resolution was not strong enough" (p. 19).

I understand that any choice foregrounding certain texts as "required" reading automatically backgrounds—and marginalizes—other texts. Just as the creators of the national voluntary history standards had to decide which narratives and "actors" they would include, so would any authors of English/language arts standards who chose to create "a partial or complete reading list" have to be sensitive to issues of inclusion and exclusion. However, I worry that the standards framers' determination not to recommend any actual "common" texts in the Common Core standards—texts that they urge all students to read at certain grade levels—runs counter to the initiative's most important goal of helping students become effective critical and analytical readers.

As anyone familiar with reading theory understands, the first move in teaching and learning reading comprehension is to "access prior knowledge." This step leads the reader to call to mind any actual experiences he or she may have previously had with the issues or ideas developed in the text at hand or, as some theorists (e.g., Egan, 2003) are now framing it, any connections to the text the reader can imagine. High school teacher and consultant Jack Farrell (2004) explains how he teaches students to tap into what they already know or can imagine as they read a text. Egan shows students how to annotate their texts, indicating

1. Some previous life experience, either vicarious or read, although this is, by no means, a pre-requisite.

2. Previous works read in this and other classes.

3. Previous concepts (or abstractions) from this and other classes.

4. Previous experiences with the language, its syntax, its rhythms, and its diction.

5. The first reading of the material. (pp. 2–3)

Educational researcher Robert Marzano (2004) is even more emphatic about the importance of tapping into prior knowledge as a vital stage in learning. Marzano expands the concept to *building* background knowledge, calling upon educators to spend time with focused instruction aimed at developing "learned intelligence": facts, generalizations, and principles that can undergird the learning of new material.

To be sure, the Common Core document is replete with language about the quality, complexity, and range of texts that educators should select for their students. (This language of agency differs from the curricular practice promoted by one of the organizations centrally involved with writing the standards: America's Choice. In this organization's curriculum, students are individually urged to select twenty-five books a year that they propose to read.) By not suggesting that any particular text, either literary or otherwise, should be read by all students at a certain grade level, the framers of the reading standards eliminate the opportunity for educators to develop and offer exemplary, large-scale lessons on *how* a reader accesses prior knowledge, imagines worlds, and builds background knowledge to construct the schemata upon which a successful reading can be constructed. I return to this sticky issue of common, required reading in the final section of this chapter.

PREPARING TO TEACH THE COMMON CORE STANDARDS: MAJOR CHALLENGES FOR TEACHERS

College faculty members who want their students to be effective readers must see their colleagues in elementary and secondary schools as allies. So the question arises: What will elementary and secondary school teachers have to do to prepare to incorporate the Common Core reading standards in their courses—in other words, to actually *teach* the ten anchor standards and the parallel twenty SLEs for literature and "informational" texts? First of all, if English teachers are to bear the bulk of the responsibility for teaching the critical and analytical reading inscribed in the standards, they will have to become more familiar with texts other than fiction, poetry, and drama, and incorporate these "informational" texts in their courses. Currently, texts other than literature have a very low profile in high school English courses. A recent study by Sandra Stotsky (2010), commissioned by the Association of Literary Scholars, Critics, and Writers, found that, of 773 ninth-, tenth-, and eleventh-grade English courses described by respondents in a national survey of high school English teachers, only five book-length works of non-fiction were assigned in fifteen or more courses: Elie Weisel's *Night* was assigned in seventy-four courses, *The Narrative of Frederick Douglass* in thirty-three, King's *I Have a Dream* in seventeen, and Thoreau's *Walden* in fifteen. The works of only sixteen authors of non-fiction prose were mentioned fifteen times or more in course descriptions: King, Lincoln, Jefferson, Emerson, Franklin, Thoreau, Patrick Henry, Barack Obama, Thomas Paine, John F. Kennedy, Maya Angelou, Frederick Douglass, Elie Weisel, Mark Twain, Jonathan Edwards, and Malcolm X (p. 73). Stotsky also found that only about a quarter of all ninth-, tenth-, and eleventh-grade courses described by respondents devoted more than twenty class periods a year to non-fiction (p. 27). (A typical high school course, in a thirty-week academic year, meets for 150 class periods.)

In addition, especially to address the language of the first three anchor standards and SLEs, teachers will apparently need to learn more about how to teach close, critical and analytical reading. Stotsky's study found that only 29% of ninth-grade, 31% of tenth-grade, and 31% of eleventh-grade English courses had "close reading" as their preferred approach to the study of literature, in contrast to 60% at ninth grade, 52% at tenth grade, and 45% at eleventh grade preferring an approach that respondents identified as "reader response." (Stotsky apparently conceives "reader-response" as an approach in which students simply share their personal, affective reaction to the text, rather than first doing a close reading, as most academic reader-response critics advocate.) Even smaller percentages of courses (22% at ninth grade, 22% at tenth grade, and 31% at eleventh grade) showed that teachers used close reading as a preferred approach to teaching non-fiction (p. 24).

An Observation and a Modest Proposal

I find it unusual and a tad ironic that while the Common Core standards document is distancing itself from any recommendation of common readings, a great many of the institutions for which the standards are allegedly preparing students (i.e., American colleges and universities) are implementing common-reading programs, in some cases for incoming, first-year students and occasionally for the entire student body, along with faculty, staff members, and community residents. A survey conducted by Andi Twinton (2007) at Gustavus Adolphus College, for example, elicited responses from 130 institutions that sponsor such programs. While I cannot delineate the specific purposes of each of these programs, I can speak for the one at the University of Arkansas that, I think, has a relatively similar purpose as other institutions. In our "One Book, One Community" project, we want all students in our introductory, first-year composition course, plus populations of students from different majors and clubs, plus faculty and staff, plus all the book clubs affiliated with the local public library, to read the same book. We sponsor campus and community events—panel discussions, art displays, film series, play readings—about issues and themes raised in the book. We bring the author to campus for two days of lectures, discussions, and class visits. Through study guides, we explicitly steer students to access their prior knowledge, to imagine other connections, and to build background knowledge about the topic of the book. We want our first-year students in particular to have, usually for the first time in their academic careers, a good experience with an entire book of non-fiction prose. We want to help everyone involved to participate in the construction of knowledge. We want people to talk collectively about what they learned from the book and how they learned it. Not everyone loves the book, but many, many people talk about it, and I can safely say that 99.9 percent of the participating population learns something valuable from the experience of common reading.

What is it that colleges and universities want to achieve with common reading programs that the framers of the Common Core standards—or even officers of state school boards—want to avoid? Is the political fallout from requiring certain works to be read by everyone so nasty that it leads educators to ignore the educational benefits of common readings?

In the face of these questions, let me offer a modest proposal.[1] What if, at the national level (or, more reasonably, at the state level) there was an appointed panel of educators and citizens who established a list of five books—say, for the sake of argument, two novels, one play or entire book of poems, and two non-fiction books—that the panel recommended every student in grades nine through twelve in the nation (or the state) read for the next five years, after which the panel would recommend a different set of five "required" books? Every effort could be made, and the provisions could even be mandated in the language establishing the panels, for the authors of selected texts to be diverse—male and female, native-born and foreign, "mainstream" and "minority." I am not talking about establishing eternal verities here—I am talking about texts being read for five years.

What would such a project yield? Teachers in grades nine through twelve would have a substantial opportunity to teach students how to build background knowledge to undergird a successful reading. Similarly, these teachers would have a collective opportunity to show students how to make text-to-text connections—the explicit goal of Anchor Standard Nine and the corresponding SLEs. Combining this common reading with an increased emphasis on teaching close, critical and analytical reading—an initiative I have promoted assiduously for the past two years (Jolliffe, 2008)—could help students build upon the Common Core standards and truly be prepared for the reading demands that college and careers hold for them.

The Common Core standards, in summary, can go a long way in preparing students to become the kinds of critical, questioning readers that college and university faculty members expect them to be. Some measure of common knowledge, now generally overlooked in educational reform movements, would be a salutary complement to such standards.

NOTE

1. Thanks to my friend Chris Goering for getting me to think seriously about this proposal.

Part III: Contexts and Resources

8 Reading and Writing Connections in College Composition Textbooks: The Role of Textbook Readers

Jimmy Fleming

College composition textbooks are a place where most first year writing students and some writing instructors are introduced to the idea of writing studies as a discipline. Inasmuch as they are used to help writing instructors meet the objectives and outcomes of their respective schools' writing programs, composition textbooks are introduced as tools for helping students learn how to write in a wide array of modes and genres and through various methods of inquiry. While designed to support the writing teacher's efforts to guide students in different ways of composing, these texts also introduce students to ways of thinking and reading critically, with varying degrees of explicit instruction.

Textbooks are successful in helping students learn how to read, think, and write critically only in the manner in which the instructor wields them, dependent on how they are used as part of the instructor's syllabus, as part of the scaffolding of writing assignments, and as part of the teacher's instruction, or ancillary to it. That said, the way composition textbooks, and composition readers in particular, represent the relationship between reading and writing can frame the way teachers and students perceive and enact these skills. In this way, composition textbooks are one site where we can examine the construction and scaffolding of reading and its relation to writing.

In advocating the close connection between reading and writing discussed throughout this volume, this chapter looks closely at how select best-selling composition readers in different market segments help students in developing critical reading skills as an extension of the reader's primary mission of providing composition instruction. I identify a select number of other influential textbooks—some readers that are not necessarily market-leaders as well as a couple of brief rhetorics—that offer instructors more unique opportunities to integrate instruction in close, critical reading skills as an integral part of writing assignments. While changes in the delivery of college textbooks means that books and texts are being published digitally, we focus here on print books and on the close reading of print texts, though some attention must be paid to how visual images are introduced as texts in composition readers.

Ways of Reading and First-Year Writing

In a meeting with graduate students and writing instructors at Georgia State University in November, 2011, Andrea A. Lunsford talked about "(Some) Ways of Reading." She spoke of different kinds of reading, including informational reading, ludic reading (playful, pure pleasure), rhetorical reading (aimed at action), aesthetic reading (deeply hermeneutical/close reading), and creative reading (the text invites readers to create on their own). Readers, she said, are reading more and different kinds of texts, especially digital texts. Writers, she said, insist on creating and producing as well as consuming text (A. Lunsford, personal communication, November 30, 2011).

College textbooks offer help to students in developing skills for some, but not all, of these kinds of reading (few, if any, help students develop a purely ludic or appreciative manner of reading, for instance). If one general aim of first year writing courses is to help students develop first as analysts and then as creators of texts, then textbooks play an important role in helping them move from being *recipients of* information, knowledge, ideas, and skills to being *participants in* the creation of *new* content, *new* knowledge, and *new* texts. The link between effective reading and writing, then, is evidenced by students' responses to assignments that show they understand what they have read and can use that understanding to create new text. If textbooks are designed to follow the arc of the writing classroom, then they must be evaluated according to the manner in which they help first year writing instructors move students from consumers to producers.

THE READING-WRITING CONNECTION IN TEXTBOOKS

The amount and kind of reading and writing instruction in college composition textbooks is disparate and wide-ranging. Textbook publishers generally categorize their books as handbooks, rhetorics, and readers. Although the distinctions among the types are often blurred, as they offer variants that combine core features of one type or the other (e.g., rhetorics with readings, rhetorics with a handbook, etc.), some generalizations hold. In some kinds of composition textbooks—most handbooks and some rhetorics—reading skills are discussed as a core set of strategies. That is, in textbooks that do not offer readings as core material to which students will refer to for analysis and re-reading, and upon which writing assignments are built, these textbooks are intended to serve as references for instruction or as the foundation for classroom work. Guided reading advice is not evident in specific applications, but rather is seen as a general set of critical thinking, analytic, and writing practices that can be applied to specific writing tasks.

So while most comprehensive handbooks on the market have abundant advice on critical reading and thinking strategies, they are best used in a skilled teacher's hands. Similar to the way instructors use handbooks for grammar instruction or advice on doing research, a full understanding of critical reading strategies extracted from these textbooks is dependent on explication by the writing instructor and on application as part of careful scaffolding in specific writing assignments of the instructor's creation.

While many handbooks cover the same material, *rhetorics* are textbooks designed to help students write effectively. They offer students an introduction to the processes of writing, and most have fully developed coverage of the writing and reading connection. They have distinctive chapters with advice on how to write fully developed, analytical papers, including: invention and revision strategies, editing advice, and writing assignments so students can practice what they are learning about the processes of writing. The reading-writing connection in some rhetorics is explicit, with separate chapters showing critical reading, thinking, and writing strategies. In others, reading advice is implicit as the textbook sends students back to texts for a closer second or third reading.

Rhetorics can be categorized by how they are used in the composition course. Ones that *structure the course* usually include core chapters organized around major writing assignments that mirror the syllabus for the course, and are often called *comprehensive rhetorics* because they have four distinct parts: a detailed rhetoric, readings, a research manual, and a handbook. These four-in-one rhetorics have detailed writing guides in chapters that correspond to specific kinds of writing assignments, such as writing a causal analysis, writing an evaluation, proposing a solution. As such, most have the word "guide" in their titles. As a group, these are the best-selling rhetorics, in part because they provide so much help for the instructor—whether he or she uses the text in class or not—but mostly because they offer step-by-step, guided writing instruction for students when they need it, inside and outside of class.

Comprehensive rhetorics generally provide a significant amount of specific reading strategies offered as an integral part of the writing guide in each chapter, and the strategies are focused on specific writing assignments. With such detailed and guided reading, and with critical thinking strategies and writing instruction specific to assignments based on rhetorical situations and/or genres, these books closely match the "Critical Thinking, Reading, and Writing" plank of the Writing Program Administrators's *WPA Outcomes Statement for First-Year Composition*, and so their advice on reading is specific to the writing assignment. In these books, the writing assignment chapters emphasize the connection between reading and writing in a particular genre. Students are introduced to a reading or a group of readings, and are asked to think about the features of the genre. The writing guide then asks them to apply what they have learned about the features of the genre or writing task to an essay of their own.

Two examples show the connectivity between reading and writing in these books. In *The St. Martin's Guide to Writing, Ninth Edition* (2011), by Rise B. Axelrod and Charles R. Cooper, each of the nine writing guide chapters follows a sequence. For example, the seventh chapter, "Proposing a Solution," opens with a brief description of the genre followed by a guide for reading that kind of essay and a discussion of its basic features. The reading guide has a focus on purpose and audience, argument and counter-argument, and a plan for reading that directs students to assess how well the author has achieved her or his goals in proposing a solution. This discussion is followed by an annotated example, three professional readings (with a careful discussion for each according to the reading plan), and a guided writing assignment (pp. 320–83).

In *The McGraw-Hill Guide: Writing for College, Writing for Life, Second Edition* (2009), by Duane Roen, Gregory R. Glau, and Barry M. Maid, the authors have explicitly crafted reading and writing instruction for each kind of writing to the WPA's learning outcomes. In the chapter "Writing to Analyze," they offer three professional essays as examples of analytical writing. Each is followed by sets of questions to guide students to a deeper reading and understanding of rhetorical knowledge (the writer's situation and rhetoric), critical thinking (guiding the student's reflective response and understanding of the essayist's ideas), composing processes and conventions (the essayist's rhetorical strategies), and inquiry and research (guiding the student's ideas for further exploration) (pp. 66–282). Since the release of the outcome statements, all other comprehensive rhetorics have expressly shown how the textbooks correspond in a correlation guide of some sort.

Some of these books also have distinct reading strategies chapters that outline specific rhetorical reading and invention advice, note-taking, or annotating strategies useful in a variety of genres and writing tasks. In *The Allyn & Bacon Guide to Writing, Fifth Edition* (2009), by John D. Ramage, John C. Bean, and June Johnson, for example, the authors offer four chapters of advice to students on how to read and think rhetorically about good writing, subject matter, how messages persuade, and style and document design. In addition, they offer two distinct chapters on seeing rhetorically, or analyzing a text (pp. 89–108), and on reading rhetorically, including advice on note-taking, using a dictionary, and re-reading advice for "first-draft reading" and "multi-draft" reading (pp. 109–49).

Other rhetorics, ones that *do not structure the course*, are often the refined best practices about teaching writing that sometimes reflect the research and/or scholarly publishing of their authors who are influential and well-regarded, if not market leaders (e.g., Peter Elbow and Pat Belanoff's *A Community of Writers* (1989) and *Being a Writer* (2002); Linda Flower's, *Problem-Solving Strategies for Writing in College and Community* (1998); and Wendy Bishop's *Reading into Writing*(2003)). Because they have an organization that does not suggest a *design* for the course, instructors can fit the books into an existing syllabus. Rather than chapters on major writing assignments, the chapters are stages of the writing process and/or on elements of writing, like purpose, tone, style, and paragraphs. While comprehensive rhetorics—the four-in-one texts—are the best-selling of the writing texts, there are other, briefer rhetorics that are notable for their distinctive way of showing students the connection between close reading and writing by helping them develop particular perspectives or ways of thinking. In the eyes of publishers, they are often called *point of view* rhetorics in that they often reflect the teaching practices and theoretical underpinnings of their authors, and thus do not invite easy categorization.

One of the most successful new textbooks in recent years, *They Say/I Say, Second Edition* (2010), by Gerald Graff and Cathy Birkenstein, is based on an assumption, implicit in its title, that students can join a larger academic conversation if they learn to place their arguments in the context of what authors have said about the topic they are writing about. It emphasizes inquiry—students have to read and decode and find out what others have to say—to assimilate other writers' voices within their own arguments. There is a give and take, a process of listening to (reading) others' arguments and responding to them. It provides templates—specific signal phrases or constructions—that help students learn transitions in their writing, moving back and forth between what they say and what others have written. The second edition added a chapter on reading, "Reading for the Conversation," with advice on helping students see that reading an academic text, or a general argument, can be broken down into patterns of "they say/I say" moves. In the chapter on reading, the authors guide students in ways of seeing both the argument that a text's author makes, but also the arguments to which he or she is responding. By recognizing the moves writers make, students can see textual elements that help them see a writer's shift in rhetorical strategy or in meaning. For some, the templates that students have worked with in their own writing provide a key to better understanding some the moves made by the authors they read.

David Rosenwasser and Jill Stephen's *Writing Analytically, Fifth Edition* (2009) has an especially targeted focus on helping students learn ways of writing and reading analytically to discover and develop ideas. The book treats writing as, "a tool of thought—a means of undertaking sustained acts of inquiry and reflection" (p. xvii). They develop strategies of rhetorical analysis based on close reading, and as such, advocate observation as a distinct form of thinking. They argue that students need more instruction on information gathering (inquiry) and evidence gathering before developing a thesis. They contend that a thesis can evolve in response to the writer's inquiries, and as such, encourage students to develop new habits of mind based on inquiry and analysis. Habits of mind include learning to read analytically by paying attention to specific skills that range from discovering meaning (by looking at word selection, entering into a dialogue with a reading, and paraphrasing), to more developed skills for summary and analysis (by freewriting in response to passages in a larger text, ranking to evaluate main ideas and evidence, and uncovering assumptions in a reading), to writing tips for deeper meaning (by applying a reading as a lens for examining something else) (pp. 205–14).

In *The Academic Writer, Second Edition* (2011), Lisa Ede places particular emphasis on helping students learn to *think* rhetorically—in terms of purpose and effect—and inasmuch as reading and writing are parallel processes, students who learn to think about writing as rhetorical processes, they learn the interconnectedness of reading and writing as they respond to the texts they read (p. 249). By thinking rhetorically, she says, students learn how to adapt to the rhetorical situation in terms of making decisions about organization, development, form, and genre. By learning how to think rhetorically, students learn how to act—that is, communicate or write as problem solvers. In arguing that reading is a situated process, Ede treats it as having common rhetorical considerations as writing. A first reading of a text is like composing a first draft; re-reading is like revising. Reading is an active process like composing, and as such, readers engage with a text and can develop "strong reading strategies" (pp. 253–72).

These brief rhetorics, "point-of-view" texts by publishers, are highly regarded for flexibility in their pedagogy. Instructors who use them are at great liberty to construct assignments around the texts, but they very much have to engage directly with the textbooks. They are explicit in making connections among thinking rhetorically, reading for meaning, analyzing texts for both rhetorical methods and arguments to engage, and writing in response to analysis and extended meaning-making.

Ways of Seeing Textbook Readers: Reading the Apparatus

Textbooks that best raise students' meta-awareness of the connection between reading and writing and that most effectively move students from consumers of texts to producers of new texts are composition *readers*, since they compel students to read and re-read texts as an integral element of writing assignments. In this kind of book, reading and writing instruction is developed in the book's apparatus and in how writing assignments are sequenced.

It is important to liberate composition readers from the misconception that all are of a kind. They are often disparaged for not having explicit treatment of critical reading skills (e.g., discerning context clues, annotating, note-taking, reading for main idea, etc.) as found in handbooks or rhetorics. Sometimes, too, they are undervalued as a tool for making explicit the connection of reading to writing, although that charge undervalues the critical thinking questions and writing sequences that are part of the book's apparatus.

A carefully chosen reader can be a valuable tool to the first year writing instructor in designing writing assignments that weave in reading and writing instruction while meeting course outcomes. The reader can, in fact, serve as the place where students and instructors alike are first shown how to closely read complex texts. In fact, as Adler-Kassner and Estrem (2007) say, "the majority of work focused on attempting to articulate various strategies for active, engaged reading is found in the prefaces and supporting material within composition readers" (p. 36).

A reader's apparatus can be evaluated on how well it helps students build reading and writing skills along a trajectory from understanding to evaluating to creating meaning. That is, a look at the apparatus shows how it helps students create writing that demonstrates a grasp of the meaning of a text (understanding), hones skills of analysis and synthesis (evaluating), and develops lines of inquiry or research (creating). Further, if it is aimed at preparing students to see new ways to inform, persuade, or determine new courses of action, then it can be evaluated on how well it helps students build reading and writing skills to use meaning and infer connections between two or more texts and to create new meaning with a rhetorical awareness of audience, purpose, and genre.

We must remember that textbook readers have the primary purposes of: (a) offering readings for use as models or analysis; (b) offering concise writing instruction for a multitude of purposes; and (c) guiding close reading instruction as part of writing assignments. The instructor choosing a textbook reader will answer the first point subjectively; it really is a matter of preference. The second point is dependent on whether the instructor will choose other textbooks, or use his or her own instruction, to introduce students to composition principles. As to the matter of integrating reading and writing, the most important consideration for any instructor choosing a reader is whether the apparatus helps him herself meet classroom goals. This might be framed as follows:

1. How is the reader/text equipped to help students understand what the essayist/writer is trying to persuade or inform in the selections? That is, how does the textbook help students learn to:

   Decode meaning;

   Understand the writer's main question (main point, thesis);

   Understand language;

   Understand audience;

   Understand context of the reading;

   See the rhetorical moves a writer makes;

   Understand the rhetorical situation;

   Summarize/paraphrase the text, and learn the difference?

2. How is the reader/text equipped to help students evaluate the text they are reading? That is, how does the textbook help students learn to:

   Compare and contrast;

   Connect to other text(s);

   Refute, based on experience or on reading of other writers;

   Synthesize;

   Analyze;

   Identify context;

   Understand counter-point;

   Argue against a main point;

   Understand the use of source material;

   Re-read;

   Understand the use of visual elements or text design;

   Understand that reading, like writing, is recursive?

3. How is the reader/text equipped to help student create new meaning, to enter the conversation—with a single reading or with multiple readings—with claims or arguments of his or her own and create meaning or extend the conversation in his or her own writing? That is, how does the textbook help students learn to:

Frame unasked questions;

Extend a writer's argument;

Extend and connect to other text(s);

Understand research strategies;

Understand voice in their writing;

Understand the rhetorical situation of their writing;

Read their writing with critical attention?

Imagine a reader's apparatus as a kind of continuum that helps students develop critical reading skills in increasing complexity, from reading as invention and discovery, to reading as a means of evaluating and analyzing, and to reading as a means to question or challenge their reading and create new meaning. It can provide *practical* tools for close reading as strategies for invention and discovery—such as annotating, note-taking, highlighting, outlining, and underlining—to address the questions of the first two criteria. More importantly, it can provide advice to help students *change their habits of mind* and *learn to ask critical questions* of a text.

The apparatus of a college textbook reader can be evaluated, then, on how it helps students develop reading skills along this sweep: recognize conventions and purposes (reading as rhetorical invention), understand content (reading for meaning), learn to synthesize and analyze (reading to evaluate), and learn to frame a question for research and inquiry in order to respond to an argument or otherwise join an academic conversation (reading to create meaning).

RHETORICAL READERS: READING AS RHETORICAL INVENTION

Among the five major publishers in composition, there are more readers published each year than any other type of textbook. With scores more available in each company's backlist, the number of viable readers available to writing instructors is staggering. It is widely believed that the reader market is roughly split: one-third rhetorically-arranged readers, one-third argument readers, and one-third "other" readers. The best-selling reader at each publisher is likely a rhetorically-arranged reader, usually deep in its revision cycle. The fastest growing segment of the market is argument-based texts and readers. The greatest diversity of readers is the "other" category, comprised of a large number of books known as cultural studies readers, most thematically organized. The vast majority of readers used in the first semester of first year writing are rhetorically-arranged readers and general thematic readers. Most argument texts and readers are used in the second-semester course of a two-course sequence.

The rhetorical reader has been the dominant best-seller for over thirty years. Every publisher offers several, all sharing the same general organization. Many rhetorical readers remain their publisher's top-selling reader. The core of today's rhetorical reader is its collection of professional (and some student) essays collected in chapters that represent traditional rhetorical patterns (narration, description, classification, comparison/contrast, etc.). All top sellers open with full coverage of critical reading and offer general rhetorical guidance on the writing process.

While the rhetorical reader, as a type of book, is sometimes defined by how much guidance on writing it offers, best-sellers have maintained their successes—most have recently published in their tenth or older editions—by responding to the needs of instructors and students. Recently, their authors have added significant amounts of guidance on critical reading that show the interconnectedness of writing and reading.

For example, two market leaders, *Patterns for College Writers, Twelfth Edition* (2012), by Laurie G. Kirszner and Stephen R. Mandell, and *Readings for Writers, Thirteenth Edition* (2010), by Jo Ray McCuen-Metherell and Anthony C. Winkler, have long been valued because of a generous amount of general guidance about the writing process in sections that their publishers call a mini-rhetoric that open the books. Here, the authors introduce writing strategies developed fully as rhetorical methods are examined and developed in writing assignments specific to the modes. In addition, each of these books (and others like them in this market segment) opens each chapter on rhetorical modes with specific and detailed advice to students about writing using that particular method of development. As the market has shifted, and demand for explicit reading instruction has increased, both the Kirszner and Mandell and McCuen and Winkler tests developed apparatuses to expressly help students read more closely.

Patterns for College Writers, first published in 1980, places a high emphasis on critical reading both as an amalgam of specific reading strategies and as an integral component of the writing process. Its apparatus is fully developed to help students use their responses to reading to move from invention and discovery to analysis and evaluation. An opening introduction, "How to Use This Book," tells students that "the study questions that accompany the essays . . . encourage you to think critically about writers' ideas" (p. 1).

A distinct chapter on critical reading, "Reading to Write: Becoming a Critical Reader," prepares students to become analytical readers and writers by showing them how to apply critical reading strategies to a typical selection and by providing sample responses to the various kinds of writing prompts in the book. It provides advice on specific reading strategies, including active reading tips about reading with a purpose, previewing, highlighting, annotating, and reading with checklists for critical reading and reading visuals. There are also annotated essays to show these processes (pp. 13–27).

Similarly, *Readings for Writers, Thirteenth Edition*, first published in 1974, is another well-established rhetorical reader. The core critical reading chapters are found in, "Part One: Reading and Writing: From Reading to Writing." The authors offer a brief discussion of four different kinds of reading—casual reading, reading for pleasure, reading for information, and critical reading—followed by guidelines for critical reading. Among the specific tips, they offer advice that helps students read actively, including: reading for rhetorical invention (demystify the author, note the author's style and words or expressions used, and understand the author's opening context); reading for meaning (understand what you read and look up facts); and reading to evaluate (imagine an opposing point of view for all opinions, look for biases and hidden assumptions, separate fact from fiction, use insights from one subject to illuminate another, evaluate the evidence, ponder the values behind an argument, and recognize logical fallacies) (pp. 3–7).

In rhetorical readers such as these, the connection between reading and writing is explicit, but the emphasis is on writing. Since rhetorical readers are always used in the first semester of a two-semester sequence in first year writing, and even though some writing assignments ask for the use of source material, the apparatus has a strong focus on helping students understand content, recognize rhetorical moves, and develop writing strategies that will be expanded in the second semester to include moves towards inquiry and research. Hence, reading strategies developed first are primarily to those of discovery and invention. Frequently, too, these questions are not always presented as writing assignments, unless they are used by the instructor as writing activities. The deeper reading strategies of analysis and evaluation are most evident in writing assignments that accompany each reading, many of which send students to outside sources.

Each selection in the modes chapters of *Patterns for College Writing*, for example, is followed by a series of reading and writing prompts that help students respond to the essay they have read. Comprehension questions call for factual responses (invention and/or discovery); vocabulary projects ask students to confirm meaning and understanding of key words; questions on purpose, audience, style, and structure help students analyze rhetorical strategies; journal entry assignments require a more reflective response (analysis and/or evaluation); and writing workshop questions send students to outside sources and call for connecting what they have read to research and/or personal experience (creating meaning) (for example, see pp. 237–39).

In *Readings for Writers*, the authors provide much of the context for each close reading in a feature called "Rhetorical Thumbnail" (for example, see McCuen-Metherell & Winkler, p. 220). The thumbnail is a preview of each reading with a brief summary of the essay writer's purpose, audience, language, and strategy, and is intended guide students to discover meaning and focus on analyzing the writer's strategies. Each reading is followed by vocabulary words and questions about the facts of the reading (understanding meaning), questions about the essayist's strategies (evaluate/analyze), questions about the issues addressed in the reading (evaluate/analyze), and is followed by writing suggestions that call for synthesis and invite reflection.

Similar to rhetorically-arranged readers are those that are organized by *rhetorical situations* or *aims* rather than rhetorical modes or methods of development. Their apparatus for teaching reading skills is more specific and developed more fully, add guidance to help students return to their own writing with strategies they used to analyze their reading, and the guided writing assignments are more clearly tied to reading responses. Rhetorical aims readers are intended for instructors who prefer readings that correspond to the kinds of assignments common in first year writing, such as observing an event, reflecting, inquiring, taking a stand, proposing a solution, and negotiating common ground. Unlike rhetorically-arranged readers that have a preponderance of classic—or "chestnut"—popular audience essays, rhetorical aims readers have a higher percentage of academic essays.

Perhaps the best-selling and longest lived of these is *Reading Critically, Writing Well: A Reader and Guide, Ninth Edition* (2011) by Rise B. Axelrod, Charles R. Cooper, and Alison M. Warner. Of all established composition readers, *Reading Critically, Writing Well* arguably has the most fully developed critical apparatus with specific, scaffolded strategies to help students learn the skills required for reading different genres of writing. The text consists of eight chapters, each focusing on a particular kind of writing assignment, from autobiography and observation, for example, to speculating about causes or effects, to writing to solve a problem (p. vi). Each chapter has a collection of student and professional essays. The student essay and the first professional piece in each chapter are annotated to show specific critical reading strategies (p. ix). The annotated professional essay in each chapter is accompanied with reading strategies that are unique to the kind of rhetorical situation being considered. For example, the fourth chapter has specific advice in its "Guide to Reading Reflective Essays" that progresses from reading for meaning (comprehending, responding, and analyzing assumptions) to reading like a writer, and sends students back to the essay for a closer reading to help them understand the writer's rhetorical moves and how they relate to the their own writing (pp. 147–206).

The connection to writing is made explicit. Each chapter has a detailed guide to writing the particular kind of essay with additional advice, distinctive in its thoroughness and specificity that guides students through a careful and critical reading of their own drafts, employing many of the strategies that they applied to the reading of the professional essay. There is also an extensive catalog of critical reading strategies—such as annotating, previewing, outlining, summarizing, paraphrasing, synthesizing, and other higher order skills—in an appendix with an annotated essay to show all critical reading strategies at work.

A similar, aims-based text and reader is *Reading Rhetorically: A Reader for Writers, Second Edition* (2005), by John C. Bean, Virginia A. Chappell, and Alice M. Gillam. Implicit in its title, the authors contend that reading rhetorically means understanding "the *how* and *what* of a text's message," that is, the author's purposes for writing and the methods used (p. xxiii). They go on to claim that "the book teaches students how to see texts as positioned in a conversation with other texts, how to recognized the bias or perspective of a given text, and how to analyze texts for both content and rhetorical method" (p. xxiii).

As a text-reader, *Reading Rhetorically* is a two-part text with an anthology of readings, grouped in chapters, devoted to aims-based college writing assignments. Text chapters guide students on how to ask rhetorical questions of the text they are reading to understand meaning, recognize different reading strategies that might be used for different kinds of writing and that will help them read difficult texts in academic disciplines unfamiliar to them, and position themselves to converse with the text and place it in conversation with other texts.

The authors provide much specific help in reading strategies that they call "listening to a text," or, "trying to understand the author's ideas, intentions, and worldview—that is, reading *with the grain* of the text, trying to understand it on its own terms" (p. 47). They explain this array of "listening"-type reading strategies as: noting organizational signals, marking unfamiliar terms and references, identifying points of difficulty, connecting the visual to the verbal, and annotating (pp. 47–52).

By showing students how to read "with the grain," Bean et al., help students develop skills in reading-for-meaning, but by offering specific reading strategies, they also help students learn to read as writers and to begin recognizing and analyzing essayists' rhetorical moves. In describing organizational signals, they advise students to note transitional phrases (much like Graf) and forecasting statements that suggest an author's intent. By suggesting students mark unfamiliar terms and references, they suggest ways for a student to mark passages or terms that require a second reading to decipher context clues or to consult with a dictionary or outside source. Similarly, by advising students to mark points of difficulty, they tell students that some passages might require they return and try to decode or rewrite the passage in their own terms, or to frame questions for further review. By connecting the visual to the verbal, they suggest seeing visuals in relation to the text (by enhancing its appeal, by supporting its claim, or by extending its meaning). All of this is summarized in their advice on annotating, accompanied by a short example (pp. 47–53). The cumulative benefit of this advice is that by helping students see how writers make their moves—make rhetorical decisions—they can apply what they learned to their own writing and learn to read their own writing more critically.

By declaring that rhetorical reading is not "a one-step process," but requires careful rereading, the authors extend their advice in a section called, "Listening As You Reread" (p. 53). The authors advise students how to map an essay to show relationships among its ideas (pp. 53–54). In a discussion of descriptive outlining, they list verbs that describe what texts do (pp. 54–56). In an interesting way to engage students directly with a text, and to show an obvious connection of the writing to the reading with a unique, skill-building exercise, they introduce students to the concept of a rhetorical précis, distinguishing it from summary. Describing a summary as a brief recapitulation of what a text says, a rhetorical précis is an analysis of how a text works rhetorically (pp. 58–62).

The tables of contents in rhetorical aims readers, as well as the manner in which their publishers categorize and market them, makes them appear as variations of traditional rhetorical readers. The more detailed apparatus that focuses equally on critical reading and writing, however, places them further along the spectrum of readers attending to the development of critical reading skills. Specifically, they assume that by assisting students in developing skills in reading rhetorically, by providing specific reading skills for different kinds of writing, and by preparing them to use their responses to their reading for the writing they undertake, this kind of text assists students in becoming more active readers, more attuned to writers' purposes and strategies, more skilled at challenging writers' claims, and therefore in a better position to write in response to other writers, to engage in an act of creation, of joining the conversation.

THEMATIC READERS: READING FOR MEANING AND ANALYSIS

Rhetorically arranged readers, including rhetorical aims readers, comprise the largest segment of the reader market. The majority of readers are organized thematically. The themes tend to be ones students are interested in—personal identity, family, popular culture, education, gender, and social and moral issues—and the themes are the chapter titles. The purpose of these readings is to give students something to write about. They are not usually used as models of writing, but as springboards to writing. As a rule, it is harder to generalize about the attention to reading that their authors provide; since each is unique, according to its themes, each has apparatus that is unique, too.

Arguably, the fastest-growing category of thematic readers are those known as cultural studies readers, most of which emerged in the past ten years or so, and reflect a shift in focus in graduate programs preparing first year writing instructors. The general aim of cultural studies readers is to help students see the contexts in which texts appear, evaluate the ways and forms that the texts' messages are presented (including print, digital, and visual texts), and use this understanding to form their own arguments and determine their own forms for writing. The challenge for cultural studies readers and for teachers who use them is to maintain focus on close reading as it influences and informs student writing. Because cultural studies as a field invites study of the contexts that generate a cultural product—such as an essay, a film, or an advertisement—it is easy for students engaged with these texts to focus on understanding or interpreting the product and its contexts rather than the elements of its construction or how a student will transfer his or her understanding to his or her own writing. Among these readers, those with a balance of print and visual texts—often called visual text readers—have become the most widely adopted. For instructors, the compelling reason for adopting these kinds of readers is that they start with texts with which today's students are familiar. If the premise is accepted that visual images are "composed" and employ similar rhetorical strategies, then students are already familiar with reading and decoding visual texts, and they can then use the same reading and writing strategies to "see" kinds of texts and "compose" using visuals as texts. For the most part, the consideration of visual texts in textbook readers is limited to developing criteria for reading and evaluating visual texts, rather than to compose them. Generally, textbook authors who have built a reading-writing apparatus around visual texts rely on concepts of "observing" and "seeing," and usually apply the same rhetorical reading concepts in "reading" visual texts. The implied concept is that, like print texts, visual images can be analyzed for elements of composition and meaning. At present, college textbook readers presume that the same methods of analysis and evaluation do indeed apply, with the exception being that they introduce concepts borrowed from other fields—like graphic arts and photography—to expand the range of rhetorical considerations. The challenge facing textbook authors—and first year writing instructors as well—is to ensure scaffolding of assignments to assume that observing does not replace analysis and that reading visual images is developed as a part of overall reading strategies and integrally linked to helping students develop writing skills. In textbooks, this must be evident in the apparatus. *Seeing and Writing 4* (2010), by Donald Mc-Quade and Christine McQuade, first published in 2000, was not the first composition textbook to use visuals as texts, but it was the first for beginning expository writing courses "grounded in a simple pedagogical premise: to invite students *to give words and images equal attention*," and intended to help students learn to think critically about visual and verbal texts and write effectively about them (p. vi, emphasis added).

Each chapter offers selections that move from the concrete to the abstract, and from readily accessible to more complex works (p. xii). Chapters progress from personal to persuasive writing, giving students the opportunity of "practicing skills of observation and inference" (p. xii). These analytic skills apply to reading both print and written texts, and support the authors' contention that "enabling students to move fluently within and among visual and verbal worlds will improve their analytic and compositional skills" (p. vi). Observational and inference skills are introduced and described in early chapters, and explored with exercises that require students to read both visual and print texts and record their observations and inferences, respectively (p. xiv). Further, rhetorical terms such as purpose, structure, audience, point of view, tone, metaphor, and context are explored as terms that apply to visual images (pp. 16–25). These concepts are explored more specifically within each chapter, in a feature called "Visualizing Composition."

The reading skills apparatus in the text is referred to as "Seeing." Paired "Seeing" and "Writing" assignments and questions follow each text. "Seeing" questions guide students back to an image or text with advice on how to closely analyze elements of its composition. That close examination, then, is the starting point for two "Writing" prompts that ask students to write about the texts or to connect to outside readings or resources.

Beyond Words: Reading and Writing in a Visual Age, Second Edition (2009) by John E. Ruszkiewicz, Daniel Anderson, and Christy Friend, claims to offer "all the support most students will require to move from reading to writing," acknowledging the breadth of that claim, the challenge of giving students something to write about, and giving them tools to respond critically and create texts of their own (p. xv).

The first two chapters introduce students to tools for reading and then composing texts, strategies developed further in the thematic readings chapters. The first chapter introduces students to rhetorical terms and concepts such as subject, audience, purpose, genre, media, context, and structure/composition. The second chapter introduces concepts of doing research, documenting sources, revising, and editing—all relevant to composing (p. xv). Thematic chapters (three through eight) include galleries of texts and visuals, clusters that give students multiple perspectives on a given topic, and assignments that ask students to compose in writing and in other media (p. xv).

Visual text readers essentially offer the same sweep of rhetorical invention reading strategies as other readers most often used in the first semester of first year writing, with the added dimension of helping student learn how to read visual texts, extending the understanding what "composition" and "reading" mean. At the moment, the consideration of how well visual text readers offer advice and refine critical reading skills must be seen on the same continuum as other textbooks. Instructors using these kinds of texts face new questions: Do students read visuals the same as they do written texts? Do the same rhetorical practices apply in understanding and analyzing visual images as texts? Are methods of research and inquiry applied similarly when visuals are considered texts?

More broadly, the same questions apply to all cultural studies readers. The challenge for cultural studies readers—visual text readers among them—and for teachers who use them is to maintain the focus on close reading as it influences and informs student writing. Because cultural studies as a field invites study of the context that generates a cultural product, such as an essay, a film, or an advertisement, it is easy for students engaged with these texts to focus on understanding or interpreting the product and its context rather than the elements of its construction or how a student transfers his or her understanding to his or her own writing. The text and the teacher must be sure that the focus of the class is on writing and not on media images or cultural artifacts or controversial issues. The focus of the book's apparatus and the teacher's scaffolding, then, must remain on helping students move from consumers to evaluators to creators of meaning.

Argument Readers: Reading to
Evaluate and Create Meaning

As students move from their first semester of composition to the second, they are often asked to do more with their reading and their writing, and are likely assigned texts that require more fully developed critical reading skills. Writing assignments have students develop lines of inquiry and compose arguments, and usually include an introduction to the research process, culminating in a paper, project, and/or presentation/publication. Textbooks for second-semester courses, therefore, are not entirely different, but are usually of a higher level of complexity in terms of content, reading, writing assignments, and strategies. As defined by market segments, the greatest number of textbooks used in second-semester composition courses is argument texts/readers.

Argument texts and readers are explicit in their attention to critical thinking, and provide ample opportunities for writing instructors to help students analyze and learn the moves in popular discourse, visual rhetoric, and academic writing that involve persuasion—from understanding rhetorical concepts such as ethos, logos, and pathos; to understanding logical fallacies; to developing ways to anticipate counter-argument; to developing lines of inquiry and research; to staking a claim and joining an ongoing debate. The purpose of the readings is both to provide models and to give students something to write about, so readings tend to be examples of argument organized into themes—such as opposing views on controversial topics like affirmative action, immigration, and euthanasia. Argument texts and readers were also the first composition textbooks in the market to introduce students to tools to analyze visual images as texts. What distinguishes them, then, is the approach they take to argument (e.g., argument and/or persuasion based on Aristotle, Rogers, Toulmin; oratorical, visual, print arguments; popular culture and academic arguments) and the amount and kind of apparatus they provide.

Two market leaders, *Everything's an Argument with Readings, Fifth Edition* (2010) by Andrea A. Lunsford, John J. Ruszkiewicz, and Keith Walters, and *Writing Arguments, Seventh Edition* (2007) by John D. Ramage, John C. Bean, and June Johnson, take a similar position that argument is an act of negotiating differences, or at least that argument is not a feat of staking didactic opposing claims. The authors of both texts suggest that the act of composing an argument, in academic or social writing, involves many ways of reading or otherwise coming to understand disparate viewpoints. If reading is the act of exploring ways of understanding, then writing is the act of extending the conversation and guiding students to the rhetorical choices of writing as a refutation of a position, an attempt to persuade, or a call for social action. Both market leaders strike a balance between the need for students to read deeply and with focus and the need to develop persuasive writing or academic writing skills—whether the outcome is writing that exemplifies personal advocacy, rhetorical analysis (including summary or synthesis of the literature on a given topic), or writing that extends or contributes to an ongoing academic debate. Thus, the close reading of arguments, regardless of the medium, form, or audience, is integral to the writing process and to the assignments offered in this kind of textbook.

Everything's an Argument with Readings, Fifth Edition (2010) by Andrea A. Lunsford, John J. Ruszkiewicz, and Keith Walters, as posited in its title, contends that all language, "including that of sounds and images or symbol systems other than writing," is persuasive and calls for a response (p. v). The authors foreground the interconnectedness of reading and writing by saying, for instance

> we aim to balance attention to critical reading (analysis) with attention to the writing of arguments (production) . . . [W]e have tried to demonstrate both activities with lively—and realistic—examples, on the principle that the best way to appreciate an argument may be to see it in action. (p. vii)

Examples are on display throughout the book, as it is often seen as both a rhetoric and a reader (the rhetoric portion is available as a separate text). Although there are scores of visual and print texts in the textbook portion, most of the analytical questions call for a student's response to both readings and to the authors' discussion of rhetorical principles that may be a discussion or writing prompt. Main writing assignments are on display in the seven thematic chapters that form the reader portion. It is important to note the distinction between the text and reader portions, in that much of the writing advice that builds on the readings sends students back to the text for deeper explanation of rhetorical concepts. There are seven to ten readings in each text, representing a wide array of genres: photographs, essays, newspaper articles and op-ed pieces, cartoons, posters, etc. Each is accompanied by marginal notes that send students to other coverage in the text for further help in understanding rhetorical concepts, such as ethos, logos, pathos, or logical fallacies. Each is followed by four to six questions that call for a student's response, usually in the form of a writing prompt or an assignment. For example, in the short essay, "English Loses Ground," by Rochelle Sharpe, a marginal note on the essayist's reliance on facts and statistics sends students to a discussion of using logos to present an argument (p. 722). The essay is followed by six response questions, including a prompt for a short essay evaluating Sharpe's argument, with directions to a chapter about evaluating arguments. *Everything's an Argument* has five chapters devoted to reading arguments, including an explanation of the claim that "everything is an argument." There is full coverage of pathos, logos, and ethos (in that order, in separate chapters) and a wide-ranging discussion of rhetorical analysis and how to think rhetorically. Each chapter concludes with expansive advice on how to respond to arguments (print and visual) presented in the text by sending students back to those texts with reading and writing prompts. In addition, the fifth chapter concludes with a detailed guide to writing a rhetorical analysis.

Writing Arguments (2007), by John D. Ramage, John C. Bean, and June Johnson, positions itself as "focusing on argument as dialogue in search of solution to problems," saying it "treats argument as a process of inquiry as well as a means of persuasion" (p. xxxvii). It strongly foregrounds the connection between reading and writing by saying, "we link the process of arguing—articulating issue questions, formulating propositions, examining alternative points of view, and creating structures of supporting reasons and evidence—with the process of reading and writing" (p. xli). *Writing Arguments* is both a rhetoric and a reader, though the bulk of writing assignments are found in the rhetoric portion. The authors offer writing assignments within or at the end of chapters that draw on discussions of the rhetorical elements of argument discussed in that chapter, and are not, as such, based on the close reading of text. For example, in the chapter on resemblance arguments, the writing assignment for the chapter asks students to write a letter to a newspaper editor to influence public opinion on an issue using persuasive analogy or precedent—topics discussed elsewhere in the chapter (p. 278).

There are different kinds of writing assignments tied to textual close reading elsewhere in the book. The reader portion is an anthology of twelve thematic chapters of seven to eight pieces, mostly essays.

The units conclude with a set of questions for classroom discussion and an optional writing prompt that asks students to consider one or more of the essays in the unit as a basis for analysis or evaluation.

In the chapter, "Reading Arguments," the authors contend that they "focus on reading arguments as a process of inquiry" (p. 22), and in keeping with the premise that students' acts of reading, research, and writing are acts of joining larger communities, they say that "because argument begins in disagreements within a social community, you should examine any argument as if it were only one voice in a larger conversation" (p. 22). To assist, they provide five reading strategies: "Read as a believer;" "Read as a doubter;" "Explore how the rhetorical context and genre are shaping the argument;" "Consider the alternative views and analyze sources of disagreement;" and "Use disagreement productively to prompt further investigation" (pp. 22–49).

Long recognized for their concise presentation of the rhetorical principles of ethos, pathos, and logos as classical types of appeals, Bean, et. al. include a discussion of *kairos*, raise the question of persuasive appeals to the writer's audience, and more closely adhere to the Toulmin system of analyzing arguments and recognizing the rhetorical and logical structures of developing "appropriate grounds and backing to support an argument's reasons and warrants" (p. xii).

WRITING ACROSS THE CURRICULUM READERS: READING AS INQUIRY

One challenge faced by publishers and textbook authors is that the focus on reading the kinds of essays most often found in composition readers—a focus on the essay as a form—does not prepare students for the kinds of reading and writing most students do in college, except in first year writing. College students are expected to write well in courses outside of college composition, sometimes without additional formal writing instruction in the classroom. They are expected, as well, to read deeply and with understanding in disciplines with which they may not be familiar, including understanding forms, jargon, content, and academic conventions. To read and write well in other disciplines, they must learn other genres, develop other rhetorical abilities, learn to develop research projects with an understanding of disciplinary research methods, and comply with disciplinary documentation standards.

In addition, in order to prepare for advanced academic pursuits, join the work force, or even take a role in any community as a citizen with public participation or advocacy, students must develop both reading and writing skills to match expectations of any audience, using various media, and in many forms and disciplines (see Alice Horning's chapter in this book).

At least implicitly, publishers understand the same need, and while textbooks on the market are not built to explicitly address issues with reading across the curriculum, by providing writing across the curriculum instruction they ask students to engage in deep reading of texts mostly unfamiliar to them in terms of complexity, discipline, content, form, and rhetorical approaches.

Writing and Reading Across the Curriculum, Tenth Edition (2008), by Laurence Behrens and Leonard J. Rosen, has long held a best-seller spot in the market niche of WAC texts/readers. The majority of its readings are collected in an anthology organized by themes and within chapter headings that reflect disciplines found in college curricula; e.g., "Sociology," "Psychology," "Biology," "American Studies," etc.

Rhetorically, the focus of the book's chapters is on summary, critique, synthesis, and analysis. Boxed inserts list specific tips for reading for each rhetorical strategy (pp. 6, 74, 144, 208). One chapter, "Critical Reading and Critique," collects reading strategies that focus a great deal on reading to understand if a writer has succeeded in achieving his/her purpose for writing and how to evaluate a text (pp. 30–75).

To write well in a discipline, a student needs to build expertise in the discipline's content and methods of synthesis, analysis, and inquiry. Authors of cross-disciplinary readers for composition courses face the peculiar challenge of helping students develop skills to read content that is complex and unfamiliar while, at the same time, provide general writing instruction and general analytic and research skills that transfer to meet the expectations of a discipline. At the same time, they must be true to disciplinary forms and scholarship while showing representative examples of "effective" writing that reflect both good rhetorical design and appropriate content from that discipline. The balance is that they must rely on students having developed some skills in reading for meaning, analysis, and evaluation, introducing rhetorical concepts that might be valued differently in different disciplines. For the most part, they recognize that students will master rhetorical skills such as synthesis and analysis while they begin developing research skills that will allow them to contribute to such scholarship.

From Inquiry to Academic Writing: A Text and Reader, Second Edition (2012), by Stuart Greene and April Lidinsky, overtly attempts to show the relationship of critical reading, thinking, inquiry, analysis, and argument. The authors show academic writing "as a collaborative conversation, undertaken in the pursuit of new knowledge," acknowledging that students must learn to write, read, and think in new ways, also showing students that "academic writing is a social act in which they are expected to work responsibly with the ideas of others" (p. v). In addition, they claim to "demystify cross-curricular thinking, reading, and writing" by breaking down students' processes into a series of manageable habits and skills they can learn and practice (p. v).

The core of the text portion of the book is a progression that helps student develop skills incrementally and cumulatively, beginning with academic thinking and proceeding to academic reading, research, and finally to academic writing. The authors place emphasis on the "recursiveness and overlapping nature" of these processes (p. vi). Describing writing as "a process motivated by inquiry," the authors attempt to show the interrelatedness of reading and writing:

> Inevitably, reading and writing processes are intertwined. Thus in Chapter 2 we encourage students to practice "writerly" reading—reading texts as writers analyzing the decisions other writers make—so that they can implement the most appropriate strategies given their own purpose for writing. (p. vi)

In addition, the authors give students opportunities to practice specific skills associated with strategies of critical reading, including activities focusing on annotating, reading rhetorically, and rhetorically analyzing an essay (pp. 29–49).

READING AND WRITING TEXT-TO-TEXT: EXTENDING THE CONVERSATION

There are some books that do not fit the categories, mostly because they are most effective at extending the sweep of writing expectations, fulfilling the broadest reach of developing critical reading skills, but also because of the specific ways they ask students to respond to texts. Those that provide scaffolded questions based on close readings of specific texts, and pose questions and prompt students to write a series of analyses and explorations of one text in reply to another, generally show students how to grapple with difficult reading. The premise is simple: Guided writing in response to reading questions helps students develop close reading skills, mastering content as a way to understand meaning and context. Furthermore, intensive writing—and re-writing—is developed through extended writing assignment sequences and as a mechanism for students to pursue a line of inquiry, build a sustained argument, or otherwise contribute to an ongoing academic conversation.

Arguably the most successful of this kind of reader, *Ways of Reading, Ninth Edition* (2011), by David Bartholomae and Anthony Petrosky (first published in 2002), landed in a market with no direct competitors, largely due to its development of ground-breaking assignment sequences and use of lengthy, challenging, academic essays. Essays by Michel Foucault, Paulo Freire, Mary Louise Pratt, and Walker Percy, among others, were seen as challenging to students in graduate school, not to mention first year writing. The authors argued, however, that the "issue is not only what students read, but what can they learn to do with what they read" (p. iii). They suggested that the problem is in the classroom, not due to the reading material or the students: "There is no better place to work on reading than in a writing course, and this book is intended to provide occasions for readers to write" (p. iii). The book's premises are that students can learn to grapple with and understand complex readings if they are guided by reading and writing assignments that help them construct their own text in response to readings. The anthology has twenty-three lengthy, challenging readings, listed alphabetically. An introductory chapter on reading provides specific advice on reading difficult texts. Each reading is accompanied by questions for a second reading, calling out that "rereading is a natural way of carrying out the work of a reader, just as rewriting is a natural way of completing the work of a writer" (p. v).

The core of the book, though, is its series of assignment sequences that group five or six readings in a broad thematic cluster, such as "The Aims of Education," "Reading Culture," and "The Uses of Reading." Each cluster has a set of assignments—reading and writing—that start students with a close reading and rereading of one core essay, then moves to a reading of another essay, and so on. The assignments lead students to read one essay in the context of, or in conversation with, another essay. Building a deep understanding of multiple essays helps students frame their own response to the questions raised, and deep understanding is achieved through a series of small and large writing assignments.

The writing assignments collected at the back of *Ways of Reading* first ask students to apply reading for meaning (i.e., synthesis) skills for each reading in an assignment sequence. The assignment sequences, though, are designed to give students a way to re-read the essays. In the assignment sequence on "The Aims of Education," students are asked to use Mary Louis Pratt's terms in "The Contact Zone" to examine a similar experience in their own schooling, to examine her explanation of "pedagogical arts," and describe how that might be put into practice in a writing class (p. 708). In a more fully developed task that looks at these two essays as well as ones by Richard E. Miller and Richard Rodriquez, students are asked to consider the authors' assertions about the limits and failures of education (especially in the humanities), about their arguments on the benefits of reading and writing, and take up the question, "[W]hat might the literate arts be said to be good for?" (p. 711). While *Ways of Reading* relies on students' general reading abilities, the cumulative effect of the assignment sequences asks students to discover meaning, and, writing from syntheses and close readings of complex texts, contribute new meaning from their own experience and analyses from multiple those close readings.

Going after the same segment of the market, and also recognizing that students can read complex texts and add meaning to their close reading through writing, *The New Humanities Reader, Third Edition* (2009), by Richard E. Miller and Kurt Spellmeyer, contends that "any text can be linked to any other text in a web of inquiry and analysis" (p. xviii). As an alphabetically arranged reader, the book collects thirty-three challenging readings selected for "creative reading," what the authors describe as moving from explicit understanding (that is, reading for content) to implicit understanding (or making connections or interpretations) (p. xviii). In that way, they say, even the act of reading for meaning has an interpretive component:

> A text becomes meaningful only through the implicit connections it motivates . . . . When we read for content, we are reading to preserve the knowledge made by others. But when we read for implicit connections, we become co-creators with the authors themselves. (p. xix)

If the idea of creative reading adds a layer of interpretation to the idea of reading for meaning, then the authors' concept of "connective thinking" adds to the basic notions of summary, synthesis, and analysis. In talking about analyzing the summaries of two texts in the reader, Miller and Spellmeyer say that "this is not the same as connecting them within the context of a larger question or debate. Yet these connections are never waiting for us fully formed already: there is always the need for a leap of imagination" (p. xxi). The leap of imagination is arrived at through writing—"writing to see," the authors say—and is a product of students developing a position, based on reading, research, connecting ideas, and learning to see that revising a position as needed has value as an act of discovery and hard work (p. xxiv). Writing activities are involved and take three distinct forms. Following each selection, the authors provide questions that ask students to see and write about connections within the readings, questions for writing that generally send the student outside the essay to write about their research or experience, and questions that send the students back to the essay and others and make connections between or among related essays. Further sequences are available on a book companion site.

The important leap of imagination suggested by Spellmeyer and Miller, as well as the habits of mind promoted by close and repeated readings of texts in Bartholomae and Petrosky, are consistent with the advocacy of the WPA Outcomes Statement, the Framework for Success, and the positions argued by Alice Horning et al. throughout this volume.

READING AND WRITING TEXT-TO-TEXT: LITERACY AND LEARNING PRACTICES

While the predominant description of first year writing in college catalogs is as a course or set of courses that focus on academic writing or argument, the general outcomes statement of first year writing is a pronouncement for a curriculum that develops research methods, explores the role of inquiry in all writing (especially academic), and as such, requires attention to developing new habits of mind, a better understanding that reading and writing are the tools of inquiry, and a recognition that exploration of literacy itself is a fundamental tact for learning and inquiry.

An under-publicized gem is *Considering Literacy: Reading and Writing the Educational Experience* (2006) by Linda Adler-Kassner. This text contends that students who work to understand the context of literacy practices (e.g., the ways of reading, writing, and thinking within different groups or communities) can more readily come to understand the practices of writing (e.g., rhetorical choices and definitions of appropriate literacies) that most effectively reach those communities (pp. vi-vii). The author sets up assignment sequences for reading and writing that are based on core assumptions, including, "writing, reading, and thinking are linked, and good writing should always be (partly) about wrestling with ideas," and that both reading and writing start with "smart (and messy) ideas" and end with "pretty (and smart) papers, and not the other way around" (pp. 1–4).

The bulk of the book is made up of readings thematically linked in broad topics about learning and learners, but its core is a series of assignment sequences that help students explore questions of education, learning, and literacies, and help them understand questions of context, place, and appropriateness in the reading they engage in and the writing they do. Sequences are grouped within four basic kinds of writing assignments: "Learning from Self;" "Learning from Others;" "Learning Through Research;" and "Speaking Out, Joining In, Talking Back." There are eight or more assignments in each category (the text focuses on similar writing strategies, so the instructor can choose), and students build on writing strategies as they move from one sequence to another. For instance, the "Learning from Self" assignments work on analysis and on working with texts; the "Learning from Others" assignments use the same strategies, but ask students also to work in interpretation and summarizing, among other skills (p. 4). As students read each essay in the sequence, they are asked to write critical reflections, make connections to other readings (in the assignment grouping), and build skills across assignment sequences.

READING AND WRITING TEXT-TO-TEXT: WRITING ABOUT WRITING

An increasing number of writing programs are moving towards writing courses that acknowledge that the study of writing itself, as a field of inquiry, affords students an advanced starting point—their own writing and literacy experiences—and thus deeper insights into how writing works. By reading about literacy and writing, and by subsuming what they learn about reading and writing practices as they develop their own reading and writing skills, students are better equipped to apply general learning outcomes to their own writing. Reading and writing about reading and writing begets opportunities to learn about reading and writing.

Most college textbooks are based on long-standing assumptions about first year writing: that it is a skill-creating course, or sequence of courses, that provide students with tools that transfer to writing in all contexts, including the workplace, and across all disciplines. In an important article in *College Composition and Communication*, Doug Downs and Elizabeth Wardle (2007) suggest, however, that learning to write in first year writing is not establishing a set of skills to be collected or taught in one or two courses early in students' careers, but that first year writing should be re-imagined to provide students an opportunity to study writing itself. Imagined as an "Intro to Writing Studies," first year writing can instead seek to "improve students' understanding of writing, rhetoric, language, and literacy in a course that is topically oriented to reading and writing as scholarly inquiry and encouraging more realistic understanding of writing" (p. 553).

Whether spurred by Downs and Wardle's assertions or arriving at similar conclusions concurrently, an increasing number of writing programs have re-cast first year writing as an introduction to writing studies. Central to these premises is the idea that in a writing studies curriculum, students become active participants in discovering and creating a writing process, thereby being active readers and active learners as they pursue lines of inquiry related to the process of critical reading and academic writing.

Elizabeth Wardle and Doug Downs developed writing about writing practices in a new textbook reader, *Writing about Writing* (2011). They tell students that they (students) should study writing as a field of inquiry because by "changing what you know about writing can change the way you write" (p. 2). Also, students see that people engage their worlds through language, reading, and writing—things they do every day. Because language, reading, and writing are subjects with which students have experience, they are more knowledgeable investigators of these subjects than they are with many other things (p. 2).

To help make the reading-writing connection, the authors selected articles (and collected them into thematic chapters) that allow students to "very consciously connect at least *some* part of each piece" to their experiences as a writer (p. 4). The authors acknowledge that both students and instructors might struggle with the content of the readings, so they scaffold questions "in ways that help make individual readings more accessible to students and that help them build toward mastery of often complex rhetorical concepts" (p. viii). Related to reading, each selection begins with opening sections that frame each reading, give background on the text and author, and suggest activities for students to do before and while they read (p. viii). Each reading is followed with questions for discussion and journal writing and reflection prompts to help focus the students' reading on important concepts.

Each reading is followed by recommendations for reading-related writing activities, some of which explore and deepen students' understanding of the very canon of scholarship attached to the processes of reading and writing. For instance, in one assignment following the Haas and Flower (1988) essay, "Reading Strategies and Construction of Meaning," Wardle and Downs suggest:

> Make a list of the rhetorical reading strategies that Haas and Flower discuss, trying to include even those they only imply without explicitly stating. Use this list to help you write a set of instructions on reading rhetorically for the next group of students who will take the class you're in now. What should they look for in texts? What questions should they ask about texts to ensure they're reading rhetorically? (p. 138)

This kind of exercise builds meta-awareness or meta-cognition. Rather than being shown how to outline, take notes, or paraphrase, students are asked to join in the discovery of these reading strategies. The act of discovery is itself participatory—and also an act of creative reading—and students are invited to join in and talk back (by writing) to scholarship in the field.

While *Writing about Writing* has writing as a primary focus, its approach to introducing students to the scholarship of the field no doubt challenges students' reading abilities. It can be assumed that most students in a writing course have not encountered this kind of material before. The book's focus on inquiry into the scholarship gives it a unique angle on the interplay of reading and writing than does most composition readers. Because the readings are about writing, they no doubt change the way students *think* about how and why writing and reading are done and what is accomplished when writing and reading are performed. This awareness suggests, too, that students will succeed in transferring reading, writing, and inquiry skills to other courses and other writing precisely because they will know the what, why, and how writing is done.

The idea of transferring an awareness of writing processes and an understanding of rhetorical choices is an important aspect of writing studies that encompasses genre-based approaches to writing. The assumption is that good writing is writing that works (or affects a response or course of action, including social action), but also recognizes that good writing is dependent on context. Students, especially in first year writing, need to be shown how to understand the rhetorical situation—the intersection of audience, purpose, form, and style—in determining what approach their writing takes.

An early entrant in the market was *Scenes of Writing: Strategies for Composing with Genres*, by Amy Devitt, Mary Jo Reiff, and Anis Bawarshi (2004). More of a rhetoric with readings, the text nevertheless has students writing in response to readings of a wide array of genres, including popular, academic, and public sources. The authors are careful to help students learn how to read scenes, that is, observe, analyze, and own the writing situations they will encounter in college and beyond. Part I is a guided analysis of genres, intended to help students observe (read) different genres and analyze the characteristics of communication within different genres, determine effective writing choices within genres, and critique scenes and genres. The steps of "observing scenes, analyzing scenes and genres, and writing within them," make up the reading and writing activities throughout the book (p. xviii). The remaining parts of the book introduce students to the kinds of writing—and the genres—they will write in college (including, argument, research, and forms of writing unique to different disciplines) and in the workplace.

The idea of exploring the moves within different genres is one of the features of another rhetorical genre text-reader: *How to Write Anything: A Guide and Reference with Readings*, by John J. Ruszkiewicz and Jay Dolmage (2010). The chapters in Parts One and Two serve as a guide to different academic and public genres and as a discussion of rhetorical choices; chapters in Parts Three through Nine are reference chapters that cover key aspects of the writing process (p. vi). The connection to reading and writing, and the idea that students can explore moves within different genres, is evident in the questions and writing assignments in the "Reading the Genre" sections that follow each reading in the chapters of Part Ten. Following a review about

The Colbert Report by television critic David Bianculli, for example, the authors ask students to do several writing tasks: re-read the review and list and discuss the essayist's use of metaphors, discuss how the essayist enumerates his main points, examine and relate an image that accompanies the text, evaluate the essayist's critique of Colbert's use of humor, and write a short essay about another cultural figure in the manner of Bianculli.

Like writing about-writing-texts, or texts that deal with literacy and learning issues, rhetorical, genre-based texts and readers help students develop a meta-awareness of their rhetorical choices. By showing students how their writing is influenced by the rhetorical choices they make, they can help them become more versatile writers, regardless of the writing task. As they become aware of audience expectations and the forms and strategies they can use in first year writing assignments, they are better prepared to transfer those learning-about-learning skills, complete the academic writing tasks they face in college, and write effectively after their college years.

WHY USE A READER: THE TRIANGULATION OF STUDENTS, TEACHERS, AND TEXTBOOKS

Instructors looking for assistance in weaving reading and writing instruction in FYW would be well served to closely examine the apparatus of a textbook reader to see how effectively it guides students to close readings and re-readings of texts and determine whether and how it prompts students to extract meaning, analyze and evaluate content, recognize a writer's rhetorical strategies, build writing assignments that allow students to respond to and argue with texts, build an extended inquiry, or otherwise create their own meaning.

It is necessary to see the college textbook reader as a component in the important triangulation of teacher, student, and writing assignment. Inasmuch as student readers may be challenged to apply what they read to what they write, whether it is an understanding of content or a reflection on the rhetorical strategies a writer has employed, the textbook can extend the instructor's pattern of connecting reading and writing to the degree that the apparatus and assignments in the book are seamlessly part of the fabric of writing assignments in the first year writing classroom.

In this way, textbook readers can assume a middle spot in the continuum from instructors to students. This can be seen in two ways. First, the textbook reader can assume a *primary* position if the reading and writing assignments in its apparatus form the basis of an instructor's syllabus, and its apparatus (assignment design) can fill core needs for the instructor, Second, it can take a *secondary* position if the readings themselves are of primary importance and if it is accepted that readings will be mediated by the instructor and used as part of a carefully scaffolded writing assignment or in classroom instruction. In either case, the textbook and the readings must have a clearly defined context for students, and that context must include carefully crafted writing assignments.

Recalling the spectrum used to consider the apparatus in textbook readers examined in this chapter—the move from reading for invention, to reading for meaning, to reading to evaluate, to reading to create meaning—we can see the kinds of textbook readers that most fully integrate reading and writing instruction. From the categories of readers we have considered, the most fully developed critical reading strategies are offered abundantly in books that require students to return to texts with guided instruction for rereading and for writing that grapples with the texts. Readers that insist on this kind of guided reading/writing sequence are those known as aims readers (Axelrod, 2011; Bean, 2011), argument readers (Lunsford, 2010; Ramage, 2007; Graff, 2010), WAC readers (Behrens, 2008; Greene, 2008), readers that invite text-to-text inquiry (Bartholomae, 2011; Miller, 2009; Adler-Kassner, 2006), and writing about writing readers (Wardle, 2011). The context in which each of these books is used, however, might distinguish the appropriate choice for a writing instructor.

The measure of success for college textbooks is market share, and as much as sales reflects the axiom of "meeting the market needs," there are no criteria to judge whether authors' abilities to weave reading and writing instruction is a primary reason for any book's success. The composition readers examined in this chapter all have top spots in their market niche, mark a shift in the way first year writing is taught, or otherwise provide a rich tapestry of critical reading strategies as an elemental thread in the pattern of guided writing instruction. As such, these are books developed with the first year writing curriculum in mind, the outcomes of which might call for a focus on critical thinking and/or critical reading in the context of academic writing. The assumption is that attention to critical, close reading skills helps students learn strategies of inquiry, research, using source material, mastering conventions of different disciplines, developing audience awareness, composing in different genres, and otherwise meeting the requirements of first year writing. That assumption is met only to the degree that the instructor has benefited from training or research in teaching reading, and/or has a fully developed plan for scaffolding reading and writing skills as an integral element of writing assignments. The success of composition textbooks, then, can best be determined by how well writing instructors in first year writing integrate the textbooks' advice and assignments in the work they do in class and in the assignments they design. This integration can be enhanced by examining how textbooks represent the relationship between reading and writing in ways that frame how teachers and students perceive and enact these skills.

Author Acknowledgments

I am deeply indebted to a large number of friends in the composition and rhetoric community who corresponded and talked with me, listened to my developing thoughts, and addressed innumerable questions as I undertook this review. If I have misrepresented anything from our conversations and correspondence or appropriated their words in an inaccurate context, the mistakes are unintentional.

I am grateful as well to colleagues at Bedford/St. Martin's for their early approval and support and for helping me frame analytical questions. None of the views in this chapter should be construed as positions held by my colleagues at Bedford/St. Martin's or as official views of the company.

9 Reuniting Reading and Writing: Revisiting the Role of the Library

Cynthia R. Haller

As discussed in this book's overview, higher education in the U.S. has historically divided reading and writing instruction. This artificial partition between them has been easily sustained—in part because theorists have not adequately addressed how the two are connected, and in part because the academy's political structure reifies their bifurcation. Reading and writing, however, need to be integrated throughout the curriculum to support students' development of critical literacy.

In this chapter, I consider how an integrated information literacy and writing model provides a strong basis for critical literacy instruction, and further, how collaborations between librarians and disciplinary faculty supports the adoption of that model. For the development of my ideas on these issues, I am grateful to Miriam Laskin, Head of Instructional Services at Hostos Community College, and Scott Sheidlower, Head of Information Literacy at York College. Conversations with both helped me understand why compositionists need to take information literacy seriously in order to re-establish lost connections between reading and writing instruction.

To unpack the role information literacy plays in fostering critical literacy, I turn first to a brief history of academic libraries in the U.S. The following overview is necessarily reductive; however, an historical and contemporary portrait of the academic library is essential to understanding how its instructional goals intersect with those of compositionists.

FROM BIBLIOGRAPHIC INSTRUCTION TO INFORMATION LITERACY: CHANGING VIEWS OF THE LIBRARY

In the U.S., both the history of academic libraries and the history of disciplinary courses are linked to the nineteenth-century rise of the modern university (Fister, 1995, p. 34; Russell, 2002, p. 21). Modeled after Germany's universities, the new institutions of higher education prized research, creating a need for textual resources. "Houses of knowledge" in a very literal sense, academic libraries were at the center of universities' intellectual activity, serving as communally shared spaces for investigation. Librarians, as overseers of rich repositories of print information, were arbiters and gatekeepers of social knowledge, determining, in cooperation with disciplinary faculty, texts belonging in the collection. Moreover, librarians archived and cataloged texts to facilitate scholarly access, often in ways that paralleled the specialized disciplinary divisions emerging in the modern university. Access, of course, was constrained by users' knowledge of the library's organizational systems. Library of Congress subject headings, for example, can both enable and prevent access to texts. Those who know how to use the taxonomy can locate sources efficiently; those who do not are hindered by their unfamiliarity with the system's language and syntax.

Fast forward to 2004. By that date, increased availability of consumer computers and mobile computing devices, coupled with the rise of the Internet and Web, had challenged information's material and spatial limitations. Alternative avenues of information dissemination, allowing information-seekers to circumvent the library as their primary access point for knowledge, threatened to squeeze libraries out of the academic information industry (think, for example, of course management systems, textbook-linked websites, Google search engines, Amazon and Google book searches, and online scholarly publications). A 2004 report from Outsell Inc., a research and advisory firm for the publication and information industries, even suggested the library was a defunct social institution: "The future of the library is that there is no library; the functions that the library performs have been blown up and are scattered throughout the universe" (as cited in Bell & Shank, 2004, p. 372).

Fast forward to 2011. Rather than marching happily toward their own extinction, however, academic libraries have been reinventing themselves. They have been diversifying the functionality of their physical spaces, with renewed attention to attractiveness and comfort. New group study and reading rooms at one of Ohio State University's libraries, for example, are also used for university receptions and events, turning the library into "the living room" of the campus. Yet, the new design has augmented rather than diminished the library's intellectual function. After the library's eleven-story stack tower (formerly enclosed brick) was converted into a six-story, glass structure, the attractive, open design drew students toward the library's print resources, many of which cannot be accessed digitally. As Carol Diedrichs, the library director, puts it, "We like to talk about how everything is digital, but it's not entirely . . . . The marriage of study spaces with a prominent place for print is like being at the intellectual crossroads of our campus" (as cited in Carlson, 2010, Quadruple the Visitors section, para. 5). Libraries, no longer "the stodgy and stuffy repositories of years past" (Carlson, 2005, para. 7), are morphing into comfortable spaces, equipped with amenities such as good lighting, cafes, lounges, conference rooms, and study areas. In some cases, they are even changing their names, calling themselves, for example, "Information Commons," but are retaining their iconic identities as intellectual centers of learning (Carlson, 2005).

More important than spatial adaptations, however—at least regarding critical literacy—is libraries' increasing focus on information literacy education. Per the American Library Association (ALA) (1989), information literacy is defined as the ability to "recognize when information is needed and have the ability to locate, evaluate, and use effectively the needed information" (para. 3). The concept of information literacy developed in part as a response to new forms of information creation, dissemination, and reception. As information resources began shifting from the relatively controlled environment of the print-based library to new, complex, and abundant "unfiltered formats," it became increasingly difficult for librarians (or anyone, for that matter) to monitor information for "authenticity, validity, and reliability" (Association of College Research Libraries, 2000, Introduction section, para.1). Through information literacy education, librarians continue to exercise their role as gatekeepers and monitors of information quality, but not simply by safe-keeping in-house collections of texts. As information literacy experts, they instruct students and faculty how best to navigate increasingly complex fields of social knowledge that might be located literally anywhere. As Miriam Laskin, a librarian at Hostos Community College/CUNY puts it

> Now, more than ever . . . each individual must be her own evaluator. Every student or person who uses the Internet and the Web to find information, must be prepared to understand that critical thinking about the source of the information is

as important as anything they are going to do with it. (M. Laskin, personal communication, January 28, 2011)

Prior to 2000, library instruction—generally known then as bibliographic instruction (BI)—consisted mostly of teaching faculty and students how to access and use the information resources physically housed in the library.[1] The logical place for BI, requiring the specialized expertise of professionals familiar with the organization of print-based social knowledge within the library, was the library itself. The logical place for information literacy (IL), however, is wherever people might need and/or encounter information: in today's world, everywhere. Information literacy can thus be seen as a critical mindset, one that facilitates people's functioning in an information-saturated environment.

Information literacy did not, of course, arrive full-blown on the library scene. From the 1980s to 2000, a number of efforts to expand and enhance library instruction were initiated at individual libraries. Additionally, a Presidential Commission on Information Literacy was formed by ALA President Margaret Chisholm in 1987, releasing its final report in 1989.[2] In 2000, the Association of College and Research Libraries (ACRL)[3] approved the *Information Literacy Competency Standards for Higher Education*, articulating and elaborating both old and new goals for library instruction. ACRL's Information Literacy Competency Standards are five in number:

1. The information literate student determines the nature and extent of the information needed.

2. The information literate student accesses needed information effectively and efficiently.

3. The information literate student evaluates information and its sources critically and incorporates selected information into his or her knowledge base and value system.

4. The information literate student, individually or as a member of a group, uses information effectively to accomplish a specific purpose.

5. The information literate student understands many of the economic, legal, and social issues surrounding the use of information and accesses and uses information ethically and legally. (ACRL, 2000, Standards, Performance Indicators, and Outcomes section, para. 1–5)

Additionally, these five standards are subdivided into twenty-two performance indicators, each of which includes behavioral outcomes. (For the full list of standards, performance indicators, and outcomes, see ACRL, 2000, or Appendix A of this volume.)

Endorsed by the American Association for Higher Education (AAHE) in 1999, and the Council of Independent Colleges in 2004, the Information Literacy Competency Standards have now been integrated into accreditation standards and principles for all institutions of higher education in the U.S.: the Middle States Commission on Higher Education (MSACS), the Western Association of Schools and Colleges (WASC), the Northwest Commission on Colleges and Universities (NWCCU), the North Central Association of Colleges and Schools (NCACS), the New England Association of Schools and Colleges (NEASC), and the Southern Association of Colleges and Schools (SACS). The ACRL website articulates where information literacy can be found within the various accreditation standards and principles of each of these organizations ("Accreditation," n.d.). This emphasis calls colleges to account for the information literacy levels of their students, furthering information literacy instruction nationwide.

Since the 2000 approval and release of the information literacy standards, ACRL has continued to work actively on their promotion. Information literacy itself is a globalized movement (Rockman, 2004, p. 6), and the ACRL website provides translations of the standards into eight different languages. Further, in 2001, ACRL followed up on the Standards with guidelines for information literacy instructors (ACRL, 2001; Gaspar & Presser, 2010, p. 156). The 2000 standards are also being adapted to a variety of specific disciplines. Standards for science and technology were approved by in 2006, and standards for anthropology, sociology, and political science came out in 2008.

Although development of the Standards was spurred on by the technological affordances of the digital age, information literacy, as defined by ACRL, is not the same thing as information technology skills. Information literacy, as "an intellectual framework for understanding, finding, evaluating, and using information" (ACRL, 2000, Introduction section, para.5), is ultimately discrete from any technology; indeed, development of the standards included deliberate incorporation of both higher and lower order thinking skills based on Bloom's Taxonomy of Educational Objectives. As Horning and Kraemer suggested in the Introduction to this volume, information literacy "can be seen as the crossroads where reading (evaluation and analysis) and writing (synthesis and incorporation) meet."

Because information literacy intersects both reading and writing processes, it has the potential to foster their reconnection in the academy. Doing so, however, requires that information literacy be construed not as a rigid set of skills and procedures—a "behavioralist framework"—but as a dynamic, generative understanding of how information is nested within and used by social communities—a "constructivist framework" (Bowles-Terry, Davis, & Holliday, 2006, p. 226). A constructivist framework supports the development of what Elmborg (2006) has called "critical information literacy" (p. 195). Like critical literacy in general, critical information literacy involves using knowledge to authentically participate in society as agents of resistance and change (p. 195).

Librarians working within a constructivist framework of information literacy do not simply teach students how to find information resources. Rather, by actively engaging students in learning how information is produced and disseminated, they support students' critical evaluation of information. Further, by teaching students how to evaluate and use the information they find, constructivist librarians "support core academic literacies, among them reading comprehension, textual analysis, research skills and strategies, the process of research and parallel (or combined) process of writing, critical thinking, and collaborative, active, inquiry-based learning" (M. Laskin, personal communication, January 28, 2011).

Optimal methods for information literacy instruction involve weaving it into curricular structures, rather than teaching it as if it were an add-on skill. It is best integrated through pedagogies that focus on student learning, especially inquiry- and problem-based learning, or those that emphasize critical thinking and require students to "expand their knowledge, ask informed questions, and sharpen their critical thinking for still further self-directed learning" (ACRL, 2000, Introduction section, para. 10). Information literacy, like critical literacy, is also not something confined to the educational arena: It is a foundation for lifelong learning and citizenship.

With their growing attention to instructing students in information literacy, libraries are moving out beyond their walls, "trying to be less constrained by their traditional physical locations and to be seen as a service that can be used in many places" (Currie & Eodice,

2005, p. 47). Librarians today are actively collaborating with disciplinary faculty, writing centers, academic learning centers, writing across the curriculum (WAC) programs, and Writing Fellows to integrate information literacy into college curricula and support services. The promise information literacy holds for reconnecting reading and writing in the academy, however, has yet to be fully realized. Information literacy, like critical literacy, is still marginalized in many colleges and universities, to the detriment of students. Its absence from the curriculum, both in composition and other disciplinary courses, contributes to the disconnection between reading and writing instruction in the academy. In the next section, I suggest that a new model for reading and writing is needed to overcome that disconnection, a model that envisions reading and writing as embedded together in the life of social communities.

READING, RESEARCH, AND WRITING: CONCEPTUAL AND THEORETICAL CONNECTIONS

As psycholinguistic activities, reading and writing are intimately connected; both are "opportunities to arrive at meaning, to reflect on that meaning, and to act" (Sheridan, 1995, p. 13). Theories about the nature of these activities differ, however, partly because of the disciplinary specialization of the modern university. Librarians and disciplinary faculty "both engage students in performing a basic activity of academia—scholarly inquiry" (Fister, 1995, p. 34), and both involve students in "discovery, questioning, organization, and process" (LaBaugh, 1995, p. 24). They have, however, developed models for research and for writing independently of one another, thus continuing to treat these processes as if they were separate. Considering disconnects in these models can point up areas that library and disciplinary faculty need to think about collaboratively, thereby developing more holistic models of critical literacy.

Earlier in this book, Horning and Kraemer offer a definition of critical literacy as a purposeful act "whereby students call on critical thinking skills to navigate, understand, transform, and apply information for their use." Reading (understanding) and writing (transforming and applying) are both nested within this definition, but the relationship between them warrants closer attention. I would argue that the nature of their relationship shifts depending on one's perspective. To an individual writing a specific text, reading and writing may appear temporally sequential, as opposite ends of a continuum of psycholinguistic activity; the continuum begins with reading and ends with writing. In actuality, however, individuals cycle iteratively and re-cursively through reading and writing processes as they generate new texts. If we view reading and writing from a socio-cultural perspective, even the illusion of a linear continuum disappears. The reception and generation of texts can no longer be seen as separate, but are instead revealed to be different aspects of one ongoing process—namely, en-gaging in the textually mediated life of the community. Critical lit-eracy, then, is the ability to participate authentically in communal life through both reading and writing. When individuals read and write, they do so within the language communities they inhabit. Whether they read or write (or both) at any given time depends on which pro-cess is warranted by the particular activity or situation.

Horning and Kraemer's earlier discussion of reading (in this vol-ume) is useful in explaining what I mean here. Decoding and deci-phering linguistic symbols, while essential to reading, is not sufficient for "true" reading, which requires making appropriate connections be-tween texts and social contexts. This kind of reading, sometimes re-ferred to by compositionists as rhetorical reading (Geisler, 1994; Haas & Flower, 1988; Penrose & Geisler, 1994), draws on extra-textual knowledge about authors, purposes, rhetorical situations, related texts, and material/social contexts to ascertain the meaning of a particular text. Skilled rhetorical readers are aware of how individual texts func-tion within specific rhetorical contexts and of how they are influenced by the material and social constraints in which they are produced, dis-seminated, and received. They understand that texts are not autono-mous and authoritative, but contingent, open to critical examination, and connected with other texts in multiple ways within various com-munities of practice.

Because a reader's expertise or domain knowledge of the context in which a text is situated enables rhetorical reading, students in low-er-division college courses tend to exhibit rhetorically naive reading practices, whereas upper-division and graduate students are better able to discern how a particular text fits within the context of the disci-pline. Nevertheless, the ability to read rhetorically is also a procedural knowledge that can be facilitated by instruction (Penrose & Geisler, 1994). Some composition textbooks reviewed earlier in this volume by

Fleming, for example, specifically address rhetorical reading strategies that can help students develop their ability to appropriately connect text and context.

Rhetorical reading enables people to construct context-appropriate meanings from print, sound, and images. They can then purposefully use this meaning in multiple ways, furthering their ability to participate in the world. Reading may be the basis for a physical action, such as when one reads a brief on a political candidate's positions to determine how to cast a vote, or more mundanely, when one reads a bus schedule to know when to go to the bus stop. Even reading that is used simply for learning, or to extend or reconstruct one's own knowledge base, prepares one for potential future action. Reading can also motivate and/or inform writing, as when one uses what is read to generate and embody new meanings in print, sound, and images.[4] Through this last use, reading and writing may fuse into authorship: the generation of new meaning embodied in shared semiotic systems and situated appropriately in existing textual networks. From a social community's perspective, reading and writing are not individually experienced psycholinguistic processes, but aspects of the cycling of knowledge within and among its members.

Critical literacy, then, requires the ability to connect what one writes with what one reads, so that any newly generated writing will be meaningful to readers. Writers do not necessarily need to incorporate specific texts into their writing for their reading to be meaningful to others, as long as they connect what they write to knowledge with which their readers are already familiar. Incorporating texts one has read into one's writing, however, can raise one's status as an author, because this incorporation explicitly situates one's own text in relation to other texts that have status and standing within a community (Rose 1996, 1999). Generating reading-informed writing appropriately designed to reach academic readers is at the heart of academic discourse, and the ability to do so is central to critical literacy.

Information literacy can further this ability because it grounds writing more obviously in existing cultural knowledge. Historically, compositionists have truncated the rhetorical canon, largely neglecting memory and delivery (Norgaard, 2003). As a result, they have misled students to perceive the writing of text as an isolated act, disconnected from the intertextual networks that underlie socio-cultural uses of language. Information literacy reconnects writing to social and cultural memory as lodged in other texts, to delivery, and as realized in the dissemination of texts for reader consumption. By making the intertextual character of knowledge more transparent, information literacy makes the purposes of writing more intelligible to students. It also enhances students' practice of the other three canons: invention, arrangement and style. Knowing how to access, evaluate, and use existing knowledge facilitates the intentional processes of discovery and inquiry. Understanding the social organization of knowledge broadens students' concept of arrangement from a concern internal to specific texts to a concern with how a particular text fits within a field of texts. Finally, knowing about stylistic variations among specific communities of practice hones awareness that disciplinary discourse conventions are determined by people, not style guides (Norgaard, 2003, pp. 128–29).

If composition instruction suffers from lack of grounding in information literacy, information literacy instruction suffers from lack of connection to the ongoing rhetorical production of knowledge. An information literacy bereft of writing can be perceived as rigid, narrow, and rule-based, and as a technical skill rather than a communication capability (Bowles-Terry, Davis, & Holliday, 2006; Elmborg, 2006). Indeed, disciplinary faculty's impression of information literacy as little more than a technical skill can be recalcitrant. A few years ago, when the librarians at one institution proposed that information literacy be considered an important competence within a new general education curriculum, one committee member on general education responded, "[W]e already have computer literacy as an outcome," and when a general invitation was sent to faculty to schedule an information literacy session for their students, one faculty member responded that he didn't want to "waste class time having my students learn computer skills" (S. Sheidlower, personal communication, October 15, 2010). If librarians conceptualize information literacy not as a rule-based skill, but as "deeply context-bound" (Norgaard, 2003, p. 126), they can help faculty understand it for what it truly is—an unfolding, developing capacity to access, use, evaluate, and apply information *for specific purposes, places, and times.* Fortunately, librarians are moving in this direction, raising the profile of information literacy in many colleges and universities.

Reintegrating information literacy and writing instruction fosters not only critical literacy, but also the activity of research. By research, I mean intentional and systematic investigation, motivated by a question or problem. Research might be considered a subcategory of reading that is intentionally, deliberately, and systematically directed toward the purpose of answering questions or solving problems. In the course of living, we read, or get meaning from pages and screens, in a somewhat serendipitous and disorganized manner, viewing advertisements, watching TV shows, surfing the net, reading a novel, or the back of a cereal box. Research as a form of reading, however, is generally both intentional and systematic.

As scientists and social scientists are quick to point out, researchers often look to experimental and empirical investigations of nontextual phenomena to answer their questions. How can this practice be reconciled with the notion of research as a subcategory of reading? If we think semiotically, these experiments and investigations involve "reading" phenomena as signs (e.g., a rise in temperature may be a sign that a chemical reaction is taking place; the body language of a teacher toward a student may be a sign of the teacher's attitude toward that student). Research, then, can include "reading" meaning in material and other phenomena.

Research and writing should be thought of and taught as parts of a single, holistic activity (Elmborg, 2005; Hook, 2005). Elmborg (2005) argues that instructional librarians and writing center professionals, by working together, can enact a "shared practice where research and writing can be treated as a single holistic process" (p. 1). Hook (2005) agrees: Separating the research process from the writing process "fractures the learning experience" of students, who experience the two processes together as an "integrated, holistic experience" (p. 25). Both advocate for a new, more integrated model of research writing, founded on the combined expertise of library and composition faculty.

Unfortunately, the political economy of the modern university, with its bifurcation of reading and writing, has segregated theoretical thinking about research and writing. Librarians often think of the research process as their purview and underestimate the importance of writing to inquiry. Conversely, writing professionals often think of the writing process as their purview, viewing the research process as subordinate to the writing process (Hook, 2005, p. 21; Fister, 1995, p. 28; Gibson, 1995, pp. 59–62). This division has led to and perpetuates discrete models for these processes. Compositionists, for instance, may look to the common, four-phase model for the writing process (pre-writing, drafting, revising, and editing), in which every stage is recursive.

Kuhlthau's (2004) model of research, however, identifies six stages in the research process: task initiation, topic selection, prefocus exploration, focus formulation, information selection, and search closure.[5] Though she does consider the research process as primarily antecedent to the writing process, Kuhlthau does view research stages as recursive, and believes that writing can be a form of "exploratory strategy" during the research process (as cited in Hook, 2005, p. 24). How might Kuhlthau's model of research articulate with compositionists' writing process models? Reconciling existing process models for research and writing, Elmborg (2005) suggests, would go far toward reuniting the "intimately intertwined" reading and writing processes in the academic work of students:

> The recursiveness of the research/writing process is related at least in part to the recurring interplay between writing and information. By segregating the research process from the writing process, we have obscured this fact and thereby impoverished both the writing process and the research process. This segregation reflects institutional division, but not the reality of student work. Composition faculty see the "writing process," whereas librarians see the "research process." This bifurcated approach fails to explain the integrated holistic experience of the student using information in the writing process. By working in collaboration, these two units can treat the research process and the writing process as a seamless whole. (p. 11)

If librarians and disciplinary faculty collaborated to better articulate reading and writing, they would also develop a shared language for scholarly inquiry that would lead to a more coherent pedagogy for research writing. Using similar terms when working with students, "teaching librarians and writing professionals [would] reinforce writing and research as shared processes" (Hook, 2005, p. 27).

For sound pedagogy, however, research and writing instruction must extend beyond the traditional "library research paper" assignment. Despite many attacks on the research paper as an academic genre, and despite the awakening understanding that both reading and writing are multimodal, the traditional "library research paper" assignment is still a staple assignment in both composition and other disciplinary courses (see Thaiss & Zawacki, 2006, p. 104 for an indication of its ubiquity in the academy). If students are to understand research and writing as a dynamic process for exploring and answering authentic questions, this addiction needs to be addressed.

In what I call the traditional research paper, students look information up and assemble it to produce an alphanumeric, print text. The history of the assignment is rooted in the late nineteenth century rise of the modern university. As Russell (2002) has explained, the research paper assignment in that context was intended for the communication of authentically original knowledge. As the pace of knowledge production in universities quickened, however, generating new knowledge became more difficult for undergraduate students. By the early part of the twentieth century, the research paper had become more a means of assessing student learning than a vehicle for communicating new knowledge. Additionally, as first year composition courses sprung up across the U.S., responsibility for teaching how to write the research paper shifted from disciplinary to English programs.

By the late twentieth century, composition instructors' dissatisfaction with the traditional research paper was on the rise. Larson (1982) argued that the so-called "generic 'research paper'" (p. 812) is actually a "non-form" of writing since it has no conceptual, substantive, or procedural identity. Further, he suggested that the assignment warps students' understanding of both research activity and writing. By implying that research activity requires only the taking of notes from books in a library, it gives students a reductive notion of what it means to do research. By implying that the research paper is the only form of writing that incorporates and uses research, it leads students to think that other genres of writing (e.g., memos, recommendations, etc.) do not rely on the incorporation of research.

Like Larson, Norgaard (2004) warns that the traditional research paper may stand in the way of good research and writing pedagogies. By divorcing research from genuine inquiry, the research paper assignment leaves only a shell product in which students assemble preexisting knowledge. Furthermore, students' production of this shell product is especially susceptible to plagiarism, as students are tempted to simply cut and paste from Internet sites to produce patchwork assemblies. To be effective, research-based assignments should call for the dialogic generation and revising of knowledge. Informational research assignments that lend themselves to cutting and pasting do not always engage students adequately in ongoing conversations about "intellectual, social and ethical issues" (p. 223).

Compositionists have developed many viable alternatives to the traditional research paper assignment, including having students engage in research activities other than reading, such as ethnography, interviews, and empirical research. As well, new ways of "writing" about the results of research activity are being explored (see Zemliansky & Bishop, 2004, for examples of both strategies). Librarians' deep understanding of research can be very helpful to composition and other disciplinary faculty seeking more authentic research writing assignments. Lutzker (1995) provides a number of suggestions for alternatives to the traditional research paper. Leckie (1996) uncovers false assumptions faculty may make about student research and provides ideas to more effectively scaffold research for novices. She also argues that the integration of information literacy into college curricula can assist students in their acculturation to research writing practices.

As has been suggested in this section, compositionists and librarians, working collaboratively, can design theories and pedagogies that reconnect reading and writing. In the next section, I consider practical ways library and disciplinary faculty can interact as they work toward achieving this goal.

CRITICAL LITERACY: CONNECTING READING, WRITING, AND DISCIPLINARY CONTENT

In Sheridan's (1995) edited volume, *Writing Across the Curriculum and the Academic Library*, Fister (1995) lamented that both bibliographic instruction (now information literacy instruction) and writing instruction were "outside the traditional political economy of the academy," in danger of becoming "a stepchild, a time-consuming, additional task shared by many, but . . . no one's primary focus" (p. 33). In a foreword to that same volume, however, Kirk (1995) offered a more positive view. In the twentieth-century university, he argued, content and process were dichotomized, and content was privileged over process, leading to the marginalization of both WAC and BI. Higher education, however, was due for a change, a "revolution in undergraduate education" that would "synthesiz[e] content and process into an integrated whole" (p. xi). WAC and BI alliances, suggested Kirk, might further that integration.

Some of this content-process synthesis has already begun. Pedagogies such as inquiry- and problem-based learning, for example, fulfill Lyotard's (1984) call for greater attention to procedural knowledge. Lyotard argued that modern conditions, where knowledge is increasingly stored in databases, require a new pedagogy that "treat[s] the teaching of content as less important than the process of inquiry and the mode of access to that content" (as cited in Elmborg, 1995, p. 2). In Lyotard's ideal pedagogy, learning content material takes a back seat to learning how to access content material or understanding "the relevant memory bank for what needs to be known" (as cited in Elmborg, 1995, p. 2). Similarly, in inquiry- and problem-based learning, the acquisition of specific content is seen not as an end in itself but as a means of solving a problem or answering a question.

In the twentieth-century university, teaching procedural knowledge was less valued, and bibliographic instruction was marginalized even more than composition instruction. Composition, at least, had a niche in academic instruction, secured by the nearly ubiquitous freshman composition course. By contrast, librarians were generally as considered service rather than instructional professionals, having second-class status to disciplinary faculty. Accordingly, much early work guiding librarians on how to promote information literacy begins from the presumption that librarians need to be especially proactive because of their "secondary" position. Thompson (1993), for instance, speaks of the need to "seduce" academic faculty at Earlham College to establish good bibliographic instruction programs (as cited in McGuinness, 2007, p. 27). *Learning to Lead and Manage Information Literacy Instruction* (Grassian & Kaplowitz, 2005) begins with a chapter on leadership qualities and strategies, tacitly sending the message that librarians be good leaders to generate and maintain successful information literacy programs. By arguing that the success of information literacy instruction depends on "how well we show how IL assists others in achieving their goals," Grassian and Kaplowitz subtly subordinate the educational agenda of librarians to that of disciplinary faculty (p. 32). Such subordination reinforces the "power deficit" between library and disciplinary faculty, giving the impression that information literacy professionals must "don their promoter's hats and hustle for business wherever they can find it" (McGuinness, pp. 27–28). It also places information literacy on a lower level than disciplinary content in a hierarchy of knowledge.

Fortunately for the future of reading and writing in the university, librarians' status in the university has been improving. Since the 1970s, ACRL has actively supported faculty rank, status, and tenure for librarians, and current growth in information literacy initiatives strengthens the argument: "With the move toward information literacy and faculty involvement, more and more librarians see themselves as equal partners with teaching faculty" (Millet, Jeremy, & Wilson, 2009, p. 180). This rise in librarian status is an encouraging sign that the twenty-first century university may indeed be in the process of re-valuing instruction in reading and writing.

As librarians have moved from "warehouse definitions of the past and toward instructional models," they have become agents of change in the university (Elmborg, 2005, p. 4). The "new" academic librarian, or what Bell and Shank (2004) call the "blended librarian," mixes the role of the traditional librarian with the information technologist's knowledge of hardware and software and the educators' expertise in teaching and learning. Librarians in this expanded role must be skilled communicators, able to "communicate easily and effectively with both teaching faculty and students, in the classroom and out" (Millet et al., 2009, p. 191). Indeed, the collaborations librarians have been actively forming with both writing and other disciplinary faculty has moved information literacy concerns from the margins of the university into its center, creating more sustainable models of information literacy instruction.

Approaches to collaboration, however, vary in how well they serve to reconnect reading and writing. In 2000, the year the Information Literacy Competency Standards were approved by ACRL, Raspa and Ward (2000) outlined three levels of potential interactions between librarians and disciplinary faculty, based on duration and intensity of the relationship, workload sharing, and commonality of goals. The first level, networking, is simply an informal and ephemeral professional sharing of information; it does not necessarily involve shared purposes. The second level, coordination, involves an identified shared purpose, but suffers from little shared activity or sustained relationships. In the third level, full collaboration, librarians and academics engage in a committed, sustained relationship, working as equal partners toward common academic goals and deciding together on how to reach those goals (pp. 4–5). Full collaboration is the most promising level for re-integrating reading and writing in the academy.

The following section describes common approaches to information literacy instruction, based on Raspa and Ward's (2009) categories of interaction. The order of presentation follows an arc of what I hope to be a movement in higher education toward greater collaboration between librarians and academy faculty, greater integration of information literacy into curricula, and a restored connection between reading and writing in the academy.

NETWORKING-COORDINATION APPROACHES

Networking and coordination approaches to information literacy instruction have the potential to reconnect reading and writing; however, lack of shared purpose and/or sustained interactions between librarians and disciplinary faculty can jeopardize their effectiveness. In the traditional library tour, for instance, classes are often brought into the library for a single session, with the librarian introducing the library resources. Such tours were common prior to and at the beginning of the digital age, when a majority of information resources were literally housed on the library's premises. Even then, the physical tour was not temporally sound, as it did not provide the "just-in-time" learning optimal for real gains in information literacy. What was learned during an overview tour would often be forgotten by the time it became useful to students.

Today, with so many information sources available only online, the tour model has, in many cases, given way to the "one-shot" information literacy session that a faculty member schedules with an information literacy instructor. In the best of circumstances, the faculty member and librarian work together to create a contextualized information literacy session specific to the needs of students in that particular course. For example, a psychology faculty member might ask students to summarize three peer-reviewed articles on a mental illness, and the information literacy instructor might teach students how to find those articles in a full-text database of psychology journals. The approach, when executed well, provides contextualized information literacy instruction, but too-cursory contact between library and disciplinary faculty can threaten its effectiveness. The faculty member, for example, may not know the available library resources sufficiently to generate an appropriate assignment, leading to the librarian experiencing difficulty in teaching the session, and student frustration in completing the assignment. Conversely, information literacy instructors may not contextualize the session appropriately to the assignment, leaving the course instructor and students frustrated.

The contextualized session approach is especially limited when only one information literacy session is given for a particular course. Scheduling at least two sessions is more pedagogically sound, given the iterative nature of research and writing. For research writing courses, Kuhlthau's (2004) research model provides good guidance for the strategic timing of sessions. Information literacy sessions are most likely to be helpful to students after topic selection, to set them up for exploring information about their topics, and also after focus formulation, when exploratory reading has sufficiently prepared them for efficient information selection. A third strategic position, not suggested by Kuhlthau's model but by writing process models, occurs after students draft their paper/research product. Drafting often reveals to writers where more information is needed to adequately develop certain ideas and arguments; and a third session can assist students in finding that information.

A common form of information literacy instruction is contact between reference librarians and individual students. Students frequently approach reference librarians with project-specific questions, sometimes at the encouragement of their instructors. If all goes well, the reference librarian guides students toward resources that help them meet the goals of the assignment. However, students are sometimes unreliable communicators of assignment guidelines and criteria. Even with the provision of faculty-written guidelines, the instructional and rhetorical purposes of the assignment may be tacit and inaccessible to the reference librarian. In such cases, intentional coordination between the disciplinary professor and the reference librarian can enhance the ability of the reference librarian to assist students appropriately.

In optimal networking and coordination approaches to information literacy instruction, synergy between disciplinary faculty, librarians, and students can connect reading and writing activities appropriately, leading to a positive experience for all. However, a number of factors can negatively affect the efficacy of these approaches. In particular, discrepancies with expectations for and terms of the interactions can lead to disappointment, frustration, and confusion on all

parts, perversely reinforcing the academy's disconnect between reading and writing.

Coordination-Collaboration Approaches: Libraries and Writing Centers

Collaborative interactions between academic librarians and student
support services, particularly writing centers, are relatively common.
These relationships tend to fall somewhere coordination and collaboration on Raspa and Ward's (2010) spectrum. Full collaborations have
often sprung up in the context of organizational proximity. Leadley
and Rosenberg (2005), for example, note that the co-membership of
both the library and the writing center in their institution's Academic
Services division facilitated their collaboration (p. 62). "Shared space,"
or the physical placement of writing centers in libraries, can also facilitate collaboration (Hook, 2005, p. 36). Currie and Eodice (2005)
explain how opening a writing center satellite in the Kansas University
Library led to the idea of cross-training peer tutors in both writing and
information literacy instruction. Since many front-line library questions could be answered by trained non-professionals, librarian time
was freed for activities and queries requiring their level of expertise.

Writing centers and librarians have also collaborated on programs
for faculty and student development. Many academic libraries sponsor workshops on research and research-related topics (e.g., plagiarism
and copyright, the language of searches, evaluation information, etc.).
Often, they collaborate with writing center professionals to develop
and offer these workshops. As Elmborg (2005) and Hook (2005) note,
however, a better theoretical reconnection between reading and writing would provide a firmer foundation for such collaborations. With
a shared understanding of inquiry as a holistic process of reading and
writing, both librarians and writing instructors might overcome their
natural territorialism (Hook, 2005, p. 28; Gibson, 1995, pp. 59–62). If
librarians stick solely to the research process and writing centers to the
writing process, however, they re-enact the academy's division of critical literacy into separate processes of reading and writing. Even when
librarians and writing centers work very effectively together conjoining
reading and writing, the absence of disciplinary faculty in the dynamic
perpetuates the academy's separation of process from content.

Collaborative Approaches: Toward an Integrated Critical Literacy

Course Integrations of Information Literacy

Fully overcoming the content-process dichotomy requires embedding information literacy instruction in courses and bringing disciplinary faculty into the collaborative loop. WAC courses are especially good candidates for this purpose. Indeed, prior to the institutionalization of the Information Literacy Competency Standards, librarians worked with writing across the curriculum programs on the co-integration of information literacy and writing in course curricula (Sheridan, 1995). When course content, information literacy, and critical reading and writing are fully incorporated in course design and delivery, content and process dovetail in the production and use of disciplinary discourse.

First year composition instructors, aware of the connection between reading and writing, have also formed effective collaborations with information literacy instructors, particularly when the course involves students in research. In a first year composition course at Cascadia College ("English 102: Writing from Research"), librarians taught one to three information literacy sessions and also collaborated with the course professor to conduct student self-assessments of information literacy (Bussert & Pouliot, 2010). At West Virginia University, faculty and librarians together developed a first year writing course with integrated sessions on evaluating internet resources and finding books and articles. They also brought the writing center into their collaboration, training writing tutors in information literacy and piloting a "Writing and Research Clinic" with combined tutor and librarian services (Brady, Singh-Corcoran, Dadisman, & Diamond, 2009).

A third locus for the active integration of information literacy is the research writing course (Isbell & Broaddus, 1995). These courses can be taught at any level. Canovan, Gruber, Knefel, and McKinlay (2010) report on the development and implementation of an interdisciplinary course, "Introduction to Research Writing," developed as part of a new core curriculum at the University of DuBuque (p. 182). The University of Washington (Bothell) has a required "Interdisciplinary Inquiry" course that is team-taught by a disciplinary instructor, a writing specialist, and a librarian (Leadley & Rosenberg, 2005). The course has evolved over time, and focuses on formulating research questions, understanding the rhetorical structure of text, evaluating and using evidence, and collaborating effectively. The first iteration was a two-course sequence that separated research and writing (the first course on focused on research, the second on writing), but later iterations of the course concentrated more heavily on teaching inquiry, creating a more unified focus.

A research writing course rich in information literacy can especially assist L2 learners with some of the difficulties they encounter while doing research, such as selecting topics; mastering sub-technical, academic vocabulary; and crediting sources appropriately (see Grabe & Zhang in this volume). Laskin and Diaz (2009) point out that L2 learners' less-developed language skills also hinder their ability to analyze, synthesis, evaluate, and use English-language texts. Much of the research reviewed by Laskin and Diaz demonstrates that information literacy instruction benefits L2 learners, increasing their vocabulary, reading comprehension, and critical thinking abilities. The authors also describe an information-literacy-integrated course, "Language, Culture, and Society," that specifically targets L2 populations. In the course, students explore sociological, anthropological, and political aspects of their own language communities, an assignment that both hones their research skills and develops pride in their language heritage.

Though embedding information literacy in curricula is increasing, librarians are generally more aware than disciplinary faculty of the pedagogical need to connect information literacy and course content. In this way, librarians resemble proponents of writing across the curriculum, envisioning writing as ideally integrated into all courses at the university rather than taught in separate composition courses. In WAC, this integration is facilitated primarily through faculty development. With information literacy, by contrast, librarians often actively participate in course instruction, a model that has drawbacks. As Laskin and Diaz (2009) point out, successful collaborations often spawn requests for further collaborations, adding to the workload of library faculty. Following Gloria Leckie, they suggest that academic librarians become "bibliographic instruction mentors, assisting and encouraging faculty with respect to integrating information literacy into their courses" (as cited in Laskin & Diaz, 2009, p. 162).

Assessment-Based Initiatives

The movement in higher education toward outcomes assessment has brought library and disciplinary faculty together to collaborate on assessment initiatives. ACRL's Information Literacy Competency Standards are clearly stated and generally understandable to outsiders, cast in language that makes them eminently assessable. Compositionists' more diversified approaches to writing instruction contrast sharply with the high level of consensus and coherence evidenced in the Standards (Fulkerson, 2005; Carter, 2003). Though the Council of Writing Program Administrators's (2000, 2008) *WPA Outcomes Statement for First-Year Composition* provides guidance on desired learning outcomes for freshman composition courses, its level of permeation into freshman composition course design is uncertain, and it deals only with first year composition.

The ACRL Standards, on the other hand, exhaustively list the qualities and behaviors of an "information-literate" individual. Further, information literacy programs are often staged in phases, moving from lower- toward higher-order competencies. No similar effort exists in composition circles to exhaustively delineate the qualities of a competent writer or the stages in becoming one. Whether it is desirable or even possible to do so is, of course, open to debate. Elmborg (2006) has criticized the strict construction of information literacy within a framework of behavioral objectives, noting that it detracts from information literacy's ability to foster critical thinking. Carter (2003) notes that postmodern perspectives challenge the notion that we can monolithically determine the definition and value of writing. A forced consensus on narrow behavioral outcomes for writing is not the answer, but engaging the question of what outcomes demonstrate writing ability in which situations may be a worthwhile enterprise.

Almost immediately after ACRL approved the Information Literacy Competency Standards, librarians began developing instruments for assessing information literacy. Two large-scale, standardized instruments were discussed earlier in this volume by Horning and Kraemer. At Kent State, a team of librarians developed the Standardized Assessment of Information Literacy Skills (SAILS), a series of multiple-choice questions using item-response theory (IRT) as its measurement model. With grant assistance and other support from the Institute of Museum and Library Services and the Association of Research Libraries (ARL), SAILS evolved into a widely-administered test, providing assessments of individual students and institutionally, bench-marking with other institutions (Project SAILS, n.d). However, SAILS measures only four of the five standards of information literacy, omitting Standard Number Four: "the information literate student, individually or as a member of a group, uses information effectively to accomplish a specific purpose" (Salem & Radcliff, 2006, p. 132). By omitting this standard, the test neglects the expressive aspect of critical literacy: critical writing.

A second large-scale assessment instrument, ETS's iSkills test, includes assessment of how students use information, but only within digital environments. Specifically, it assesses students' ability to use Information and Communication Technologies (ICT) for research and for writing (Katz, 2007). The iSkills test analyzes how students respond to fifteen information-based tasks in a Web environment. It is designed to assess students' ability to define an information need, access information using digital environments, evaluate information, and manage or organize information; it also addresses students' ability to integrate knowledge, to create information, and to effectively communicate information to particular audiences in digital environments. These latter three are clearly capabilities relevant to writing. The iSkills test, however, is limited to Web-mediated reading, research, and writing.

Apart from the standardized approach of SAILS and iSkills, localized assessments of information literacy are plentiful. As with writing assessment, localizing information literacy assessment strengthens its authenticity and face validity. Mackey and Jacobson (2010) report on localized information literacy assessment in a number of disciplines. Some of these assessments build on work in writing assessment, using rubric-based scoring of research papers.

When library and disciplinary faculty collaborate in defining assessment outcomes, the goal of reconnecting reading with writing is often furthered. For a theme-based, first year writing course at George Washington University, for instance, a cross-disciplinary assessment committee created the following list of course outcomes:

1. To read, think, and write critically and analytically

2. To gain a functional grasp of rhetorical principles

3. To acquire the ability to explore, use, and analyze information resource to meet research objectives

4. To demonstrate the habit and discipline of careful editing and proofreading

5. To develop an effective writing process. (Gaspar & Presser, 2010, p. 159)

It took the committee five meetings to complete the outcomes list and a rubric draft (p. 163); as a result of this intensive interdisciplinary work, the final list incorporated both reading and writing competencies.

By contrast, when information literacy assessment is handled separately from writing assessment, it may be less effective. Bussert and Pouliot (2010) report on a project in which students self-assessed their information literacy learning in four sections of "English 102: Writing from Research." One to three information literacy sessions were offered in each section, and students completed an information literacy self-assessment three times during the semester. The instrument used was based on SAILS, and mirrored information literacy standards rather than integrating information literacy and writing competencies. The only writing competencies the instrument asked students to assess were those already present within the Standards, such as citing sources and the ability to organize, synthesize, and incorporate information into one's knowledge base (p. 136).

Students reported improvements over the course of the semester, and they commented on the usefulness of the IL instruction. Teachers also reported stronger research reports, with more "As" assigned. However, students also complained that the terminology in the instrument was confusing, even after the language of the instrument was revised in the second semester (p. 145). This confusion may reflect a partition between the desired outcomes of information literacy and those of writing in the course. As discussed earlier in this chapter, separate languages have evolved in library and composition scholarship for discussing reading-writing processes. The language of the self-assessment instrument, grounded in information literacy, may not have sufficiently dovetailed with the language used by the composition instructor, reducing the instruments' intelligibility to students.

Sustainable Information Literacy

Course-integrated information literacy instruction has served as a powerful instrument of change in the university. However, integrations based on sheer personal power—the librarian leadership model—are not sufficient to institutionalize information literacy instruction. As Currie and

Eodice (2005) point out, librarian-writing instructor partnerships ultimately need to answer questions of sustainability. Infrastructures need to be put in place so that collaborations do not die off as the individuals that instigate them move on (p. 52). Librarians agree. McGuiness (2007) offers many potential "top-down" strategies for information literacy, suggesting that librarians exploit opportunities created by innovative pedagogical initiatives and institutional transformation (p. 33).

For instance, as mentioned earlier, information literacy is now considered in accreditation criteria for all accrediting bodies of higher education in the U.S. This connection to accreditation provides a key opportunity to institutionalize information literacy. At Trinity College in San Antonio, an initiative to fully integrate information literacy into the college won funding from a presidential call for proposals supporting the college's accreditation efforts (Millet et al., 2009). The resulting five-year program, "Expanding Horizons: Using Information in the Twenty-First Century," focuses on five key aspects of information literacy. Trinity's information-literacy-across-the-curriculum effort joins others at various institutions, including one in biology and history at Wartburg College; one in a general education curriculum at Augustana College; and the Mellon-funded project at Five Colleges of Ohio (p. 181). At Trinity, the president's grant funded annual workshops, course development, and symposia; initial reports are promising. Nine courses were piloted during the fall 2008 semester, and another ten were introduced in the spring of 2009. Trinity librarians have served as embedded librarians in various courses or have taught or co-taught regular courses.

A sustainable infrastructure for information literacy can help narrow the status gap between librarians and disciplinary faculty. As Millet et al. (2009) point out, equal footing with faculty course instructors is crucial to achieving the outcomes of information-literacy enhanced courses or assignments (p. 190). To work effectively together, librarians, disciplinary faculty, and even students "must revise the notion of fixed roles for themselves within the academy, and instead embrace a dynamic where the emphasis falls on learning goals and solutions to challenges for learners" (p. 191).

CONCLUSION: OPENING A BLIND EYE

Given how productive collaboration with librarians can reconnect reading and writing in the academy, the composition field's lack of attention to theorizing libraries and information literacy is somewhat puzzling. Although WAC programs provide instructional models in information literacy and though WAC professionals understand the need of making connections with other teaching initiatives across the institution, "its advocates have not given much consideration to the value of collaborating with librarians" (Leadley & Rosenberg, 2005, p. 65). It is not that compositionists have failed to establish collaborations with librarians and information literacy instructors. Quite the contrary: Publications for library and information literacy professionals abound with examples of such collaborations, and many of these publications are either written or co-written by writing professionals.

The richness of this literature in library and information science publications, however, has no parallel in rhetoric and composition publications. In the course of doing research for this chapter, I was surprised at how little has been written in composition journals and books about the library and information literacy.[6] *Composition Forum* recently published a profile of a collaborative information literacy program (Brady, Singh-Corcoran, Dadisman, & Diamond, 2009); and Sheridan's (1995) book on WAC and the library, published by Greenwood Press, reaches beyond a library audience. Generally, however, conversations about reconnecting research and writing take place in the Burkean parlors of library and information science. Librarians have been very proactive in bringing composition theory into the arena of information literacy. By contrast, very little work on information literacy has been published in mainstream composition journals and book series.

Academic librarians' aggressive agenda for incorporating composition scholarship may be explained in part by librarians' historically lower status in the political economy of the university. As discussed earlier, information literacy instruction, compared to composition instruction, is the new kid on the block, and librarians have worked hard to raise its profile in the university. Building connections with disciplinary faculty, especially writing programs and writing centers, was a logical avenue toward a fuller integration of information literacy within college curricula. Composition instruction, though it has its own issues of marginalization, enjoys a slightly more secure perch within the disciplinary structure of the university, perhaps making compositionists less motivated to explore the value of information literacy.

Compositionists' relative silence about library and information literacy may also be a symptom of a general neglect of the connections between reading and writing. In ignoring information literacy and the library, composition scholars devalue one of the two legs of meaning-making: reading. Research on rhetorical reading in the 1990s brought attention to connections between reading and writing, but it did not consider how bibliographic instruction might support rhetorical reading. Today, compositionists' appear unaware of how work on multimodal composing and digital literacy can be enhanced by conversations about information literacy. Information literacy supports the kind of rhetorical reading we want our students to do—whatever the medium.

As Norgaard (2003) points out, compositionists pay a cost for neglecting information literacy: namely, the continued, unjustified separation of writing from reading instruction in the academy that hinders students' development of critical literacy. Composition instruction without an information literacy perspective encourages the writing of solipsistic texts that cannot reference and be appropriately taken up within communities of practice. This crippled approach contributes to the reading-writing disconnect often experienced by students.

Neglecting reading-writing connections is costly for librarians as well. Information literacy instruction bereft of a locus and a practice becomes a narrow skill, and implications for broader intellectual endeavors remain hidden (Norgaard, 2003). For several years, however, library professionals have actively worked on reconnecting reading and writing, integrating perspectives from the field of composition into their own work. Norgaard, a compositionist, was invited to write two guest columns in *Reference and User Services Quarterly*. Why have we not had a similar guest column, written by an information literacy professional, in *College Composition and Communication*? Elmborg and Hook's (2005) edited volume on collaborations between libraries and writing centers was published in an information literacy book series. Where are the books on information literacy in our composition series?

The easy answer is to say that librarians are not interested in publishing in our field, while we have willingly been publishing in theirs. Such a rationalization lets us off too easily. It is more likely that the publishing imbalance is an effect of institutional history and disciplinary power structures. Composition instruction has had a home in the university for a long time, whereas information literacy instruction is just lately coming into its own. Compositionists may feel they have much to teach information literacy instructors and little to learn from them. If so, they are wrong. Integrating information literacy instruction in composition and other courses can revitalize and restore connections between reading and writing in the academy.

As librarians continue to work more closely with disciplinary faculty in designing and delivering curriculum, questions will surely arise. Who, eventually, will be responsible for teaching hybrid courses generated by these collaborations? Will disciplinary instructors, in both composition and otherwise, simply appropriate the role of information literacy instructors? Will librarians and disciplinary faculty team teach courses? Will both composition and information literacy professionals become obsolete as disciplinary faculty integrate process and content more fully in their pedagogy? Perhaps the discipline-based university, as we know it today, will evolve into a new, interdisciplinary institution that foregrounds reading and writing. Whatever the future, building bridges between information literacy and writing instruction fosters the critical literacy of our students today.

Notes

1. As late as 1995, teaching students how to use the library was known as bibliographic instruction (BI), as evidenced by the use of the term in Sheridan's (1995) collection of essays, *Writing-Across-the Curriculum and the Academic Library*.

2. For a concise summary of the early evolution of information literacy, see Rockman (2004), pp. 4–6.

3. The Association of College and Research Libraries (ACRL) is the largest division of the American Library Association (ALA). At the time of the writing of this chapter, its membership was estimated at around 12,000.

4. Though most composition scholars and instructors recognize that "writing" is not limited to generating alphanumeric text, it is worth mentioning that I define writing in its broadest sense, involving any or all of the modes identified by the New London Group as the "New Literacies." See Horning and Kraemer, in this book, for a thorough discussion of these literacies.

5. Other models of research were developed by librarians, but Kuhlthau's (2004) is one of the first to be developed and is widely known.

6. Brady, Singh-Corcoran, Dadisman, and Diamond (2009) express similar surprise at the relative absence of information literacy articles in composition literature.

10 Undergraduate Research and Information Literacy in the Digital Environment

Erik D. Drake

The digital delivery of both traditional publications such as journal articles and new media resources has moved to the digital environment a significant portion of reading for the purpose of conducting research. This trend has changed multiple aspects of the undergraduate research experience—from habits of annotating while reading to selecting passages for synthesizing into creative works such as research papers. Digital access to resources makes them immediately and easily available for consumption, exposing students to a wide variety of publications for any research project they confront. These efficiencies bring reading and writing ever closer temporally, while also posing urgent pressures for critical judgment and the assimilation of new ideas. Information literacy skills become paramount in such an environment due to the demand of evaluating materials and incorporating them in one's work cogently and ethically.

As the research process has increasingly become understood as conflated with reading, the relationship between research and writing remains relatively unexplored in the literature. While research for writing (that is, conducting research and then presenting the results) is almost always an expected outcome of the research process, writing for research is mentioned frequently in the literature, but almost never discussed in more than a cursory way. Indeed, conducting research generally requires reading in some format, while writing is essential for organizing new knowledge acquired through the research process and for organizing the process itself. Research, then, is a domain in which reading and writing are connected in practice, but that connection is not well-established in theory. This chapter briefly reviews models of information seeking, explores literature related to technology and reading for research, points out practical connections between reading and writing through the research process in a digital context, discusses the importance of information literacy skills for reading and writing, and highlights the role of libraries in supporting the development of those skills.

MODELS OF INFORMATION SEEKING

The process of seeking information for the purpose of synthesizing information and producing a product—commonly referred to as research—is often called "information seeking" in the literature. Researchers have long sought to construct a model of the research process to better understand the processes people follow as they conduct research. Although information seeking has been studied at least since the 1950s, James Krikelas (1983) was the first to propose a research model applicable to the general population. Krikelas's model included four linear steps, beginning with an information need and ending when the perception of that need no longer exists. Kuhlthau's (1985) model of the information process, like Krikelas's, appears in the literature as a linear model. Unlike Krikelas, whose model was described behaviorally, Kuhlthau incorporated affective and cognitive theory into her model. Further, her model was research-based, whereas Krikelas's was primarily practice-based (Weiler, 2005). Kuhlthau's model has been validated among many different types of researchers, including college students (Kuhlthau, Turock, George, & Belvin, 1990). For a more detailed discussion of information seeking, see Haller's chapter in this volume.

Scholars of information seeking have commented repeatedly that the linearity of both Krikelas's and Kuhlthau's models does not accurately reflect the non-linear nature of most research, although Kuhlthau (1991) did note that she envisioned her model to be an iterative process. Weiler (2005) observed that Eisenberg and Berkowitz's (1990) component-based information seeking model, based on their "Big6 Skills," was intended to offer a flexible, non-linear representation of the research process, and therefore may be more consistent with the dynamic nature of learning in the age of constructivist learning theory and the flexible nature of hypertext. Like Krikelas and

Kuhlthau, the Big6 Skills present a series of steps that researchers generally follow, but are presented a non-linear fashion. Instead, the Big6 Skills are portrayed as an interconnected web that more accurately conveys the iterative and hypertextual nature of information seeking in today's world. Like other models of information seeking, the Big6 Skills are comprised of a series of steps or stages that researchers move through as they seek information: definition of the task and development of information seeking strategies; the location and use of information; synthesis of information into a written or other creative product to be shared with others; and evaluation of the product and process (see Lamb, 2001, for a comparison of a number of information seeking models). It should be noted that Krikelas's model is not included in Lamb's comparison. His was one of the earliest models, providing a conceptual framework for others that followed. In addition, Lamb presents the Big6 Skills as linear to facilitate comparison (Weiler, 2005, includes a discussion and references to resources about the webbed nature of Big6).

Most information seeking models begin with a stage involving the formulation of an idea and ending with a product. Traditionally, the product would have been a research paper. Although, in an increasingly technological world, the product could be any number of electronic, print, or visual creations. In Kuhlthau's model, the production stage is called "Presentation," and the rise of electronic publishing tools, including applications as diverse as word processing software, presentation software, blogs, video production software, and social media offer many opportunities for electronic publishing. The literature does not discuss the use of these or any writing technologies in information seeking in theoretical or empirical ways. It includes only discussions of practice. Much research is needed to better understand the relationships between information seeking and writing technologies.

The transition from linear to iterative (or webbed) models of information seeking is parallel to a similar paradigm shift in models of writing from process to post-process. Post-process models view writing as iterative, synthetic, situated, and personally constructed (Kent, 1999). Ideally, the presentation stage of information seeking results in a creative product that synthesizes new knowledge from a variety of sources. In this way, information seeking can also be seen as exactly equating with the writing process. As Berthoff (1970) noted, teachers "design sequences of assignments which let our students discover what language can do, what they can do with language" (p. 70).

Reading is an explicit and integral part of all of major information seeking models. Reading from print was the primary method of gathering information when all of major information seeking models were developed; therefore, it is almost inextricably integrated into the research process. Writing, however, is a secondary consideration in all of major information seeking models in the sense that the writing process itself is never discussed in detail. In Kuhlthau's model, for example, the entire writing process is encapsulated within "Presentation," the last stage of information seeking. This is not to suggest that writing plays no role in information seeking. Kuhlthau (1994) and Eisenberg and Berkowitz (1990) have designed activities to assist students as they move through the stages of research. Many of those activities incorporate writing or other creative methods. Such activities might include guiding students to brainstorm ideas for research topics, helping to refine research foci, writing research questions, note-taking, or outlining. These activities are always framed by authors of information seeking models in the context of conducting research, however, and never as steps in the writing process, although it is clear that such activities are essential—indeed, integral—to the writing process.

In many ways, writing for research (as opposed to research for presentation, often through writing) really is the same as the early stages of the writing process. Typical writing activities during research include brainstorming, note-taking, annotating, and outlining the same artifacts that might be produced in the early stages of writing a research paper. The writing process does not occur in the final stage of research, but instead, like reading, is an integral component of research. Certainly, the production of polished writing occurs after information seeking is mainly complete, and the process of writing for an audience is outside the scope of information seeking models. However, research and writing are closely linked, and much more discussion of this relationship in the literature is necessary to reconnect reading and writing through information seeking.

INFORMATION SEEKING AND INFORMATION LITERACY

While the role of technology in the information search process has been considered by many of the researchers who have developed information search models, all of the widely recognized models were developed prior to the rise of the highly technological society in which we now live. Because they were developed in theory, in research, and in practice, all of the models discussed above have proven themselves to be, for the most part, robust across a wide array of information types, resources, and formats. Researchers have increasingly become interested in the relationship (if any) between information seeking behavior and ubiquitous access to technology.

To navigate the research process and craft a quality product, information seekers require a set of skills. The fluency of researchers with respect to seeking information has come to be widely known as information literacy. In a highly technological world, the necessity for students to use digital resources effectively, as well as increased access to information in many formats, has given rise to literacies with a variety of names. Mackey and Jacobson (2011) describe five different literacies, in addition to information literacy, found in the literature: media literacy, digital literacy, visual literacy, cyberliteracy, and information fluency. All of these different literacies arose from the differing goals, objectives, beliefs, and the needs of various professional and discipline-based organizations. Interestingly, Mackey and Jacobson, in support of the various literacies, tend to focus on the technologies that are in or out of favor within the disciplinary context of a given literacy.

Mackey and Jacobson (2011) proposed a reframing of information literacy from skills-based to "collaborative production and sharing of information using particularly interactive technologies" (p. 70). They proposed the word "metaliteracy" (p. 70) to describe a re-conceptualized information literacy that is technology agnostic and encompasses all of the literacies listed above. It is useful to observe that the acquisition of information is suggested by the incorporation of the world "literacy" in all of the constructs just described. A more holistic view of literacy would incorporate writing, as described in Chapter One of this volume. Such a construct would encapsulate the reciprocal nature of the acquisition and creation of information as modeled by the research process. Further, new technologies as described later in this chapter hold the potential to operationalize a metaliteracy that embraces both reading and writing situated in the same time and place.

INFORMATION SEEKING IN DIGITAL ENVIRONMENTS

Many of the positive influences of technology on information seeking are numerous, well-documented, and, for the most part, self-evident. For example, an extensive digital archive of historical materials available online can be accessed at any time, from almost any place, and searched in seconds. To access an equivalent print collection, a researcher might have had to travel long distances to one or more repositories, access the materials only during the repositories' open hours, and spent long periods of time searching for information relevant to the researcher's need. Dalton and Charnigo (2004) observed that some historians organize their research around travel considerations. Speed, immediate access, and self-service are the primary affordances of technology discussed relative to information seeking. This is likely because, as Weiler (2005) found, many scholars place the highest priority on time when searching for information.

Like all prioritizations, priorities in information seeking come with tradeoffs. Researchers who prioritize time over other aspects of research do so at the expense of such important matters as authority, accuracy, relevance, breadth, and depth of resources. While all of these tradeoffs required consideration prior to the advent of ubiquitous technology, technological advances have made it easier for researchers to prioritize time over the quality of information. This is not to suggest that there is evidence of a widespread decline in the quality of scholarship due to technological advances. Rather, technology presents educators and librarians with new challenges in helping students understand the standards for scholarly research.

The Internet search engine is the epitome of the balance between researchers' time and almost all standards for scholarly research. Educators and librarians often express anxiety that search engines have reduced the quality of research, particularly among undergraduate and younger students. Indeed, entering a phrase in a search engine often yields thousands or millions of results, some relevant or not, some accurate or not, some authoritative or not. The use of search engines for scholarly research raises many important questions: How do researchers know when they have "found enough"? How does immediate access to information influence researchers' self-perception of information seeking competence? How are researchers informed about the validity and authority of information resources? How do researchers conduct an organized and logical search, and what is the role of haphazard searching and serendipitous finds? How do researchers perceive the role of educators and librarians as intermediaries in online searching? What are discipline-based differences in the use of technology for information seeking? Research has been conducted to address all of these questions. However, as technology evolves, so do any potential answers.

One of the greatest challenges facing users of online search engines is knowing when they have found enough resources to address their information needs. In a print environment where collections, for the most part, have bounds, this can be a daunting question when presented with millions of hits after entering keywords in a search engine. Herbert Spencer (1955) coined the term "satisficing" to describe a decision-making strategy whereby people make a choice when they perceive they have adequately met a need rather than finding the optimal solution.

Prabha, Connaway, Olszewski, and Jenkins (2007) conducted a study to understand how the concept of "satisficing" applies to information seeking behavior among academic users of libraries. The study consisted of focus groups in which undergraduate and graduate students and faculty members were asked about their criteria for terminating information searches. The authors found that undergraduates stopped looking for resources when they perceived that they had met the requirements of the assignments, including the number of citations, the number of pages written, or meeting criteria for a certain letter grade or score on the assignment. The study supports a similar finding by Barrett (2005) that undergraduate students stopped searching when they perceived that they had met course requirements.

Both studies support the idea that undergraduates satisfice their research around their role as students meeting course requirements. It is incumbent upon instructors, then, to design writing assignments in ways that clearly define content, writing and research requirements, and increase the likelihood that students successfully meet those requirements. Further, the cognitive complexity required by research-based writing assignments may require the support of content-based instructors, writing instructors, and librarians working collaboratively toward students' intellectual growth and development.

Bodi's (2002) analysis of the literature indicated that undergraduate students struggle with research in a few particular areas: topic selection and narrowing, selecting subject headings for searching, and evaluating resources during their searches. She noted that undergraduates, as novice researchers, lack an awareness of scholarly research methods, and therefore must develop strategies to deal with the ambiguity inherent in the research process. Bodi argued that research instruction in libraries generally is not tailored to specific disciplinary needs or the abilities of students. She further argued that librarians should develop new strategies for teaching search strategies at a level appropriate to undergraduates in the context of disciplinary research at the novice level. Bodi proposed that asking questions of students is an effective strategy for helping undergraduates develop information seeking abilities, particularly for moving through the most challenging stages of information seeking. Questioning also helps students better understand the context of scholarly communication within the disciplines.

Bodi observed that students often appear to search haphazardly, as "happy to find whatever" (Bodi, 2002, p. 110). This observation supports the notion of students' satisficing for information resources, studied by Prabha, Connaway, Olszewski, and Jenkins (2007). If students' primary concern in searching for information is to meet assignment or course requirements, and an effective search process is neither one of those requirements, or if they are not taught appropriately by librarians, there is no rational reason for them to conduct a search in anything other than haphazardly. This also explains why undergraduate students perceive little need for involving librarians in their information searching.

The literature indicates that one of the challenges facing undergraduate students conducting research is in understanding methods of scholarly communication. One particularly challenging skill to acquire is the ability to evaluate the quality of an information resource and the authority of its author. As novice researchers, "even when students find the information they need, they have difficulty evaluating it and choose quantity over quality" (Bodi, 2002, p. 111). Searching for journal articles online can exacerbate this challenge. Articles found in a print journal have a contextual basis for evaluation. Researchers can readily see what organization is responsible for publishing a journal. Often, the title of the journal can be recognized as reputable, although most undergraduates likely lack this knowledge, particularly early in their academic careers. Browsing through the publication provides a sense of the affiliations and reputations of the authors and offers a glimpse into the state of knowledge in the discipline.

O'Brien and Symons' (2007) study of undergraduates found that some students appeared to have difficulty distinguishing between websites and electronic databases. They further note that libraries and the literature often does not differentiate between the library's physical and online presence, making it even more difficult for students to understand the contextual basis for the information they find online. Research by Cockrell and Jayne (2002) supports the idea that librarians' attempts to design library websites very precisely actually confuses students, who expect to be able to find a variety of resources of different types and formats with few searches—or, preferably, a single search.

As interfaces for locating journal articles online improve, they increasingly appear as virtual manifestations of print copies. However, scholarly communication is likely to continue to move toward a Web-first or Web-only publication model. The hypertextual nature of Web-based publication increases the likelihood that scholarly work will look less like a printed publication in the future. As that trend evolves, it is essential that online authors and publishers develop new ways to contextualize publications in order for novice researchers to develop an understanding of a discipline's scholarly publications. This trend will almost assuredly affect the writing process in the future, as students have more and more opportunities to break down the traditional constraints of publishing in print. Technological innovations in writing will allow more flexibility and creativity in the design, layout, and order of text. In turn, such innovations may have an effect on writing content. The convergence of online reading and writing could also affect the research process. Time and research are necessary to better understand how technology is influencing the interaction of reading, writing, and research.

In addition to changing undergraduates' perceptions of scholarly publication, the rise of technology has changed the types of information resources available to students, as well as how they access and use those resources in collecting information for creative work, such as research papers. A number of studies have been published that examine the role of multimedia in undergraduate research. Chen and Macredie (2010) reviewed the literature regarding Web-based interaction as it relates to three human factors: gender differences, prior knowledge, and cognitive styles. Regarding gender differences, they found that most studies indicated a difference between males and females in Web-based interactions: "In particular, females encountered more disorientation problems and had more negative attitudes then men" (p. 385). The authors did note, however, that some studies reported no gender-based differences in Web interactions.

The literature suggests that there are differences in Web-based interactions between novices and experts, particularly regarding Web-based instruction and Internet searching. Flexible paths are beneficial to experts participating in Web-based instruction, while novices benefit from structured content, such as hierarchical maps. Similar differences were found regarding Internet searching. Experts demanded more sophisticated search tools and time-saving measures to locate information, although one study suggested that experts are more likely to miss some highly relevant sites. Novices, on the other hand, use search engines more than experts and prefer structure and hypertext to help them navigate the Web. In addition, novices take more time than experts to complete broad searching tasks (Chen & Macredie, 2010).

Finally, regarding cognitive style, the literature is inconclusive about any relationship between field dependency and learning performance with respect to Web-based instruction. Field dependency is a cognitive style characterized by a tendency to experience surroundings in a relatively global manner, and to struggle with individual elements. Field independent users tend to experience their surroundings analytically, and are comfortable dealing with elements out of their context. Field dependency does appear to affect users' learning preferences. In particular, field dependent learners tended to prefer linear learning, while field independent students preferred non-linear learning. In addition, field dependent subjects in one study tended to use teaching notes and other class resources more often than did field independent students (Chen & Macredie, 2010).

The findings of Chen and Macredie (2010) are consistent with those of researchers interested in the information search process cited earlier in this chapter. The novice versus expert differences found by Chen and Macredie (2010), with respect to Web-based instruction and Internet searching, for example, parallel the differences in searching expertise found by Bodi (2002), as well as comparisons of novice and expert writers. Becker (2006), for example, reviewed the literature comparing novice and expert writers with respect to textual revision. She found wide differences in the process, perceptions, and product quality between novice and expert writers. This suggests that the preferences, perceptions, and practices of information seekers persist in both their reading and their writing endeavors, even as the use of technology has increased dramatically over the past decade. This literature, taken together, suggests that the process of conducting research has become increasingly empowering to students at the cost of greater complexity in the sub-processes of research; therefore, greater support for students is required as they become expert seekers of information.

Chen and Macredie's (2010) findings also support the idea that libraries must take into consideration the widely varying needs of users when designing computer interfaces. As Chen and Macredie observed, however, inconsistencies and gaps in the literature require additional research on human differences in computer interaction, including the three factors that they studied, in addition to others, such as affective factors, age differences, and cultural background.

Researchers have increasingly taken interest in the design of online information sources and its effect on reading comprehension and information seeking. Vaughan and Dillon (2006), for example, studied the structure and genre of online newspapers and how users interacted with them. The authors solicited input from experts to develop criteria for an online newspaper genre, after which they designed an online newspaper conforming to their genre criteria and a separate online newspaper not conforming to the genre. For example, the experts determined that a quality online newspaper should include a menu of navigation links in the left-hand column. Several similar criteria were selected to design the genre-conformed newspaper. The criteria were ignored in the genre-violating newspaper.

After creating the online newspapers, the authors conducted a longitudinal experiment with users to understand whether any interactions existed between the two different newspapers and users' comprehension of the news content, the usability of the website, and user navigation. Results showed that users of the genre-conforming newspaper performed significantly better in all three areas (comprehension, usability, and navigation) than users of the genre-violating newspaper. Over time, users of both newspapers significantly improved their performance in all three areas (Vaughan & Dillon, 2006).

This study has a number of interesting implications for both practice and research. First, it is clear that genres can develop in relatively short amounts of time. Some genre theorists view the lifetime of a genre as over many, many years—even as long as centuries (Vaughan & Dillon, 2006). Second, adhering to genre conventions in designing online resources may improve users' comprehension of content. Third, maintaining a consistent site promotes user comprehension and site use. Finally, the fact that all factors in both groups improved over time suggests that traditional website usability studies may not provide an accurate representation of the user's experience. Users' abilities related to a website may improve over time; thus, usability studies may need to be conducted repeatedly, or after user have had time to learn to navigate the site. Library researchers and practitioners should attend to these implications when designing Web interfaces and when evaluating websites for use by students.

In addition to the structural and generic context of websites, the visual appeal of websites may impact their use, particularly for members of Generation Y, or today's college students. Djamasbi, Siegel, and Tullis (2010) conducted a study of Generation Y'ers related to their perceptions and viewing of several websites. The first phase of the study consisted of a survey to rate the visual appeal of various websites. This portion of the study resulted in identifying four characteristics of websites present on sites that participants rated as significantly higher than pages not including these elements. The four characteristics were a main large picture, pictures of celebrities, a search feature, and little text. For phase two, three web pages featuring the four characteristics, and three pages lacking all of the characteristics, were shown to a different group of Generation Y participants. Eye movements were tracked using an unobtrusive eye-tracking device. Heat mapping of the data showed that participants fixated the longest on, and in order, the four characteristics identified in the first study (Djamasbi et al., 2010).

The results of this study, taken together with those of Vaughan and Dillon (2006), suggest very specific information about the expectations, preferences, and needs of undergraduates when using websites to access information. The findings of Djamasbi et al. (2010), in particular, present a strong challenge for librarians, who tend to be very textual in their work.

Although much of the literature reviewed in this section discusses scholarly communication, little or no reference was made to the production of knowledge in written or other formats. The research is clear that students increasingly reject reading large blocks of text on web pages. This finding is directly related to composition and rhetoric in the context of reading and writing as a sort of supply and demand economy. If readers increasingly demand smaller blocks of text and more visual rhetoric, authors of texts will need to shift their design and composition to be read, whether the reader and the author are the same or different people. As Wysocki (2004) noted, effective composition is the direct result of careful analysis of visual and textual elements of one or more genres, and considering the intended audience. A high comfort level with reading short blocks of text may result in preferences to write in a similar fashion. Indeed, blogs, microblogs, and other social media are one indication that students' writing habits are already changing.

INFORMATION SEEKING BY ACADEMIC DISCIPLINE

A large body of research indicates that there are disciplinary differences in information seeking behaviors. In the context of information seeking as a unification of reading and writing, disciplinary differences are not unexpected given that research in both reading and writing has revealed disciplinary differences in the ways people read and write. The literature in this area generally takes three forms: (1) comparative studies of information seeking across many disciplines; (2) studies of information seeking within a specific discipline; and (3) studies that examine disciplinary differences incidental or tangential to non-disciplinary aspects of information seeking. Because the body of literature is so large, much of it conflicting, this section focuses on relatively recent research related specifically to undergraduate information seeking by discipline.

Whitmire (2002) conducted a study of undergraduates' information seeking behaviors. Biglan's (1973a, 1973b) model of disciplinary differences, categorizing academic disciplines along three dimensions, was the theoretical framework of the study (Whitmire, 2002, p. 631). The three dimensions are: (1) hard versus soft; (2) pure versus applied; and (3) life versus nonlife. "Hard" disciplines are those in which members of the discipline are more likely to agree about the important research questions of the field than those in "soft" disciplines. Hard disciplines include the physical sciences and engineering, while soft disciplines include fields in the humanities and social sciences (Whitmire, 2002). "Pure" disciplines, according to Biglan, include those in which research tends to be more theoretical, such as the physical sciences, humanities, and social sciences, versus the "applied" disciplines, where research is often more practical. Such fields include engineering, business, and education. The third dimension describes the discipline's relationship to living organisms. This dimension categorizes disciplines as "life" versus "nonlife." "Life" disciplines include the social sciences and education, whereas "nonlife" disciplines include the physical sciences and engineering. Biglan's framework has been the basis of many studies related to higher education. Whitmire (2002) cited a selection of studies based on Biglan in her conceptual framework.

Whitmire (2002) used ten survey questions about information seeking activities to compare information seeking behaviors among undergraduate students along the three Biglan dimensions. She found a number of significant relationships between the various disciplines and information seeking behavior. For example, in the hard versus soft disciplines, participants "in the soft disciplines engaged in more information-seeking activities with the exception of using the library as a place to read or study" (Whitmire, 2002, p. 634). Similar results were found with students in the pure and life disciplines who engaged in more information seeking behavior than did students in applied and nonlife disciplines.

Whitmire (2002) noted that the population she studied, unlike previous studies of disciplinary differences in information seeking, was undergraduate students. She cited many previous studies of graduate students and faculty, and some of her results differed from previous findings. She attributes the differences to those in the populations studied. Whitmire, unlike several other authors, found that humanities students used indexes to locate journal articles and sought assistance from reference librarians. Whitmire's study validated previous research that showed that "physical science majors used indexes to find journal articles" (Whitmire, 2002, p. 636). Social science majors, on the other hand, sought information through citation chaining and browsing library collections. Whitmire's study contradicted another part of that prior research that showed no difference in the information seeking behaviors of social and physical scientists. As Whitmire noted, the difference in disciplinary expertise between the undergraduate students she studied, and the more expert scholars studied previously, accounted for differences in the findings over prior research.

Whitmire's study provides further evidence that librarians must tailor instruction to meet the information seeking needs of novice and expert users, and must address the differences in research needs across the academic disciplines.

While the literature reviewed thus far in this chapter provides a strong indication of the ways in which undergraduate students locate and use digital resources, none of this literature provides any insight into the impact of electronic research on writing across the disciplines. Since writing has played such a minimal role in the literature on information seeking in general, this is not surprising. However, it is reasonable to hypothesize that with dramatic changes in the ways undergraduates seek information, the ways they write for research have changed as well. Software productivity packages often include outlining functionality that, presumably, saves students time in organizing their research notes. How does such software affect students' analysis and synthesis of their research data? Conversely, how do the disciplinary conventions of reading and writing affect students' use of technological information sources? The needs of writers with respect to disciplinary standards for evidence and citation, for example, are likely affected by such things as the citation functionality of online databases, or the citation software embedded in writing software. These and similar important questions about the relationships between technology, research, and writing continue to be explored in the literature. Answers are crucial if we are to reconnect reading and writing.

SCREEN-BASED READING BEHAVIORS

With an understanding of how technology has changed the ways people seek information, and how information seeking differs by academic discipline, it is necessary to examine changes in the ways people read after they have found information they sought. Reading is by far the most common method of gathering information for research. The role of writing is secondary to reading in the process of information gathering. Writing tasks such as note-taking, outlining, and annotating help readers organize their ideas. While the focus of this section is on reading, writing as it assists in reading is discussed briefly as well.

Widespread access to technology has fundamentally changed the ways users, particularly younger users, read. Some scholars have argued that digital texts threaten literacy. A more convincing argument, it seems, is that technology has changed reading, in some ways for the better. Certainly, digital texts afford many benefits that print documents do not, including searchability, hypertextuality, multimedia formats, and even the ability to magnify the text from the reading device. Researchers are increasingly interested in the effects that on-screen texts might have on reading behaviors.

Liu (2005) surveyed professionals and graduate students to better understand reported changes in reading behaviors over the previous ten years. Participants reported a number of changes in their reading behaviors over that period, many of which can be identified as technology related. Interestingly, no participants in the study reported reading less than they had ten years previous; in fact, the majority reported reading more. This suggests that technology is not the death knell of reading, as has been suggested by some scholars. *What* and *how* participants in Liu's study read changed dramatically over the decade. A large majority (83.2%) reported spending more time reading electronic documents. Reading behaviors that increased during the study period included: browsing and scanning, keyword spotting, one-time reading, reading selectively, and non-linear reading. Reading behaviors that decreased included sustained attention, in-depth reading, and concentrated reading (Liu, 2005). While Liu did not discuss the ways in which changes in reading behavior might impact writing, it seems logical to conclude that the reading behaviors he observed might negatively impact scholars' writing. Less concentrated reading likely reduces a researcher's ability to analyze and synthesize the information to the extent required to produce scholarly writing.

Liu is one of the few authors who examined both reading and writing behaviors in the context of technological advancements by studying the annotating habits of participants. More than 50% of participants reported never highlighting or annotating documents, while all reported highlighting or annotating printed documents at least occasionally. Regarding printing for reading, all participants reported printing electronic documents for reading at least occasionally, and more than 71% reported doing so frequently. Liu cited previous research indicating that people frequently search or browse electronic documents, but are more likely to print documents for in-depth reading.

What is not clear is whether people print documents for the purpose of highlighting or annotating, or if they print them because they prefer to read the printed documents, and therefore highlight or annotate in the format in which they happen to be reading. Liu cited several studies indicating that people have strong preferences for reading printed rather than electronic documents, that reading from a monitor is slower than reading printed text, and that readers find online text to be more difficult to understand, less interesting, and less credible than printed versions. All of this suggests that readers have strong preferences for reading in print; however, further research is necessary to understand whether those preferences might be cultural, generational, or mitigated by improvements in screen quality and portability of electronic devices. Throughout history, the most successful and enduring technologies have been those with pages that provide the reader a sense of the length of a document, allow leafing through pages, and allow the reader to hold the document at a comfortable reading distance from the eyes.

Annotation is a key activity related to the connection between reading and writing. It is an act that allows the reader to write about what they read contemporaneously and in the same medium. While most annotations are brief and unedited, the act of annotating brings together reading and writing in a way that most other writing cannot. Annotation helps the reader understand and contextualize the text, and provides notes that may lead to more complete writing at some point in the future. This relationship between reading and writing may help explain why annotation is so important to scholarly researchers.

Given the dramatic increase in the amount of online reading, it is useful for librarians, educators, and web designers to understand how students navigate full-text databases when searching for journal articles. Interestingly, the distinction between searching for resources and reading online has blurred. Although several of the studies discussed next might appear to be about searching for texts, they actually focus on how people navigate through texts online. This distinction will continue to fade as more and more texts are published online and as the act of reading increasingly becomes an issue of online navigation.

Nicholas et al. (2008) studied the transactional logs of several electronic journal libraries to learn about students' use of the libraries to read and download articles, and followed up with a questionnaire about online search behaviors. The authors found that students spend much of their time navigating electronic journal libraries, evidenced by the number of times they clicked on navigational pages, such as menus, lists, and search pages. This suggests that web designers must attend to the organizational and navigational structures of digital libraries to help users efficiently locate information.

Nicholas et al. (2008) also found that students, more than faculty, were likely to view the full text of articles rather than abstracts. While the authors did not discuss the implications of this point in detail, it seems of great importance to librarians and educators. As novice researchers, students may need the entire context of an article to determine whether it is relevant to their search, whereas faculty may feel they have the expertise know whether they wish to read the full-text article from the content of the abstract, or to continue with their search. Faculty need to understand that this is one of the many ways their search strategies differ from those of their students. Librarians can develop instruction to reflect students' research practice and to help them develop a research strategy using abstracts as their research experience increases. The authors noted that most electronic journal libraries require users to access full-text articles through an abstract page. This could discourage students from navigating further if abstracts are not perceived as being important to their search.

Transaction log data showed that users viewed full-text articles, on average, for less than two minutes. As they pointed out, this is clearly not enough time to carefully read a typical scholarly article. A follow-up survey of students and faculty found that 43% of faculty reported reading in print format their last article searched, suggesting a large proportion of articles being printed for reading rather than read online (Nicholas et al., 2008). This is a likely explanation for relatively short online reading times.

The study found that "scholars at research universities spent longer viewing an article than their counterparts in teaching universities" (Nicholas et al., 2008, p. 196). Overall, students spent more time reading online than did faculty. This result was supported by both the log and survey data, suggesting that students may be more inclined generally to read online than faculty. Finally, the authors found evidence that students and faculty alike may avoid reading more online than necessary. Shorter articles tended to receive relatively longer online reading time, and longer articles were more likely to be read as an abstract and less likely to be read online (Nicholas et al., 2008).

E-readers, Reading and Writing

With the recent rise in popularity of e-readers, it is becoming increasingly necessary to understand how previous research on reading remains valid; since e-reader manufacturers continue to improve the technology in an attempt to make reading electronic books simulate reading on paper. E-readers such as the Nook and Kindle, replicate for the first time the size, shape, and weight of paper books as an electronic technology, and screens have improved such that readability is far superior to older technologies. A key question is whether the affordances of e-readers are such that they offset readers' negative perceptions about reading online, including lower comprehension, speed, and credibility than their printed counterparts. The popularity of e-readers suggests that they may be the first digital technology that offers serious competition to the printed book.

E-readers and other tablet computing devices have the exciting potential to provide a technological means to reconnect reading and writing. With built-in annotation and highlighting functionality, they integrate reading and writing in a single document. Word processing applications are often available for tablet devices. While this integrated reading and writing functionality is not new to computing technology, the advantage of e-readers and tablet devices is their portability and ease of use. The remainder of this section examines questions related to the use of e-readers in reading and writing.

Very few empirical studies have been published about the potential influences of e-readers on reading. The majority of the literature around e-readers takes two forms: (1) opinion pieces that either attempt to predict the future of e-readers in libraries or lament the impending death of the printed book as a result of the rise of e-readers, or (2) non-scientific case study articles describing the use of e-readers in libraries (see Dougherty, 2010, and Gielen, 2010, for examples of such literature). It is characteristic of the literature related to any new technology takes this form. Over time, the literature begins to shift from descriptive and prescriptive to research. E-readers are such a new technology that it is likely that studies are in progress but have not yet made their way into scholarly journals.

Because empirical research on e-readers is currently lacking, this section provides a summary of questions raised in the literature about the potential impact of e-readers on reading. Dougherty (2010) published a comprehensive summary of the benefits and problems about the potential use of e-readers in libraries. A number of the issues discussed could potentially change users' reading behaviors. First, Dougherty described the display technologies and compared them with older technologies and books. Unlike other hand-held devices and computers, e-readers are not backlit, making them easier on the eyes. He noted that the disadvantage is that, like printed books, an external light source is required for reading. Other improvements in display technology have also made e-readers easier to read.

Dougherty (2010) also raised the universal problem of content. First, some e-readers are proprietary. Although many e-readers are compatible with some standard formats, users are often required to purchase much of their content through the manufacturer's online store. Second, e-books do not fit well with traditional library purchasing models. Under current sales models, a library would need to license them like software. Libraries and distributors will continue to develop models for the shared use of e-books. Third, e-readers allow users to carry with them hundreds or thousands of books, dramatically changing the way they access information. All of these issues have the potential to change information seeking, reading behaviors, and library use.

A number of academic libraries have deployed e-books and e-readers. Dougherty (2010) provided several, brief examples. Technological compatibility, user support, security, and Web design became more important in libraries supporting e-readers, and must be considered to maximize user benefit. Users, it appears, are not completing rejecting other formats in favor of e-books. It is difficult to understand how much of this dynamic can be accounted for by the affordances of non-digital reading formats versus the simple lack of availability of many information resources in digital formats. Time and research may tell.

Research on the use of e-readers had primarily been conducted by digital content providers and manufacturers, such as eBrary and Sprinter. One notable exception is a study conducted by the American Council of Learned Societies (ACLS), an organization of American societies interested in humanities scholarship. The ACLS maintains a digital collection of nearly 2,800 scholarly works in the humanities. The Council studied the viability of constituent reading of scholarly monographs using e-readers. ACLS converted three of the titles in their collection into several electronic formats commonly read by e-readers, and then surveyed users about their experiences reading the scholarly works using e-readers (Gielen, 2010).

While the study sample consisted of users of the ACLS digital collection—and was made up of more than 60% librarians and only 4% students—the study produced some interesting results, even if they cannot be extrapolated beyond the sample. More than 90% of participants reported satisfaction with simply reading books on a digital reader. However, for scholarly research, only 13% of respondents reported preferring e-readers over more traditional sources of information. Challenges reported by users included difficulty in navigating the text, in highlighting and annotating, and in using equipment features. Gielen (2010) found no clear preference for a digital book format, although XML was dropped as a format early in the study due to navigation problems on certain e-readers. Neither did participants indicate a clear preference for one type of digital reader over another (Gielen, 2010).

Generalizability of the study results is questionable due to sampling bias. It seems likely that librarians, the majority of the study sample, might be more comfortable with the technology and reading formats studied. The general population would likely have more difficulty than the study participants in completing the study activities. Undergraduate students, however—presumably younger than the 96% of the sample reported not as students—might be more comfortable with the technology and in strategizing ways to overcome the challenges of reading digitally.

Gielen's (2010) results indicate that many of the problems related to reading in electronic formats discussed earlier in this chapter persist, even with e-readers. While many of the issues related to the display have been resolved by e-readers, and the use of electronic reading devices in scholarly research continues to be hampered by difficulties with highlighting and annotating in particular. This suggests that researchers have a need for technology that helps them integrate reading and writing, particularly through annotation functionality. Gielen expressed optimism that future improvements to e-readers may alleviate some of the challenges found by the study. Much research is needed to understand how younger readers, undergraduates in particular, interact with e-readers, and to compare reading behaviors and preferences with e-readers versus older technologies.

Empirical research on e-readers as writing devices is also lacking. Faris and Selber (2011) raised a number of important questions related to the use of e-readers in undergraduate composition classes. The majority of their review focused on issues of reading and navigation discussed earlier in this chapter. They found that students often struggled with technical and navigation issues related to e-readers, such as file naming conventions, but that they adapted to the constraints of the product to meet their learning needs. The authors were also surprised to find that students used e-readers conservatively, primarily using only the functions necessary to meet assignment requirements. This may indicate that college students have not made the transition from print to electronic texts as completely as we may have previously thought.

Regarding writing and e-readers, Faris and Selber (2011) noted that the e-reader they tested did not include an annotation feature. Students improvised a variety of methods to meet their annotating needs, both in print and digitally. The authors saw both positive and negative aspects of students' workarounds for annotation. Students reported being more engaged with the text after devising annotation systems, but they also reported avoiding writing down long quotes that they otherwise might have highlighted (Faris & Selber, 2011).

While not an empirical study, Faris and Selber's review reinforces the results of previous research, including the importance of annotation and highlighting while reading in either print or digital formats. It also supports the idea that students are highly adaptive when using new or challenging technologies to meet course requirements. In addition, it shows that many of the questions related to digital reading and writing remain unanswered. The review ends with a long list of technology, pedagogical, and institutional questions about e-readers, many of which have been raised in this chapter.

Newer tablet computing devices such as the iPad have the potential to reconnect reading and writing in ways that e-readers have not been able to. With virtual keyboards, the ability to capture handwriting and computing resources more like full-sized computers, electronic tablets allow annotation and the electronic integration of reading and writing in ways that older technologies, including e-readers, have not been able to accomplish successfully.

Digital Information Literacy Instruction and Libraries

It is clear that changes in technology have dramatically changed the way users seek, access, and read information, and have begun affecting writing as well. Some authors have seen these changes as a threat to books and libraries. In actuality, as much of the literature cited earlier in this chapter has shown, technological advancements have changed, and perhaps increased, the need for librarians as intermediaries in the information search process. Instead of being gatekeepers of information, users need librarians to act as search experts who can help them navigate the vast, disorganized array of information resources available at their fingertips.

As the role of the librarian changes, so does the need for information literacy instruction. Traditional information literacy instruction has been linear and de-emphasizes the complexity of both digital information and the devices used to access it (Bodi, 2002). Further, librarians have often taught classes on a one-size-fits-all basis, while research and anecdotal evidence clearly show that scholars have always searched for information in ways unique to their discipline. In a world of print resources, essentially bound by library walls, this method worked because students had little other choice for seeking assistance with accessing information. This model of information literacy instruction is not likely to be sustainable going forward, as students will increasingly go elsewhere for assistance if the instruction provided by libraries is not tailored to them, their discipline, and their specific information needs.

Further, research by Kuhlthau (1991) and others has shown that information-seeking is a highly personal, non-linear, subjective, and developmental process (Weiler, 2005). The process can change for an individual and even from one search to another. Users are more likely to perceive value in information literacy instruction that takes into account these factors and provides particular attention to users as they move through the more difficult stages of the information search process.

Developing such information literacy instruction might seem a daunting task. Conceptually, however, it is congruent with the user-centric movement advocated by library and information theorists since at least the 1980s, and aligns well with the constructivist movement in education. A common question raised in response to calls for user-oriented services is how libraries, with limited resources and serving large populations, can offer what seem to be highly customized services. There are ways to meet the increasing demands of users, even within the constraints of most library staff budgets. The most fundamental—and arguably the most challenging—change required is in staff thinking. No longer does the library provide services to the student body, but to the student. Such a fundamental shift is never easy, requiring professional development, professional dialog, strategic thinking, case studies, pilot programs, and visitations to help staff visualize user-oriented services.

Library staff must also re-conceptualize how they deliver instruction. In-person classes are becoming less desirable to students, particularly if they are not required. Information literacy instruction lends itself well to delivery via technology, including podcasts and Webinars. Librarians can design short instructional modules on specific topics tailored to users in specific disciplines or with different levels of expertise. The modules can be recorded and made available on the Web for use when and where students need them. Instructional modules must be kept updated as technology and resources change; this is not dissimilar to updating in-person instructional materials before offering a live class. One of the questions often raised about asynchronous delivery of instruction is the inability of students and faculty to interact with librarians in real time. With the widespread use of chat reference services, often on a twenty-four hour basis, assistance for students accessing online instruction can be delivered as needed. A continuing challenge for libraries is in marketing online instruction to students. Many libraries have long struggled with marketing in-person instruction. Making access and content more relevant and attractive to students will help in those marketing efforts.

Yet another challenge facing librarians in promoting information literacy in a digital world is the often complex nature of searching multiple online resources simultaneously. Users' standards for searching has become a simple, single search box characteristic of search engines such as Bing or Google. In many academic libraries in particular, searching the many available databases requires multiple searches, understanding different search strategies and thesauri, and navigating results in various formats. Way (2010) observed that, until recently, federated searching was the most promising solution to this problem. However, even federated searching presents challenges to users, including limitations on results retrieved, speed, and integrating search results in a single list with de-duplicated results (Way, 2010).

Over the last few years, new commercial products have become available to address concerns with federated searching. One of the earliest was Serials Solutions' *Summon*, referred to as a "Web-scale discovery tool" (Way, 2010, p. 214). Other competing products include EBSCO's *Discovery Service* and *Ex Libris* from Primo Central. Way (2010) writes: "Unlike federated search tools which search across a limited number of individual resources simultaneously, these web-scale resources pre-harvest content into one single index, allowing users to search across a greater amount of content" (p. 214). Web-scale discovery tools are faster than federated searches, and they merge, de-duplicate, and rank results from multiple databases in one results list. Unlike products like Google Scholar that search the entire Web, Web-scale discovery tools can be limited to search the resources available through a library (Way, 2010).

Way (2010) conducted a study of library resource use after implementing *Summon* at Grand Valley State University. He analyzed database usage statistics prior to and after *Summon* became the main search box on the university libraries' home page. Way reported a steady increase in the use of the libraries' online databases from 2006 through 2008. In 2009, there was an unexpected and unexplained drop in usage of those same databases; however, during the study period, usage statistics did show a steady use increase of certain databases, certain online newspapers, and the library's online catalog of monographs through *Summon* (Way, 2010).

Way's (2010) results indicated that *Summon* broke down the "silos that existed based on subject content, publisher or content provider" (p. 219). Further, the Web-scale discovery service directed users to content that they might otherwise have not found, away from general databases of popular literature from which many undergraduates had previously started their research, despite the questionable content of those databases for scholarly research. Way was concerned, however, about the drop in use of more specialized, subject-oriented databases. Further research is necessary to better understand the nature of the decrease. In the meantime, Way recommended that information literacy instruction direct users to the content from those databases.

While libraries and librarians traditionally have focused their work around conducting research, primarily through reading, the shift toward librarians as teachers of information literacy has resulted in a larger focus on writing as an integral part of information seeking. It would do little good for a student to conduct research and not produce a means of sharing that research with other scholars. Further, writing provides the framework for conducting research in at least two ways: as a course writing assignment and as a mechanism to organize students' thoughts as they read and gather information to meet course requirements. Librarians have increasingly become partners in writing instruction through information literacy instruction in much the same way that they traditionally have been involved in reading instruction. This shift is an important reconnection of reading and writing.

An emerging technology trend that is assisting librarians and other faculty members reconnect reading and writing is the explosive increase of social media. Blogs and microblogs, for example, situate reading, writing, and publishing in time and space. Their use as tools for scholarly research and writing are somewhat limited currently, however. Information sources and scholarly writing products generally require much larger quantities of text than the amount of information that blogs and microblogs are generally used to convey. Scholars use these and other social media for scholarly communication in ways that were not previously feasible. The inevitable evolution of social media will surely continue to reconnect reading and writing, in many unpredictable ways. The work of librarians with respect to information literacy will need to evolve as well.

Conclusion and Implications for Research

It is clear that technology has profoundly changed how users seek, access, and read information. It has also altered their needs related to information literacy. The rise of social media, for example, is a clear reconnection of reading, writing, and information seeking. Exactly how, and to what extent, technology has influenced reading and writing for the purposes of information seeking is not as well understood. It is fluid and changes with continual technological advancements. Much additional research is necessary to understand the exact nature of the relationships between reading, writing technology, and digital literacy in the context of information seeking. As with all research related to technology, research questions and methods must be updated continually to track the rapidly changing nature of technology use.

It is also not clear whether technology has changed the fundamental nature of information seeking. Because most models of the information search process are based on conceptualizations of psychology and learning, any indication that technology might be changing the information search process suggest that technology could be changing the ways in which people think. Clearly, there could be many other explanations for such changes, including information search models that are ill-defined relative to technology. However, it will be useful to continue to study information seeking to monitor such changes and to understand the origins of changes in information seeking behavior.

Many models of the information search process that originated in print-dominated environments have been criticized as being overly linear. This has become even more apparent as text has become less linear. Research is needed to better understand whether the underlying constructs of existing models are valid in highly technological environments, or if new models are required to more accurately represent information seeking in the digital age.

Extensive research has been, and continues to be, conducted relative to reading digital texts. As technology changes, scholars must continue to understand the nature of online reading and the mutual evolution of reader, medium, and text. As the newest devices for reading electronic text, tablet computing devices hold tremendous promise for changing reading, presenting the first real technological challenge to print books. Further, such devices offer the potential to reconnect reading and writing via technology. This technology is so new that little research has yet been published on the subject. More studies on tablets and their influence on reading and research are needed, and likely are forthcoming.

Rapid advances in technology have created new opportunities and challenges for libraries in developing programs of information literacy instruction for students. Much of the literature on information literacy instruction is descriptive or prescriptive. More research is needed to help librarians understand effective instructional methods as they re-conceptualize their information literacy instruction for digitally-oriented students. One of the challenges in delivering information literacy instruction is related to the disparate and often confusing nature of searching multiple online databases. This chapter cited one study of Web-scale discovery services as a method of assisting librarians and students to navigate an increasingly complex digital universe of information resources. Much additional research is needed to help librarians understand how such tools can assist them in meeting students' information needs, and also to help developers improve and design tools that meet similar needs.

Notably absent from the literature is research on the relationships between social media, reading, writing, and scholarly communication. For example, scholars are increasingly reading scholarly journals by receiving journal tables of contents through many different technological means, including RSS feeds and text messages. Technologies such as Facebook could become methods for disseminating scholarly information; they are already are devices for scholarly communication. Social media hold tremendous potential for reconnecting reading and writing, as both are necessary and integral to participation in the communities that have formed around social media. Additional research will help scholars better understand how such technologies affect scholarly research and communication, and what impact they might have on reading and information seeking behaviors.

The digital age has introduced much uncertainty and change in the interactions between students, librarians, information, and media. This dynamic presents many opportunities for research, and exciting opportunities to better meet students' information needs. The ever-evolving nature of technology necessitates continual research and changes in the work of librarians to meet the equally fluid expectations of students. The work of librarians is as important, if not more so, than it ever has been. Librarians will continue to evolve to provide quality services to their constituents, as they have done throughout history.

Research necessarily connects reading and writing. Indeed, one could make a strong argument that reading and writing have never become disconnected in the domain of information seeking. It is clear that writing has been overshadowed by reading in scholarly discussions of information seeking; therefore, librarians and educators have been delivering an incomplete product to students. A variety of technologies—in particular tablet computing devices, web publishing, and social media—offer real potential to reconnect reading and writing. Librarians and educators must leverage these and future technologies to help students connect reading and writing to actively contribute to scholarly discourse of the future.

Appendices

Appendix A: The Association of College and Research Libraries Information Literacy Competency Standards for Higher Education [Excerpt]

(The complete document is available at http://www.ala.org/acrl/standards/informationliteracycompetency)

STANDARD ONE

The information literate student determines the nature and extent of the information needed.

Performance Indicators:

1. The information literate student defines and articulates the need for information.

Outcomes Include:

   a. Confers with instructors and participates in class discussions, peer workgroups, and electronic discussions to identify a research topic, or other information need
   b. Develops a thesis statement and formulates questions based on the information need
   c. Explores general information sources to increase familiarity with the topic
   d. Defines or modifies the information need to achieve a manageable focus
   e. Identifies key concepts and terms that describe the information need

    f. Recognizes that existing information can be combined with original thought, experimentation, and/or analysis to produce new information

2. The information literate student identifies a variety of types and formats of potential sources for information.

Outcomes Include:

    a. Knows how information is formally and informally produced, organized, and disseminated
    b. Recognizes that knowledge can be organized into disciplines that influence the way information is accessed
    c. Identifies the value and differences of potential resources in a variety of formats (e.g., multimedia, database, website, data set, audio/visual, book)
    d. Identifies the purpose and audience of potential resources (e.g., popular vs. scholarly, current vs. historical)
    e. Differentiates between primary and secondary sources, recognizing how their use and importance vary with each discipline
    f. Realizes that information may need to be constructed with raw data from primary sources

3. The information literate student considers the costs and benefits of acquiring the needed information.

Outcomes Include:

    a. Determines the availability of needed information and makes decisions on broadening the information seeking process beyond local resources (e.g., interlibrary loan; using resources at other locations; obtaining images, videos, text, or sound)
    b. Considers the feasibility of acquiring a new language or skill (e.g., foreign or discipline-based) in order to gather needed information and to understand its context
    c. Defines a realistic overall plan and timeline to acquire the needed information

4. The information literate student reevaluates the nature and extent of the information need.

Outcomes Include:

    a. Reviews the initial information need to clarify, revise, or refine the question
    b. Describes criteria used to make information decisions and choices

Standard Two

The information literate student accesses needed information effectively and efficiently.

Performance Indicators:

1. The information literate student selects the most appropriate investigative methods or information retrieval systems for accessing the needed information.

Outcomes Include:

    a. Identifies appropriate investigative methods (e.g., laboratory experiment, simulation, fieldwork)

    b. Investigates benefits and applicability of various investigative methods

    c. Investigates the scope, content, and organization of information retrieval systems

    d. Selects efficient and effective approaches for accessing the information needed from the investigative method or information retrieval system

2. The information literate student constructs and implements effectively-designed search strategies.

Outcomes Include:

    a. Develops a research plan appropriate to the investigative method

    b. Identifies keywords, synonyms and related terms for the information needed

    c. Selects controlled vocabulary specific to the discipline or information retrieval source

    d. Constructs a search strategy using appropriate commands for the information retrieval system selected (e.g., Boolean operators, truncation, and proximity for search engines; internal organizers such as indexes for books)

    e. Implements the search strategy in various information retrieval systems using different user interfaces and search engines, with different command languages, protocols, and search parameters

    f. Implements the search using investigative protocols appropriate to the discipline

3. The information literate student retrieves information online or in person using a variety of methods.

Outcomes Include:

   a. Uses various search systems to retrieve information in a variety of
      formats
   b. Uses various classification schemes and other systems (e.g., call num-
      ber systems or indexes) to locate information resources within the
      library or to identify specific sites for physical exploration
   c. Uses specialized online or in person services available at the institu-
      tion to retrieve information needed (e.g., interlibrary loan/document
      delivery, professional associations, institutional research offices, com-
      munity resources, experts and practitioners)
   d. Uses surveys, letters, interviews, and other forms of inquiry to
      retrieve primary information

 4. The information literate student refines the search strategy if necessary.

Outcomes Include:

   a. Assesses the quantity, quality, and relevance of the search results to
      determine whether alternative information retrieval systems or inves-
      tigative methods should be utilized
   b. Identifies gaps in the information retrieved and determines if the
      search strategy should be revised
   c. Repeats the search using the revised strategy as necessary

 5. The information literate student extracts, records, and manages the
    information and its sources.

Outcomes Include:

   a. Selects among various technologies the most appropriate one for the
      task of extracting the needed information (e.g., copy/paste software
      functions, photocopier, scanner, audio/visual equipment, or explor-
      atory instruments)
   b. Creates a system for organizing the information
   c. Differentiates between the types of sources cited and understands
      the elements and correct syntax of a citation for a wide range of
      resources
   d. Records all pertinent citation information for future reference
   e. Uses various technologies to manage the information selected and
      organized

Standard Three

The information literate student evaluates information and its sources critically and incorporates selected information into his or her knowledge base and value system.

Performance Indicators:

1. The information literate student summarizes the main ideas to be extracted from the information gathered.

Outcomes Include:

    a. Reads the text and selects main ideas
    b. Restates textual concepts in his/her own words and selects data accurately
    c. Identifies verbatim material that can be then appropriately quoted

2. The information literate student articulates and applies initial criteria for evaluating both the information and its sources.

Outcomes Include:

    a. Examines and compares information from various sources in order to evaluate reliability, validity, accuracy, authority, timeliness, and point of view or bias
    b. Analyzes the structure and logic of supporting arguments or methods
    c. Recognizes prejudice, deception, or manipulation
    d. Recognizes the cultural, physical, or other context within which the information was created and understands the impact of context on interpreting the information

3. The information literate student synthesizes main ideas to construct new concepts.

Outcomes Include:

    a. Recognizes interrelationships among concepts and combines them into potentially useful primary statements with supporting evidence
    b. Extends initial synthesis, when possible, at a higher level of abstraction to construct new hypotheses that may require additional information
    c. Utilizes computer and other technologies (e.g. spreadsheets, data-

bases, multimedia, and audio or visual equipment) for studying the
interaction of ideas and other phenomena

4. The information literate student compares new knowledge with prior
   knowledge to determine the value added, contradictions, or other
   unique characteristics of the information.

Outcomes Include:

   a. Determines whether information satisfies the research or other
      information need
   b. Uses consciously selected criteria to determine whether the informa-
      tion contradicts or verifies information used from other sources
   c. Draws conclusions based upon information gathered
   d. Tests theories with discipline-appropriate techniques (e.g., simula-
      tors, experiments)
   e. Determines probable accuracy by questioning the source of the data,
      the limitations of the information gathering tools or strategies, and
      the reasonableness of the conclusions
   f. Integrates new information with previous information or knowledge
   g. Selects information that provides evidence for the topic

5. The information literate student determines whether the new knowledge has an impact on the individual's value system and takes steps to
   reconcile differences.

Outcomes Include:

   a. Investigates differing viewpoints encountered in the literature
   b. Determines whether to incorporate or reject viewpoints encountered

6. The information literate student validates understanding and interpretation of the information through discourse with other individuals,
   subject-area experts, and/or practitioners.

Outcomes Include:

   a. Participates in classroom and other discussions
   b. Participates in class-sponsored electronic communication forums
      designed to encourage discourse on the topic (e.g., email, bulletin
      boards, chat rooms)
   c. Seeks expert opinion through a variety of mechanisms (e.g., inter-
      views, email, listservs)

7. The information literate student determines whether the initial query
   should be revised.

Outcomes Include:

a. Determines if original information need has been satisfied or if additional information is needed
b. Reviews search strategy and incorporates additional concepts as necessary
c. Reviews information retrieval sources used and expands to include others as needed

STANDARD FOUR

The information literate student, individually or as a member of a group, uses information effectively to accomplish a specific purpose.

Performance Indicators:

1. The information literate student applies new and prior information to the planning and creation of a particular product or performance.

Outcomes Include:

a. Organizes the content in a manner that supports the purposes and format of the product or performance (e.g. outlines, drafts, storyboards)
b. Articulates knowledge and skills transferred from prior experiences to planning and creating the product or performance
c. Integrates the new and prior information, including quotations and paraphrasings, in a manner that supports the purposes of the product or performance
d. Manipulates digital text, images, and data, as needed, transferring them from their original locations and formats to a new context

2. The information literate student revises the development process for the product or performance.

Outcomes Include:

a. Maintains a journal or log of activities related to the information seeking, evaluating, and communicating process
b. Reflects on past successes, failures, and alternative strategies

3. The information literate student communicates the product or performance effectively to others.

Outcomes Include:

    a. Chooses a communication medium and format that best supports the purposes of the product or performance and the intended audience

    b. Uses a range of information technology applications in creating the product or performance

    c. Incorporates principles of design and communication

    d. Communicates clearly and with a style that supports the purposes of the intended audience

STANDARD FIVE

The information literate student understands many of the economic, legal, and social issues surrounding the use of information and accesses and uses information ethically and legally.

Performance Indicators:

    1. The information literate student understands many of the ethical, legal and socio-economic issues surrounding information and information technology.

Outcomes Include:

    a. Identifies and discusses issues related to privacy and security in both the print and electronic environments

    b. Identifies and discusses issues related to free vs. fee-based access to information

    c. Identifies and discusses issues related to censorship and freedom of speech

    d. Demonstrates an understanding of intellectual property, copyright, and fair use of copyrighted material

    2. The information literate student follows laws, regulations, institutional policies, and etiquette related to the access and use of information resources.

Outcomes Include:

    a. Participates in electronic discussions following accepted practices (e.g. "Netiquette")

    b. Uses approved passwords and other forms of ID for access to information resources

c. Complies with institutional policies on access to information resources

d. Preserves the integrity of information resources, equipment, systems and facilities

e. Legally obtains, stores, and disseminates text, data, images, or sounds

f. Demonstrates an understanding of what constitutes plagiarism and does not represent work attributable to others as his/her own

g. Demonstrates an understanding of institutional policies related to human subjects research

3. The information literate student acknowledges the use of information sources in communicating the product or performance.

Outcomes Include:

a. Selects an appropriate documentation style and uses it consistently to cite sources

b. Posts permission granted notices, as needed, for copyrighted material

Appendix B: Research-Based Recommendations for Effective Instruction in 21st-Century Literacies: A Policy Research Brief produced by the National Council of Teachers of English [Excerpt]

(The complete document is available at http://www.ncte.org/library/
NCTEFiles/Resources/Positions/Chron1107ResearchBrief.pdf.)

For teachers . . .

Research shows that effective instruction in 21st-century literacies takes an integrated approach, helping students understand how to access, evaluate, synthesize, and contribute to information. Furthermore, as Web 2.0 demonstrates, participation is key, and effective teachers will find ways to encourage interaction with and among students. Recommendations include:

- Encourage students to reflect regularly about the role of technology in their learning.
- Create a website and invite students to use it to continue class discussions and bring in outside voices.
- Give students strategies for evaluating the quality of information they find on the Internet.
- Be open about your own strengths and limitations with technology and invite students to help you.
- Explore technologies students are using outside of class and find ways to incorporate them into your teaching.

- Use a wiki to develop a multimodal reader's guide to a class text.
- Include a broad variety of media and genres in class texts.
- Ask students to create a podcast to share with an authentic audience.
- Give students explicit instruction about how to avoid plagiarism in a digital environment.
- Consult the resources on the Partnership for 21st-Century Skills website at http://www.21stcenturyskills.org.

FOR SCHOOLS AND POLICYMAKERS . . .

Teachers need both intellectual and material support for effective 21st-century literacy instruction. Accordingly, schools need to provide continuing opportunities for professional development as well as up-to-date technologies for use in literacy classrooms.

- Address the digital divide by lowering the number of students per computer and by providing high quality access (broadband speed and multiple locations) to technology and multiple software packages.
- Ensure that students in literacy classes have regular access to technology.
- Provide regular literacy-specific professional development in technology for teachers and administrators at all levels, including higher education.
- Require teacher preparation programs to include training in integrating technology into instruction.
- Protect online learners and ensure their privacy.
- Affirm the importance of literacy teachers in helping students develop technological proficiency.
- Adopt and regularly review standards for instruction in technology.

Appendix C: Conference on College Composition and Communication Position Statement on Teaching, Learning, and Assessing Writing in Digital Environments [Excerpt]

(The complete statement is available at http://www.ncte.org/cccc/ resources/positions/digitalenvironments)

ASSUMPTIONS

Courses that engage students in writing digitally may have many features, but all of them should

1. introduce students to the epistemic (knowledge-constructing) characteristics of information technology, some of which are generic to information technology and some of which are specific to the fields in which the information technology is used;

2. provide students with opportunities to apply digital technologies to solve substantial problems common to the academic, professional, civic, and/or personal realm of their lives;

3. include much hands-on use of technologies;

4. engage students in the critical evaluation of information (see American Library Association, "Information Literacy"); and

5. prepare students to be reflective practitioners.

As with all teaching and learning, the foundation for teaching writing digitally must be university, college, department, program, and course learning goals or outcomes. These outcomes should reflect current knowledge in the field (such as those articulated in the "WPA Outcomes Statement"), as well as the needs of students, who will be expected to write for a variety of purposes in the academic, professional, civic, and personal arenas of life. Once programs and faculty have established learning outcomes, they then can make thoughtful decisions about curriculum, pedagogy, and assessment.

Writing instruction is delivered contextually. Therefore, institutional mission statements should also inform decisions about teaching writing digitally in the same ways that they should inform any curricular and pedagogical decisions.

Regardless of the medium in which writers choose to work, all writing is social; accordingly, response to and evaluation of writing are human activities, and in the classroom, their primary purpose is to enhance learning.

Therefore, faculty will

1. incorporate principles of best practices in teaching and learning. As Chickering and Ehrmann explain, those principles are equally applicable to face-to-face, hybrid, and online instruction

   - Good Practice Encourages Contacts Between Student and Faculty
   - Good Practice Develops Reciprocity and Cooperation Among Students
   - Good Practice Uses Active Learning Techniques
   - Good Practice Gives Prompt Feedback
   - Good Practice Emphasizes Time on Task
   - Good Practice Communicates High Expectations
   - Good Practice Respects Diverse Talents and Ways of Learning

2. provide for the needs of students who are place-bound and time-bound.

3. be guided by the principles outlined in the CCCC "Writing Assessment: A Position Statement" for assessment of student work in all learning environments—in face-to-face, in hybrid, and in online situations. Given new genres, assessment may require new criteria: the attributes of a hypertextual essay are likely to vary from those of a print essay; the attributes of a weblog differ from those of a print journal (Yancey). Because digi-

tal environments make sharing work especially convenient, we would expect to find considerable human interaction around texts; through such interaction, students learn that humans write to other humans for specific purposes. Good assessment requires human readers.

Administrators with responsibilities for writing programs will

1. assure that all matriculated students have sufficient access to the requisite technology, thus bridging the "digital divide" in the local context. Students who face special economic and cultural hurdles (see Digital Divide Network) as well as those with disabilities will receive the support necessary for them to succeed;

2. assure that students off campus, particularly in distance learning situations, have access to the same library resources available to other students (see American Library Association, "Guidelines for Distance Learning");

3. assure that reward structures for faculty teaching digital writing value such work appropriately. Department, college, and institutional policies and procedures for annual reviews and for promotion and tenure should acknowledge the time and intellectual energy required to teach writing digitally (see CCCC "Promotion and Tenure" and "Tenure and Promotion Cases for Composition Faculty Who Work with Technology"). This work is located within a new field of expertise and should be both supported—with hardware and software—and recognized. Similarly, institutions that expect faculty to write for publication must have policies that value scholarly work focused on writing in digital environments—the scholarship of discovery, application/engagement, integration, and teaching (see Boyer; Glassick, Huber, and Maeroff; Shulman);

4. assure that faculty have ready access to diverse forms of technical and pedagogical professional development before and while they teach in digital environments. Such support should include regular and just-in-time workshops, courses, individual consultations, and Web resources;

5. provide adequate infrastructure for teaching writing in digital environments, including routine access to current hardware; and

6. develop equitable policies for ownership of intellectual property that take effect before online classes commence

Writing Programs, in concert with their institutions, will

1. assess students' readiness to succeed in learning to write in digital environments. Programs should assess students' access to hardware, software and access tools used in the course, as well as students' previous experience with those tools. In order to enhance learning, programs may also assess students' attitudes about learning in online environments; and

2. facilitate the development of electronic portfolios where such programs are in place or are under consideration. As important, writing programs will work to help develop the infrastructure and the pedagogy to assist students in moving their portfolios from one course to another, one program to another, one institution to another, as well as from educational institutions to the workplace, working to keep learning at the center of the enterprise and to assure that students learn to use the technology, not just consume it. To accomplish this goal, institutions need to work with professional organizations and software manufacturers to develop portfolio models that serve learning.

Appendix D: Writing Program Administrators' First Year Writing Outcomes [Excerpt]

(The complete statement is available at http://wpacouncil.org/positions/outcomes.html)

Rhetorical Knowledge

By the end of first year composition, students should
- Focus on a purpose
- Respond to the needs of different audiences
- Respond appropriately to different kinds of rhetorical situations
- Use conventions of format and structure appropriate to the rhetorical situation
- Adopt appropriate voice, tone, and level of formality
- Understand how genres shape reading and writing
- Write in several genres
- Faculty in all programs and departments can build on this preparation by helping students learn
- The main features of writing in their fields
- The main uses of writing in their fields
- The expectations of readers in their fields

Critical Thinking, Reading, and Writing

By the end of first year composition, students should
- Use writing and reading for inquiry, learning, thinking, and communicating

- Understand a writing assignment as a series of tasks, including finding, evaluating, analyzing, and synthesizing appropriate primary and secondary sources
- Integrate their own ideas with those of others
- Understand the relationships among language, knowledge, and power
- Faculty in all programs and departments can build on this preparation by helping students learn
- The uses of writing as a critical thinking method
- The interactions among critical thinking, critical reading, and writing
- The relationships among language, knowledge, and power in their fields

Processes

By the end of first year composition, students should
- Be aware that it usually takes multiple drafts to create and complete a successful text
- Develop flexible strategies for generating, revising, editing, and proof-reading
- Understand writing as an open process that permits writers to use later invention and re-thinking to revise their work
- Understand the collaborative and social aspects of writing processes
- Learn to critique their own and others' works
- Learn to balance the advantages of relying on others with the responsibility of doing their part
- Use a variety of technologies to address a range of audiences
- Faculty in all programs and departments can build on this preparation by helping students learn
- To build final results in stages
- To review work-in-progress in collaborative peer groups for purposes other than editing
- To save extensive editing for later parts of the writing process
- To apply the technologies commonly used to research and communicate within their fields

Knowledge of Conventions

By the end of first year composition, students should
- Learn common formats for different kinds of texts
- Develop knowledge of genre conventions ranging from struc-
  ture and paragraphing to tone and mechanics
- Practice appropriate means of documenting their work
- Control such surface features as syntax, grammar, punctuation,
  and spelling.
- Faculty in all programs and departments can build on this
  preparation by helping students learn
- The conventions of usage, specialized vocabulary, format, and
  documentation in their fields
- Strategies through which better control of conventions can be
  achieved

Appendix E: Common Core Standards in English Language Arts [Excerpts]

(The full standards documents can be found at http://www.corestandards.org/)

The CCR anchor standards and high school grade-specific standards work in tandem to define college and career readiness expectations—the former providing broad standards, the latter providing additional specificity.

Key Ideas and Details

RI.11–12.1. Cite strong and thorough textual evidence to support analysis of what the text says explicitly as well as inferences drawn from the text, including determining where the text leaves matters uncertain.

RI.11–12.2. Determine two or more central ideas of a text and analyze their development over the course of the text, including how they interact and build on one another to provide a complex analysis; provide an objective summary of the text.

RI.11–12.3. Analyze a complex set of ideas or sequence of events and explain how specific individuals, ideas, or events interact and develop over the course of the text.

Craft and Structure

RI.11–12.4. Determine the meaning of words and phrases as they are used in a text, including figurative, connotative, and technical meanings; analyze how an author uses and refines the meaning of a key term or terms over the course of a text (e.g., how Madison defines faction in Federalist No. 10).

RI.11–12.5. Analyze and evaluate the effectiveness of the structure an author uses in his or her exposition or argument, including whether the structure makes points clear, convincing, and engaging.

RI.11–12.6. Determine an author's point of view or purpose in a text in which the rhetoric is particularly effective, analyzing how style and content contribute to the power, persuasiveness or beauty of the text.

Integration of Knowledge and Ideas

RI.11–12.7. Integrate and evaluate multiple sources of information presented in different media or formats (e.g., visually, quantitatively) as well as in words in order to address a question or solve a problem.

RI.11–12.8. Delineate and evaluate the reasoning in seminal U.S. texts, including the application of constitutional principles and use of legal reasoning (e.g., in U.S. Supreme Court majority opinions and dissents) and the premises, purposes, and arguments in works of public advocacy (e.g., The Federalist, presidential addresses).

RI.11–12.9. Analyze seventeenth-, eighteenth-, and nineteenth-century foundational U.S. documents of historical and literary significance (including The Declaration of Independence, the Preamble to the Constitution, the Bill of Rights, and Lincoln's Second Inaugural Address) for their themes, purposes, and rhetorical features.

Range of Reading and Level of Text Complexity

> RI.11–12.10. By the end of grade 11, read and comprehend literary nonfiction in the grades 11–CCR text complexity band proficiently, with scaffolding as needed at the high end of the range.

By the end of grade 12, read and comprehend literary nonfiction at the high end of the grades 11–CCR text complexity band independently and proficiently

Excerpt 2. English Language Arts Standards » Writing » Grade 11–12

The CCR anchor standards and high school grade-specific standards work in tandem to define college and career readiness expectations— the former providing broad standards, the latter providing additional specificity.

Text Types and Purposes

> W.11–12.1. Write arguments to support claims in an analysis of substantive topics or texts, using valid reasoning and relevant and sufficient evidence.
>
> - Introduce precise, knowledgeable claim(s), establish the significance of the claim(s), distinguish the claim(s) from alternate or opposing claims, and create an organization that logically sequences claim(s), counterclaims, reasons, and evidence.
> - Develop claim(s) and counterclaims fairly and thoroughly, supplying the most relevant evidence for each while pointing out the strengths and limitations of both in a manner that anticipates the audience's knowledge level, concerns, values, and possible biases.
> - Use words, phrases, and clauses as well as varied syntax to link the major sections of the text, create cohesion, and clarify the relationships between claim(s) and reasons,

between reasons and evidence, and between claim(s) and counterclaims.

- Establish and maintain a formal style and objective tone while attending to the norms and conventions of the discipline in which they are writing.
- Provide a concluding statement or section that follows from and supports the argument presented.

W.11–12.2. Write informative/explanatory texts to examine and convey complex ideas, concepts, and information clearly and accurately through the effective selection, organization, and analysis of content.

- Introduce a topic; organize complex ideas, concepts, and information so that each new element builds on that which precedes it to create a unified whole; include formatting (e.g., headings), graphics (e.g., figures, tables), and multimedia when useful to aiding comprehension.
- Develop the topic thoroughly by selecting the most significant and relevant facts, extended definitions, concrete details, quotations, or other information and examples appropriate to the audience's knowledge of the topic.
- Use appropriate and varied transitions and syntax to link the major sections of the text, create cohesion, and clarify the relationships among complex ideas and concepts.
- Use precise language, domain-specific vocabulary, and techniques such as metaphor, simile, and analogy to manage the complexity of the topic.
- Establish and maintain a formal style and objective tone while attending to the norms and conventions of the discipline in which they are writing.
- Provide a concluding statement or section that follows from and supports the information or explanation presented (e.g., articulating implications or the significance of the topic).

W.11–12.3. Write narratives to develop real or imagined experiences or events using effective technique, well-chosen details, and well-structured event sequences.

- Engage and orient the reader by setting out a problem, situation, or observation and its significance, establishing one or multiple point(s) of view, and introducing a narrator and/or characters; create a smooth progression of experiences or events.
- Use narrative techniques, such as dialogue, pacing, description, reflection, and multiple plot lines, to develop experiences, events, and/or characters.
- Use a variety of techniques to sequence events so that they build on one another to create a coherent whole and build toward a particular tone and outcome (e.g., a sense of mystery, suspense, growth, or resolution).
- Use precise words and phrases, telling details, and sensory language to convey a vivid picture of the experiences, events, setting, and/or characters.
- Provide a conclusion that follows from and reflects on what is experienced, observed, or resolved over the course of the narrative.

Production and Distribution of Writing

W.11–12.4. Produce clear and coherent writing in which the development, organization, and style are appropriate to task, purpose, and audience. (Grade-specific expectations for writing types are defined in standards 1–3 above.)

W.11–12.5. Develop and strengthen writing as needed by planning, revising, editing, rewriting, or trying a new approach, focusing on addressing what is most significant for a specific purpose and audience.

W.11–12.6. Use technology, including the Internet, to produce, publish, and update individual or shared writing products in response to ongoing feedback, including new arguments or information.

Research to Build and Present Knowledge

W.11–12.7. Conduct short as well as more sustained research projects to answer a question (including a self-generated question) or solve a problem; narrow or broaden the inquiry when appropriate; synthesize multiple sources on the subject, demonstrating understanding of the subject under investigation.

W.11–12.8. Gather relevant information from multiple authoritative print and digital sources, using advanced searches effectively; assess the strengths and limitations of each source in terms of the task, purpose, and audience; integrate information into the text selectively to maintain the flow of ideas, avoiding plagiarism and overreliance on any one source and following a standard format for citation.

W.11–12.9. Draw evidence from literary or informational texts to support analysis, reflection, and research.

- Apply grades 11–12 Reading standards to literature (e.g., "Demonstrate knowledge of eighteenth-, nineteenth- and early-twentieth-century foundational works of American literature, including how two or more texts from the same period treat similar themes or topics").
- Apply grades 11–12 Reading standards to literary non-fiction (e.g., "Delineate and evaluate the reasoning in seminal U.S. texts, including the application of constitutional principles and use of legal reasoning [e.g., in U.S. Supreme Court Case majority opinions and dissents] and the premises, purposes, and arguments in works of public advocacy [e.g., The Federalist, presidential addresses]").

Range of Writing

W.11–12.10. Write routinely over extended time frames (time for research, reflection, and revision) and shorter time frames (a single sitting or a day or two) for a range of tasks, purposes.

Appendix F: Other Writing Textbooks of Note

Handbooks

Far and away, the most frequently used college writing textbook is the *handbook*. The traditional definition is that handbooks are intended primarily to help students write correctly. Though many of the larger handbooks offer detailed writing advice, handbooks are generally used for help in conventions of grammar, style, usage, punctuation, and mechanics as well as advice on research and documenting papers. All provide some help with general reading skills, such as previewing or observing a text; active reading skills, such as annotating, underlining, and note-taking; and connect those activities to general advice on rhetorical strategies, such as analyzing, reflecting, informing, and arguing. Handbooks do not provide as much help with close reading of specific texts as other textbooks do. Instructors may use handbooks in class or assign reading from them, though most are used as reference books intended for students to consult on their own.

"Comprehensive" handbooks form the foundation of each publisher's handbook franchises (associated with the author), offer the most detailed coverage of critical reading, and are the explicit in making the connection to writing. Most offer distinct chapters on critical reading as part of their coverage of analyzing and writing arguments. They introduce students to strategies for previewing, active reading, summarizing, and analyzing a text, numerous exercises, and offer abundant annotated examples from several genres, including text, photographs, and Web pages. Because of the placement of reading chapters in the context of chapters about analyzing and constructing arguments, these handbooks explicitly show the connection of critical thinking, reading, and writing. Examples are abundant, and the advice is well-grounded. The student, however, must rely on an instructor's use of this advice to ensure her understanding of critical reading strategies transfers to her writing assignments. Some offer discreet sections that include specific advice on critical reading skills with print and visual examples, usually accompanied by chapters or sections covering reading and writing arguments, or as a component of critical thinking. All have examples of critical reading strategies in action that are often annotated, and that often show synthesis and analysis. Though most include annotated student essays depicting a close reading, none includes full readings as part of scaffolded writing assignments.

Top-selling, full-sized handbooks include *Writing: A Manual for the Digital Age, Second Edition* by David Blakesley and Jeffrey L. Hoogeveen, *The Penguin Handbook, Fourth Edition*, by Lester Faigley; *The Little, Brown Handbook, Twelfth Edition*, by H. Ramsey Fowler and Jane E. Aaron; *The Hodges Harbrace Handbook, Eighteenth Edition*, by Cheryl Glenn and Loretta Gray; *The Bedford Handbook, Eighth Edition*, by Diana Hacker and Nancy Sommers; *Writing Matters*, by Rebecca Moore Howard; *The St. Martin's Handbook, Seventh Edition*, by Andrea A. Lunsford; *The McGraw-Hill Handbook, Third Edition*, by Elaine Maimon, Janice Peritz, and Kathleen Yancey; *The Scott, Foresman Handbook for Writers, Ninth Edition*, by John J. Ruszkiewicz, Christy E. Friend, Daniel E. Seward, and Maxine Hairston; *The Simon & Schuster Handbook for Writers, Ninth Edition*, by Lynn Q. Troyka and Doug Hesse; and, *The DK Handbook, Second Edition*, by Anne Frances Wysocki and Dennis A. Lynch.

RHETORICS

Top-selling comprehensive rhetorics include *The St. Martin's Guide to Writing, Ninth Edition*, by Rise B. Axelrod and Charles R. Cooper; *The Curious Writer, Third Edition*, by Bruce Ballenger; *The Norton Field Guide to Writing with Readings and Handbook, Second Edition*, by Richard Bullock, Maureen Daly Goggin, and Francine Weinberg; *The Allyn & Bacon Guide to Writing, Sixth Edition*, by John D. Ramage, John C. Bean, and June Johnson; *The Prentice Hall Guide for College Writers, Ninth Edition*, by Stephen Reid; and *The McGraw-Hill Guide: Writing for College, Writing for Life, Second Edition*, by Duane Roen, Gregory R. Glau, and Barry M. Maid.

READERS

Argument Readers

As the fastest growing segment of the reader market, there are dozens of competitive argument texts and readers on the market, including *Envision: Writing and Researching Arguments*, Third Edition, by Christine Alfano and Alyssa O'Brien; *Current Issues and Enduring Questions: A Guide to Critical Thinking and Argument with Readings*, Ninth Edition, by Sylvan Barnet and Hugo Bedau; *Aims of Argument: A Text and Reader*, Seventh Edition, by Thomas Crusius and Carolyn Channel; *Good Reasons: Researching and Writing Effective Arguments*, Fifth Edition, by Lester Faigley and Jack Selzer; *Dialogues: An Argument Rhetoric and Reader*, Seventh Edition, by Gary J. Goshgarian and Kathleen Krueger; *Practical Argument: A Text and Anthology*, by Laurie G. Kirszner and Stephen R. Mandell; *Inventing Arguments*, Second Edition, by John Mauk; *Elements of Argument: A Text and Reader*, Tenth Edition, by Annette T. Rottenberg and Donna Haisty Winchell; and *Perspectives on Argument*, Seventh Edition, by Nancy V. Wood.

Inquiry-Based Readers

There are other readers that focus on inquiry, both for academic writing and writing for other purposes. Some of these are *The Curious Reader: Exploring Personal and Academic Inquiry*, Second Edition, by Bruce Ballenger and Michelle Payne; *Inquiry: Questioning, Reading, Writing*, Second Edition, by Lynn Z. Bloom and Edward M. White, with Shane Borrowman; and *Composing Inquiry: Methods and Readings for Investigation and Writing*, by Margaret J. Marshall.

Glossary

Academic critical literacy—Best defined as the psycholinguistic processes of getting meaning from or putting meaning into print and/or sound, images, and movement, on a page or screen, and used for the purposes of analysis, synthesis, and evaluation, these processes develop through formal schooling and beyond—at home and at work, in childhood and across the lifespan—and are essential to human functioning in a democratic society. There are two points to be made for present purposes from this definition. First, notice that this definition includes perception and production as well as text and visual elements, and that it focuses on the key skills of analysis, synthesis, and evaluation. This proposed definition suggests that readers must be able to go significantly beyond getting meaning from print to using that meaning in very specific ways. This proposal furthermore suggests that reading is the same fundamental activity, whether it is carried out with paper or digital texts and whether it entails topics like theoretical physics or trash novels. By implication, that reading must be closely integrated with writing in critical literacy.

Blended librarian—An academic librarian who blends the traditional skills of librarians with knowledge of information technology and the ability to apply that knowledge effectively in the teaching-learning process (see Bell & Shank, 2004).

Common Core Standards—A set of guidelines developed by a panel commissioned by the National Governors' Association and the Council of Chief State School Officers to support the teaching and learning of reading, writing, speaking, language awareness, and mathematics in U.S. elementary and high schools.

Contrastive rhetoric—The study of how a person's first language discourse practices and culture socialization influence his or her writing in a second language. The first formally published research on this issue was by Robert Kaplan (1966). His published study, showing that students from different cultural backgrounds use different paragraph organizational patterns, pioneered attention to cultural and linguistic differences in the writing of ESL students. Since that time, the area of study has had a significant impact on the teaching of writing in both English as a second language (ESL) and English as a foreign language (EFL) classes.

Critical literacy—The proficiency beyond basic comprehension of text, wherein the reader is able to question, transform, and draw unwritten intent from text.

Critical reading—The ability to not just understand texts, but also to interpret texts based on societal context.

Discourse community—A distinctive cultural group whose members dictate the unwritten rules and mores of communication—what things should be said and how. Most people move within and among several discourse communities every day.

Discourse synthesis—"The process in which writers are engaged when they read multiple texts and produce their own related texts" (Spivey, 1997, p. 146), particularly for the purpose of the writing task, and in which they use the texts they have read in some direct way.

Embedded librarian—A librarian who collaborates with academic faculty to provide extended information literacy instruction within the context of a particular course.

EFL—English as a foreign language. Indicates the use of English in a non-English speaking region. EFL instruction occurs in the student's home country, as part of the normal school curriculum, and can refer to English language instruction from elementary grades through graduate school. At the university level in home countries, it can also be referred to as EAP instruction.

ESL—English as a second language (may also be referred to as ESOL—English for speakers of other languages). Refers to the use or study of English (in a native, English-speaking country) by speakers with a different native language.

EAP—English for academic purposes. Entails training students—usually in a higher education setting—to use language appropriately for academic learning. It is a challenging and multi-faceted area within the wider field of English language learning and teaching (ELT), and is one of the most common forms of English for specific purposes (ESP).

Foundational literacies—Thecore skills needed to comprehend and utilize written text, including reading and writing.

Generation 1.5 students—May also be called *immigrant generation students*. Primarily refers to people who immigrate to a new country before or during their early teens. They earn the label "Generation 1.5" because they bring with them characteristics from their home country, but continue their assimilation and socialization in the new country. Their identity is thus a combination of new and old cultures and traditions. Their experiences, characteristics, and educational needs lie somewhat between those of first-generation adult immigrants and the U.S.-born, second generation children of immigrants. In some cases, it is not clear that these students are L2 students if they have been living in the U.S. most of their lives. The title designation itself is controversial.

Global strategies—Also known as *top-down reading strategies*. These are the strategies that include setting appropriate goals, identifying main ideas, recognizing discourse organization, and using appropriate background knowledge in the reading process.

iBT TOEFL—Internet-based Test (iBT) TOEFL is a revised version of the TOEFL test. Since its introduction in late 2005, iBT TOEFL has progressively replaced previous test formats (computer-based tests (CBT) and paper-based tests (PBT)), although paper-based testing is still used in select areas. The four-hour test consists of four sections, each measuring one basic language skill (with some tasks requiring integrating multiple skills). All tasks focus on language used in an academic, higher-education environment.

ICT—Information and communication technologies. This abbreviation refers to all forms of electronic communication.

IELTS—International English Language Testing System. This is an international standardized test of English language proficiency. It is jointly managed by the University of Cambridge ESOL Examinations, the British Council and IDP Education Pty Ltd, and was established in 1989. IELTS is accepted by most Australian, British, Canadian, Irish, New Zealand, and South African academic institutions, over three thousand academic institutions in the United States, and various professional organizations. It is also a requirement for immigration to Australia and Canada.

Information literacy—A set of capabilities that enables an individual to "recognize when information is needed and have the ability to locate, evaluate, and use effectively the needed information" (ALA, 1989, para. 3).

Metacognition—The awareness and/or examination of one's own mental processes, and is often referred to as "thinking about thinking" or "knowing about knowing."

Mining—A reading strategy in which a reader looks at a text to find particular information that can be used in writing or some other appropriate task.

MMORPG—Massively multiplayer online role-playing games. A genre of computer role-playing games in which a very large number of players interact with one another within a virtual game world.

Multiliteracies—Coined by The New London Group in the mid-1990s to address the increasing impact of technology on communication, this term refers to the ability to comprehend meaning in a variety of delivery formats, including printed text, oral language, audio-visual representations, musical works, etc.

Multimodality—The ability to understand and use text in multiple sign systems.

New literacies—This term encompasses the range of proficiencies that grow from continually-developing information and communication technologies, such as digital literacy, computer literacy, technology literacy, etc.

Pre-university intensive language programs—International students who do not meet the university's English proficiency requirement are required to study in a program that provides intensive instruction in English. Generally, the Intensive English Program (IEP) helps students master English language writing, reading, listening, speaking, and grammar skills.

Polymorphic literacy—Reading and writing that draw on verbal and non-verbal ways of shaping meaning. Concepts of place play a role in literacy practices.

RAC—Reading across the curriculum. This abbreviation refers to the idea that reading should be taught in every discipline, as part of the teaching or instructional goals or student outcomes of every course.

Reading—Reading is variously defined, usually as getting meaning from print. In other words, just being able to pronounce aloud the

words that appear on a page is not reading, according to this definition. At the very least, readers must get the meaning for their
activity to qualify as reading. To be successful in college and beyond, on paper and on screen, students must be able to go well beyond just getting meaning and well beyond just being able to work
with printed texts. Reading is a psycholinguistic process, involving the interaction of readers' thinking with the language of the
text. It must involve getting meaning, but in addition, it must also
entail moving beyond meaning to analysis, synthesis, and evaluation. That is, as I and a number of other scholars have proposed,
reading must function as part of critical literacy.

Reading guide—A handout reading teachers give to students, especially English L2 students, that contains questions about general or
specific information from the reading to help students comprehend the reading or focus on particular key information in the
reading article.

Recitation of text—A teaching practice common in advanced ESL and
EFL classes in many countries around the world. The teacher explains an English text paragraph by paragraph, explaining difficult vocabulary and complex grammar in each sentence. This
process is repeated through the entire text. Explanations are most
often given in the students' L1, and students are often not asked to
identify or explain main ideas in the text.

Rhetorical reading—Reading that considers a text's author, purpose,
and rhetorical situation to ascertain meaning.

Satisficing—Accepting a satisfactory rather than optimal result; i.e., in
library research, the practice of selecting the first or most convenient items in a set of database results, rather than seeking out the
most *relevant* items from among the results.

Second language (L2)—A second language (L2) is any language learned
after the first language, or mother tongue (L1).

Social knowledge—Knowledge that has been disseminated sufficiently
enough to be shared by a group or groups of people within society. Social knowledge is part of the shared cultural knowledge of
a community or society.

Sub-technical vocabulary—Words critical for academic writing, but
are not subject-specific words, including words and phrases such
as: analyze, interpret, consider, suggests, hierarchy, results in, pre-
dicts, alternative, the foregoing, the fact that, etc.

Symptomatic reading—To read texts not only for what they say literally, but for symptoms of larger cultural tensions. Also, to read a text for "what it does not say" and "what it did not want to say," but is nonetheless part of its ideological underpinning.

Think aloud protocol—A research methodology where study participants are asked to say aloud what they are thinking and/or feeling as they read, write, or perform some other task.

TOEFL—Test of English as a Foreign Language. Evaluates the ability of an individual to use and understand English in an academic setting. It sometimes is an admission requirement for non-native English speakers at many English-speaking colleges and universities. The TOEFL test is the most widely respected English-language test in the world, recognized by more than 7,500 colleges, universities, and agencies in more than 130 countries.

Writing across the curriculum (WAC)—"[R]efers specifically to the pedagogical and curriculum attention to writing occurring in university subject matter classes other than those offered by composition or writing programs . . . to increase the amount and quality of writing occurring in such courses as history, science, mathematics and sociology" (Bazerman et al., 2005, pp. 9–10).

Writing in the disciplines (WID)—"[R]efers to both a research movement to understand what writing actually occurs in the different disciplinary areas and a curricular reform movement to offer disciplinary related writing instruction but within a program designed for that purpose" (Bazerman et al., 2005, pp. 9–10).

References

Adler-Kassner, L. (1998). Ownership revisited: An exploration in progressive and expressivist composition scholarship. *College Composition and Communication, 49*(2), 208–33.

Adler-Kassner, L. (2006). *Considering literacy: Reading and writing the educational experience.* New York, NY: Pearson Longman.

Adler-Kassner, L., & Estrem, H. (2005). Critical thinking, reading, and writing: A view from the field. In S. Harrington, K. Rhodes, R.O. Fischer, & R. Malenczyk (Eds.), *The outcomes book: Debate and consensus after the WPA Outcomes Statement* (pp. 60–71). Logan, UT: Utah State University Press.

Adler-Kassner, L., & Estrem, H. (2007). Reading practices in the writing classroom. *WPA: Writing Program Administrators, 31*(1), 35–47.

Alexander, J. (2009). Gaming, student literacies, and the composition classroom: Some possibilities for transformation. *College Composition and Communication, 61*(1), 35–63.

Alliance for Excellent Education. (2006). Learning what's at stake. Retrieved from http://www.all4ed.org/adolescent_literacy/index.html.

Allison, D., Berry, V., & Lewkowicz, J. (1995). Reading-writing connections in EAP classes: A content analysis of written summaries produced under three mediating conditions. *RELC Journal, 26,* 25–43.

American College Testing. (2006). *Reading between the lines: What the ACT reading test reveals about college readiness: Executive summary.* Retrieved from http://www.act.org/research/policymakers/pdf/reading_report.pdf.

American College Testing. (2010). *A first look at the Common Core and college and career readiness.* Retrieved from ACT Research reports http://www.act.org/research/policymakers/pdf/FirstLook.pdf.

American Library Association. (1989). *Presidential committee on information literacy: Final report.* Retrieved from http://www.ala.org/ala/mgrps/divs/acrl/publications/whitepapers/presidential.cfm.

Anderson, L. W., & Krathwohl, D. R. (Eds.). (2001). *A taxonomy for learning, teaching, and assessing: A revision of Bloom's Taxonomy of Educational Objectives.* New York, NY: Longman.

Angelova, M., & Riazantseva, A. (1999). "If you don't tell me, how can I know?": A case study of four international students learning to write the U.S. way. *Written Communication, 16,* 491–525.

Association of College and Research Libraries. (2000). *Information literacy competency standards for higher education.* Retrieved from http://www.ala. org/ala/mgrps/divs/acrl/standards/informationliteracycompetency.cfm.

Association of College and Research Libraries. (2001). *Objectives for information literacy instruction: A model statement for academic librarians.* Retrieved from http://www.ala.org/ala/mgrps/divs/acrl/standards/objectivesinformation.cfm.

Association of College and Research Libraries. (2007). *Association of College & Research Libraries guidelines for academic status for college and university librarians.* Retrieved from http://www.ala.org/ala/mgrps/divs/acrl/standards/guidelinesacademic.cfm.

Association of College and Research Libraries. (2010). What is the Association of College & Research Libraries? Retrieved from http://www.ala.org/ala/mgrps/divs/acrl/about/whatisacrl/index.cfm.

Axelrod, R., Cooper, C., & Warriner, A. (2011). *Reading critically, writing well* (9th ed.). Boston, MA: Bedford/St. Martin's.

Aydelott, S. (1998). A study of the reading/writing connection in a university writing program. In B. Sturtevant, J. Dugan. P. Linder, & W. Linek (Eds.), *Literacy and community: The twentieth yearbook of the College Reading Association* (pp. 101–14). Carrollton, GA: College Reading Association.

Baba, K. (2009). Aspects of lexical proficiency in writing summaries in a foreign language. *Journal of Second Language Writing, 18,* 191–208.

Badley, G. (2008). Developing (authentic?) academic writers. *Quality Assurance in Education: An International Perspective, 16*(4), 363–74.

Barrett, A. (2005). The information-seeking habits of graduate student researchers in the humanities. *Journal of Academic Librarianship, 31*(4), 324–31.

Barritt, L. S. & Kroll, B. M. (1978). Some implications of cognitive-development psychology for research in composing. In C. R. Cooper & L. Odell (Eds.), *Research on composing: Points of departure* (pp. 49–58). Urbana, IL: National Council of Teachers of English.

Bartholomae, D. (1995). Writing with teachers: A conversation with Peter Elbow. *College Composition and Communication, 46,* 62–71.

Bartholomae, D. & Petrosky, A. (2005). *Ways of reading: An anthology for writers* (7th ed.). Boston: Bedford/St. Martin's.

Bartholomae, D., & Petrosky, A. (2011). *Ways of reading: An anthology for writers* (9th ed.). Boston, MA: Bedford/St. Martin's.

Batelle, J. (2005). *The search: How Google and its rivals rewrote the rules of business and transformed our culture.* New York: Penguin Books.

Bazerman, C. (1980). A relationship between reading and writing: The conversational model. *College English, 41*(6), 656–61.

Bazerman, C. (1988). *Shaping written knowledge: The genre and activity of the experimental article in science.* Madison, WI: University of Wisconsin Press.

Bazerman, C. (2009). 2009 CCCC chair's address: The wonder of writing. *College Composition and Communication 61*(3), 571–80.

Bazerman, C., Little, J., Bethel, L. Chavkin, T., Fouquette, D. & Garufis, J. (2005). *Reference guide to writing across the curriculum.* West Lafayette, IN: Parlor Press.

Bean, J. C. (2001). *Engaging ideas: The professor's guide to integrating writing, critical thinking, and active learning in the classroom.* San Francisco, CA: Jossey-Bass.

Bean, J. C., Chappell, V. A., & Gillam, A. M. (2005). *Reading rhetorically: A reader for writers* (2nd ed.). New York, NY: Pearson Longman.

Bean, J. C., Chappell, V. A., & Gillam, A. M. (2011). *Reading rhetorically* (3rd ed.). Boston, MA: Pearson Longman.

Bean, J. & Weimer, M. (2011). *Engaging ideas: The professor's guide to integrating writing, critical thinking, and active learning in the classroom* (2nd ed.). San Francisco: Jossey-Bass.

Becher, T. (1989). *Academic tribes and territories: Intellectual enquiry and the cultures of disciplines.* Milton Keynes, England: Open University Press.

Becker, A. (2006). A review of writing model research based on cognitive processes. In A. Horning & A. Becker (Eds.), *Revision: History, theory, and practice* (pp. 25–49). West Lafayette, IN: Parlor Press.

Behrens, L., & Rosen, L. J. (2008). *Writing and reading across the curriculum* (10th ed.). New York, NY: Pearson Longman.

Belanger, J. F. (1978). *Reading skill as influence on writing skill* (Doctoral dissertation). Retrieved from ERIC. (ED163409)

Bell, S. J., & Shank, J. (2004). The blended librarian: A blueprint for redefining the teaching and learning role of academic librarians. *College & Research Libraries News, 65*(7), 372–75.

Berthoff, A. E. (1970). *The resolved soul: A study of Marvell's major poems.* Princeton, NJ: Princeton University Press.

Biglan, A. (1973a). The characteristics of subject matter in different academic areas. *Journal of Applied Psychology 57,* 197–203.

Biglan, A. (1973b). Relationships between subject matter characteristics and the structure and output of university departments. *Journal of Applied Psychology 57,* 204–13.

Birnbaum, J. C. (1986). Reflective thought: The connection between reading and writing. In B. Petersen (Ed.), *Convergences: Transactions in reading and writing* (pp. 30–45). Urbana, IL: National Council of Teachers of English.

Bitter, G. & Pierson, M. (2004). *Using technology in the classroom.* Boston: Allyn & Bacon.

Bizzell, P. (1992). *Academic discourse and critical consciousness.* Pittsburgh, PA: University of Pittsburgh Press.

Björk, L. & Brauer, G. (2003). *Teaching academic writing in European higher education.* Dordrecht, The Netherlands: Kluwer Academic.

Block, C. & Cameron, D. (2002). *Globalization and language teaching.* London: Routledge.

Block, C. (2004). Globalization and language teaching. *ELT Journal, 58*(1), 75–77.

Bloch, J. (2008). Plagiarism in an intercultural rhetoric context. In U. Connor, E. Nagelhout, & W. Rozycki (Eds.), *Contrastive rhetoric: Reaching to intercultural rhetoric* (pp. 257–74). Philadelphia: J. Benjamins.

Bodi, S. (2002). How do we bridge the gap between what we teach and what they do? Some thoughts on the place of questions in the process of research. *Journal of Academic Librarianship, 28*(3), 109–14.

Booth, W. C. (1982). Presidential address: Arts and scandals. *PMLA, 98*(3), 312–22.

Bosley, L. (2008). "I don't teach reading": Critical reading instruction in composition courses. *Literacy Research and Instruction, 47*, 285–308.

Bowles-Terry, M., Davis, E., & Holliday, W. (2010). "Writing information literacy" revisited: Application of theory to practice in the classroom. *Reference and User Services Quarterly, 49*(3), 225–230.

Boyarin, J. (1993). *The ethnography of reading.* Berkeley: University of California Press.

Brady, L., Singh-Corcoran, N., Dadisman, J. A., & Diamond, K. (2009, Spring). A collaborative approach to information literacy: First-year composition, writing center, and library partnerships at West Virginia University. *Composition Forum, 19.* Retrieved from http://compositionforum.com/issue/19/west-virginia.php.

Brandt, D. (1986). Notes on social foundations of reading and writing. In B. Petersen (Ed.), *Convergences: Transactions in Reading and Writing* (pp. 99–114). Urbana, IL: National Council of Teachers of English.

Brandt, D. (2001). *Literacy in American lives.* New York: Cambridge University Press.

Breivik, P. S. & Gee, E. G. (2006). *Higher education in the Internet age: Libraries creating a strategic edge.* Westport, CT: American Council on Education and Praeger Press.

Bullock, R., Goggin, M. D., & Weinburg, F. (2010). *The Norton field guide with readings and handbook.* New York: W. W. Norton & Company.

Buschman, J. & Warner, D. (2006). *Innovation or tradition? Information literacy and its foundation: A critical library view.* Paper presented at the 4th International Conference on the Book. 22 October 2006. Boston, MA.

Bussert, L., & Pouliot, N. (2010). A model for information literacy self-assessment: Enhancing student learning in writing courses through collaborative teaching. In T. P. Mackey & T. E. Jacobson (Eds.), *Collaborative information literacy assessments: Strategies for evaluating teaching and learning* (pp. 131–54). New York: Neal-Schuman Publishers, Inc.

Callahan, M., Griffo, V. B., & Pearson, P. D. (2009). Teacher knowledge and teaching reading. In F. Falk-Ross, S. Szabo, M. B. Sampson, & M. M. Foote (Eds.), *Literacy issues during changing times: A call to action* (pp. 37–62). Texas A&M University-Commerce: The College Reading Association.

Canovan, B., Gruber, A. M., Knefel, M. A., & McKinlay, M. (2010). Many voices, one goal: Measuring student success through partnerships in the core curriculum. In T. P. Mackey & T. E. Jacobson (Eds.), *Collaborative information literacy assessments: Strategies for evaluating teaching and learning* (pp. 175–211). New York: Neal-Schuman Publishers, Inc.

Carlson, S. (2005, September 30). Thoughtful design keeps new libraries relevant. *The Chronicle of Higher Education.* Retrieved from http://chronicle.com/article/Thoughtful-Design-Keeps-New/16326/.

Carlson, S. (2010, May 30) A place to see and be seen (and learn a little, too): $109-million renovation of Ohio State's library reinforces its role in connecting the campus. *The Chronicle of Higher Education.* Retrieved from http://chronicle.com/article/Do-Libraries-Still-Matter-/65708/.

Carmichael, S. B., Martino, G., Porter-Magee, K., & Wilson, W. S. (2010). *The state of state standards.* Washington, DC: Thomas B. Fordham Institute.

Carter, M. (1988). The role of invention in belletristic rhetoric: A study of the lectures of Adam Smith. *Rhetoric Society Quarterly, 18*(1), 3–13.

Carter, M. (2003). *Where writing begins: A postmodern reconstruction.* Carbondale, IL: Southern Illinois University Press.

Casanave, C. (2004). *Controversies in second language writing.* Ann Arbor, MI: University of Michigan Press.

Chen, S. Y., & Macredie, R. (2010). Web-based interaction: A review of three important human factors. *International Journal of Information Management, 30*(5), 379–87.

Christensen, N. L. (2003). The master double frame and other lessons from classical education. In Helmers, M. (Ed.) *Intertexts: Reading pedagogy in college writing classrooms* (pp. 71–100). Mahwah, NJ: Erlbaum.

Cockrell, B. J., & Jayne, E. A. (2002). How do I find and article? Insights from a Web usability study. *The Journal of Academic Librarianship, 28*(3), 122–32.

Coiro, J. (2011). Talking about reading as thinking: Modeling the hidden complexities of online reading comprehension. *Theory into Practice, 50*(2), 107–15. doi:10.1080/00405841.2011.558435

College Board. National Commission on Writing. (2003). *The neglected "R": The need for a writing revolution*. Retrieved from http://www.collegeboard.com/prod_downloads/writingcom/neglectedr.pdf.

College Board. National Commission on Writing. (2004). *Writing: A ticket to work or a ticket out*. Retrieved from http://www.collegeboard.com/prod_downloads/writingcom/writing-ticket-to-work.pdf.

College Board. National Commission on Writing. (2005). *Writing: A powerful message from state government*. Retrieved from http://www.collegeboard.com/prod_downloads/writingcom/powerful-message-from-state.pdf.

Common Core State Standards. (2010). Washington, DC: National Governors Association & National Council of State School Officers. Retrieved from http://www.corestandards.org/.

Conference on College Composition and Communication. (2004). *Position statement on teaching, learning and assessing writing in digital environments*. Retrieved from http://www.ncte.org/cccc/resources/positions/digitalenvironments.

Connor, U. (1996). *Contrastive rhetoric*. New York: Cambridge University Press.

Connor, U. (2002). *Contrastive rhetoric: Cross-cultural aspects of second-language writing*. Stuttgart: Klett.

Connor, U. (2004). Intercultural rhetoric research: Beyond texts. *Journal of English for Academic Purposes, 3*, 291–309.

Connor, U. (2008). Mapping multidimensional aspects of research: Reaching to intercultural rhetoric. In U. Connor, E. Nagelhout, & W. Rozycki (Eds.), *Contrastive rhetoric: Reaching to intercultural rhetoric* (pp. 299–315). Philadelphia: J. Benjamins.

Cope, B. & Kalantzis, M. (2000). *Multiliteracies: Literacy learning and the design of social futures*. London: Routledge.

Council of Writing Program Administrators. (2000/2008). *WPA outcomes statement for first-year composition*. Retrieved from http://www.wpacouncil.org/positions/outcomes.html.

Council of Writing Program Administrators. (2010, February 14). The Outcomes Statement History [Fact sheet]. In *The Outcomes Statement History*. Retrieved from http://comppile.org/archives/WPAoutcomes/continue.html.

Council of Writing Program Administrators, National Council of Teachers of English, & National Writing Project. (2011). *Framework for success in postsecondary writing*. Retrieved from http://www.wpacouncil.org.

Crick, N. (2003). Composition as experience: John Dewey on creative expression and the origins of "mind." *College Composition and Communication, 55*(2), 254–75.

Currie, L., & Eodice, M. (2005). Roots entwined: Growing a sustainable collaboration. In J. K. Elmborg & S. Hook (Eds.), *Centers for learning: Writing centers and libraries in collaboration.* (pp. 42–60). Chicago: Association of College and Research Libraries.

Dalton, M. S., & Charnigo, L. (2004). Historians and their information sources. *College and Research Libraries, 65*(5), 400–25.

Deans, T. (2000). *Writing partnerships: Service-learning in composition.* Urbana, IL: National Council of Teachers of English.

Dehaene, S. (2009). *Reading in the brain: The science and evolution of a human invention.* New York: Penguin.

Delaney, Y. A. (2008). Investigating the reading-to-write construct. *Journal of English for Academic Purposes, 7,* 140–50.

DeVido Tetrault, D., & Center, C. (2009). But I'm not a reading teacher! *Open Words: Access and English Studies, 3*(1), 45–61. Retrieved from http://www.pearsoncomppro.com/open_words_journal/index.php.

Devitt, A., Reiff, M. J., & Bawarshi, A. (2004). *Scenes of writing: strategies for composing with genres.* New York, NY: Pearson/Longman.

DeWitt, S. L. (2001). *Writing inventions: Identities, technologies, pedagogies.* Albany: State University of New York Press.

Djamasbi, S., Siegel, M., & Tullis, T. (2010). Generation Y, Web design, and eye tracking. *International Journal of Human-Computer Studies, 68*(5), 307–23.

Donahue, C. (2009). "Internationalization" and composition studies: Reorienting the discourse. *College Composition and Communication, 61*(2), 212–43.

Dougherty, W. C. (2010). E-readers: Passing fad or trend of the future? *Journal of Academic Librarianship, 36*(3), 254–56.

Downs, D. (2010, September). Writing-about-writing curricula: Origins, theories, and initial field-tests. *WPA-CompPile Research Bibliographies,* No. 12. Retrieved from http://comppile.org/wpa/bibliographies/Bib12/Downs.pdf.

Downs, D., & Wardle, E. (2007). Teaching and writing, righting misconceptions: (Re)envisioning "first-year composition" as "introduction to writing studies." *College Composition and Communication, 58*(4), 552–84.

Eakle, J. A. & Garber, A. M. (2003) International reports on literacy research: Mexico, Colombia, Brazil, Argentina, Chile. *Reading Research Quarterly. 38*(4), 524–28.

Ede, L. (2011). *The academic writer* (2nd ed.). Boston, MA: Bedford/St. Martin's.

Educational Testing Service. *iSkills.* Retrieved from http://www.ets.org/s/icriticalthinking/pdf/13134_iCriticalThinkingTable.pdf.

Egan, K. (2003). Start with what the student knows or what the student can imagine. *Phi Delta Kappan, 84,* 443–45.

Eisenberg, A. (2011, December 18). When science leaps from the page. *New York Times,* p. 4.

Eisenberg, M. & Berkowitz, R.E. (1990). *Information problem solving: The Big Six skills approach to library & information skills instruction.* Norwood, NJ: Ablex.

Elbow, P. (1995). Being a writer vs. being an academic: A conflict in goals. *College Composition and Communication, 46,* 72–83.

Elbow, P. (2000). *Everyone can write: Essays toward a hopeful theory of writing and teaching writing.* Cary, NC: Oxford UP.

Elbow, P. (2002). The cultures of literature and composition: What could each learn from the other? *College English 64*(5), 533–46.

Elley, W. (1991). Acquiring literacy in a second language: The effect of book-based programs. *Language Learning, 41,* 375–411.

Elley, W. (2000). The potential of book floods for raising literary levels. *International Review of Education, 46,* 233–55.

Ellis, R., & Loewen, S. (2005). Second language vocabulary and academic achievement in undergraduate university students. In E. Manalo & G. Wong-Toi (Eds.), *Communication skills in university education: The international dimension* (pp. 260–76). Auckland, New Zealand: Pearson Education New Zealand.

Elmborg, J. K. (2005). Libraries and writing center professionals in collaboration: Complementary practices. In J. K. Elmborg & S. Hook (Eds.), *Centers for learning: Writing centers and libraries in collaboration* (pp. 1–20). Chicago: Association of College and Research Libraries.

Elmborg, J. K., & Hook, S. (Eds.) (2005). *Centers for learning: Writing centers and libraries in collaboration.* Chicago: Association of College and Research Libraries.

Emanuel, R., Adams, J., Baker, K., Daufin, E. K., Ellington, C., Fitts, E., Himsel, J., Holladay, L. & Okeowo, D. (2008). How college students spend their time communicating. *International Journal of Listening, 22*(1), 13–28.

Emig, J. (1971). *The composing processes of twelfth graders.* Urbana: NCTE.

Emig, J. (1983). *The web of meaning: Essays on writing, teaching, learning, and thinking.* Upper Montclair NJ: Boynton/Cook Publishers.

Ensslin, A. (2007). *Canonising hypertext: Explorations and constructions.* London: Continuum International Publishing Group.

Faris, M. J., & Selber, S. A. (2011). E-book issues in composition: A partial assessment and perspective for teachers. *Composition Forum,* 24. Retrieved from http://compositionforum.com/issue/24/ebook-issues.php.

Farrell, J. (2004). *What exactly is prior knowledge?* Retrieved from http://www.readfirst.net/prior.htm.

Ferris, D. (2009). *Teaching college writing to diverse student populations.* Ann Arbor, MI: The University of Michigan Press.

Ferris, D., & Hedgcock, J. (2005). *Teaching ESL composition.* Mahwah, NJ: L. Erlbaum.

Fish, S. (1980). *Is there a text in this class? The authority of interpretive language communities.* Cambridge, MA: Harvard UP.

Fishman, J., Lunsford, A., McGregor, B., & Otuteye, M. (2005). Performing writing, performing literacy. *College Composition and Communication, 57*(2), 224–52.

Fister, B. (1995). Connected communities: Encouraging dialogue between composition and bibliographic instruction. In J. Sheridan (Ed.), *Writing-across-the-curriculum and the academic library: A guide for librarians, instructors, and writing program directors* (pp. 33–51). Westport, CT: Greenwood Press.

Fitzgerald, J. & Shanahan, T. (2000). Reading and writing relations and their development. *Educational Psychologist, 35*(10), 39–50.

Fleckenstein, K. S. (2004). Words made flesh: Fusing imagery and language in a polymorphic literacy. *College English 66*(6), 612–31.

Flower, L. (1990). Introduction: Studying cognition in context. In L. Flower, V. Stein, J. Ackerman, M.J. Kantz, K. McCormick, & W.C. Peek (Eds.), *Reading-to-write: Exploring a cognitive and social process* (pp. 3–32). New York, NY: Oxford University Press.

Flower, L. (1994). *The construction of negotiated meaning: A social cognitive theory of writing.* Carbondale: Southern Illinois University Press.

Flower, L. & Hayes, J. R. (1981). A cognitive process theory of writing. *College Composition and Communication, 32*(4), 365–87.

Flower, L., Stein, V., Ackerman, J., Kantz, M., McCormick, K. & Peck, W. (1990). *Reading-to write: Exploring a cognitive and social process.* New York: Oxford University Press.

Foster, D. (1997). Reading(s) in the writing classroom. *College Composition and Communication, 48*(4), 518–39.

Foster, D. & Russell, D. R. (Eds.). (2002). *Writing and learning in cross-national perspective: Transitions from secondary to higher education.* Urbana, IL: National Council of Teachers of English.

Fowler, H. R., & Aaron, J. E. (2012). *The Little, Brown handbook* (12th ed.). Boston, MA: Pearson.

Fox, H. (1994). *Listening to the world: Cultural issues in academic writing.* Urbana, IL: National Council of Teachers of English.

Freire, P. (1968/2007) *Pedagogy of the oppressed.* New York: Continuum.

Friedman, T. L. (2006). *The world is flat: A brief history of the twenty-first century, updated and expanded edition.* New York: Farrar, Straus and Giroux.

Fulkerson, R. (2005). Composition at the turn of the twenty-first century. *College Composition and Communication, 56*(4), 654–87.

Gaspar, D. B., & Presser, P. S. (2010). Vampires, philosophers, and graphic novels: Assessing thematic writing courses in "The Big Read." In T. P. Mackey & T. E. Jacobson (Eds.), *Collaborative information literacy assessments: Strategies for evaluating teaching and learning.* (pp. 155–74). New York: Neal-Schuman Publishers, Inc.

Gee, J. P. (1999). The future of the social turn: Social minds and the new capitalism. *Research on Language and Social Interaction, 32*(1&2), 61–68.

Gee, J. P. (2003). *What video games have to teach us about learning and literacy.* New York: Palgrave Macmillan.

Geisler, C. (1994). *Academic literacy and the nature of expertise: Reading, writing, and knowing in academic philosophy.* Hillsdale, NJ: Erlbaum.

George, A. L. (1998). Grounds of assent in Joseph Priestley's *A Course of Lectures on Oratory and Criticism. Rhetorica: A Journal of the History of Rhetoric, 16*(1), 81–109.

Gibson, C. (1995). Research skills across the curriculum: Connections with writing-across-the-curriculum. In J. Sheridan (Ed.), *Writing-across-the-curriculum and the academic library: A guide for librarians, instructors, and writing program directors* (pp. 57–69). Westport, CT: Greenwood Press.

Gielen, N. (2010). *Handheld e-book readers and scholarship: Report and reader survey.* New York, NY: American Council of Learned Societies.

Gleason, B. (2001). Teaching at the crossroads: Choices and challenges in college composition. *The Writing Instructor.* Retrieved from http://www.writinginstructor.com/reflections/gleason.html.

Glenn, W. J. (2007). Real writers as aware readers: Writing creatively as a means to develop reading skills. *Journal of Adolescent & Adult Literacy 51*(1), 10–20.

Goodman, K. S. (1996). *On reading.* Portsmouth, NH: Heinemann.

Grabe, W. (2003). Reading and writing relations: Second language perspectives on research and practice. In B. Kroll (Ed.), *Exploring the dynamics of second language writing* (pp. 242–62). Cambridge: Cambridge University Press.

Grabe, W. (2009). *Reading in a second language: From theory to practice.* New York: Cambridge University Press.

Grabe, W., & Kaplan, R. B. (1996). *Theory and practice of writing: An applied linguistic perspective.* New York: Longman.

Grabe, W., & Stoller, F. (2011). *Teaching and researching reading* (2nd ed.). New York: Longman.

Graff, G., & Birkenstein, C. (2010). *They say/I say: The moves that matter in academic writing* (2nd ed.). New York: W. W. Norton & Company.

Graham, S., & Hebert, M. A. (2010). *Writing to read: Evidence for how writing can improve reading.* A Carnegie Corporation Time to Act Report. Washington, DC: Alliance for Excellent Education.

Grant, L., & Ginther, A. (2000). Using computer-tagged linguistic features to describe L2 writing differences. *Journal of Second Language Writing, 9,* 123–45.

Grassian, E. S., & Kaplowitz, J. R. (2005). *Learning to lead and manage information literacy instruction.* New York: Neal-Schuman Publishers Inc.

Greene, S., & Lidinsky, A. (2012). *From inquiry to academic writing: A text and reader* (2nd ed.). Boston, MA: Bedford/St. Martin's.

Haas, C. (1993). Beyond "just the facts": Reading as rhetorical action. In A. M. Penrose & B. M.

Sitko (Eds.), *Hearing ourselves think: Cognitive research in the college writing classroom* (pp. 19–32). New York: Oxford University Press.

Haas, C., & Flower, L. (1988). Rhetorical reading strategies and the construction of meaning. *College Composition and Communication, 39*(2), 167–83.

Hagood, M. (2002). Critical literacy for whom? *Reading Research and Instruction, 41,* 247–64.

Hairston, M. (1982). The winds of change: Thomas Kuhn and the revolution in the teaching of writing. *College Composition and Communication, 33*(1), 76–88.

Hale, G. A., Taylor, C., Bridgeman, B., Carson, J., Kroll, B., & Kantor, R. (1996). *A study of writing tasks assigned in academic degree programs.* ETS Research Report. No. RR-95–44. TOEFL-RR–54. Educational Testing Service, Princeton, NJ 08541.

Hall, S. T. & Lewis, M. W. (2008). *Education in China: 21st century issues and challenges.* New York: Nova Science.

Haller, C. R. (2010). Toward rhetorical source use: Three student journeys. *WPA: Writing Program Administration, 34*(1): 33–59.

Harkin, P. (2005). The reception of reader-response theory. *College Composition and Communication, 56*(3), 410–25.

Harkin, P. & Sosnoski, J. J. (2003). Whatever happened to reader-response criticism? In M. Helmers (Ed.), *Intertexts: Reading pedagogy in college writing classrooms* (pp. 101–22). Mahwah, NJ: Erlbaum.

Harklau, L., Losey, K., & Siegal, M. (1999). *Generation 1.5 meets college composition: Issues in the teaching of writing to U.S.-educated learners of ESL.* Mahwah, NJ: Erlbaum.

Haswell, R. (1991). *Gaining ground in college writing: Tales of development and interpretation.* Dallas: SMU Press.

Haswell, R. H., Briggs, T. L., Fay, J. A., Gillen, N. K., Harrill, R., Shupala, A. M., et al. (1999). Context and rhetorical reading strategies. *Written Communication, 16*(1), 3–27.

Hautecoeur, J. (2000). Literacy in the age of information: Knowledge, power or domination? *International Review of Education, 46*(5), 357–65.

Hawisher, G. E. (1992). Electronic meetings of the mind: Research, electronic conferences, and composition studies. In G. E. Hawisher & P. LeBlanc, (Eds.), *Re-imagining computers and composition: Teaching and research in the virtual age* (pp. 81–101). Portsmouth: Heinemann.

Hawisher, G., & Selfe, C. (2006). Globalization and agency: Designing and redesigning the literacies of cyberspace. *College English, 68*(6), 619–36.

Hawisher, G., & Selfe, C. (2007). *Gaming lives in the 21st century: Literate connections.* New York: Macmillan.

Hawisher, G. E., Selfe, C. L., Moraski, B. & Pearson, M. (2004). Becoming literate in the information age: Cultural ecologies and the literacies of technology. *College Composition and Communication 55*(4), 642–92.

Head, A.J. & Eisenberg, M.B. (2010). Truth be told: How college students evaluate and use information in the digital age. Retrieved from http://projectinfolit.org/pdfs/PIL_Fall2010_Survey_FullReport1.pdf.

Helmers, M. (Ed.). (2003). *Intertexts: Reading pedagogy in college writing classrooms.* Mahwah, NJ: Erlbaum.

Herber, H. L. (1978). *Teaching reading in the content areas* (2nd ed.). Englewood Cliffs, NJ: Prentice-Hall.

Hill, C. A. (2003). Reading the visual in college writing courses. In M. Helmers (Ed.), *Intertexts: Reading pedagogy in college writing classrooms.* (pp. 123–50). Mahwah, NJ: Erlbaum.

Hillesund, T. (2010). Digital reading spaces: How expert readers handle books, the Web and electronic paper. *First Monday, 15*(4–5). Retrieved from http://firstmonday.org/htbin/cgiwrap/bin/ojs/index.php/fm/article/view/2762/2504.

Himley, M. (2007). Response to Phillip P. Marzluf, "Diversity writing: Natural languages, authentic voices." *College Composition and Communication, 58*(3), 449–69.

Hirvela, A. (2004). *Connecting reading and writing.* Ann Arbor, MI: University of Michigan Press.

Hook, S. (2005). Teaching librarians and writing center professionals in collaboration: Complementary practices. In J. K. Elmborg & S. Hook (Eds.), *Centers for learning: Writing centers and libraries in collaboration* (pp. 21–41). Chicago: Association of College and Research Libraries.

Horning, A. (1978). The connection of writing to reading: A gloss on the gospel of Mina Shaughnessy. *College English, 40*(3), 264–68.

Horning, A. S. (1987). *Teaching writing as a second language.* Carbondale, IL: Southern Illinois University Press.

Horning, A. S. (2007). Reading across the curriculum as the key to student success. *Across the Disciplines, 4*. Retrieved from http://wac.colostate.edu/atd/articles/horning2007.cfm.

Horning, A. (2010). A potential [solution] to the plagiarism problem: Improving reading. *Journal of Teaching Writing, 25,* 143–75.

Horning, A. S. (n.d.). *Reading, writing and digitizing: Understanding literacy in the electronic age.* Book manuscript in preparation.

Horowitz, D. (1986). What professors actually require: Academic tasks for the ESL classroom. *TESOL Quarterly, 20,* 445–62.

Howard, R. M. (1995). Plagiarisms, authorships, and the academic death penalty. *College English, 57*(7), 708–36.

Huffman, D. (2010). Towards modes of reading in composition. *Reader: Essays in reader-oriented theory, criticism, and pedagogy 60,* 162–88.

Huot, B. (2007). Consistently inconsistent: Business and the Spellings Commission report on higher education. *College English 69*(1), 512–25.

International Reading Association. (2006). Retrieved from http://www.reading.org/.

Intersegmental Committee of the Academic Senates of the California Community Colleges, the California State University, and the University of California. (2002). *Academic literacy: A statement of competencies expected of students entering California's public colleges and universities.* Berkeley, CA: University of California.

Irwin, J., & Doyle, M. A. (1992). *Reading/writing connections: Learning from research.* Newark, DE: International Reading Association.

Isbell, D., & Broaddus, D. (1995). Teaching writing and research as inseparable: A faculty-librarian teaching team. *Reference Services Review, 23*(4), 51–62.

Jackson, J. M. (2009). Reading/writing connection. In R. F. Flippo and D. C. Caverly (Eds.), *Handbook of college reading and study strategy research* (2nd ed.) (pp. 145–73). New York: Routledge.

James, K. H., & Gauthier, I. (2009). When writing impairs reading: Letter perception's susceptibility to motor inference. *Journal of Experimental Psychology 138*(3), 416–31.

Jarvis, S. (2002). Short texts, better-fitting curves and new measures of lexical diversity. *Language Testing, 19,* 57–84.

Jarvis, S., Grant, L., Bikowski, D., & Ferris, D. (2003). Exploring multiple profiles of highly rated learner compositions. *Journal of Second Language Writing, 12,* 377–403.

Jiang, X., & Grabe, W. (2007). Graphic organizers in reading instruction: Research findings and issues. *Reading in a Foreign Language 19*(1), 34–55.

Johns, A. (1993). Reading and writing tasks in English for academic purposes classes: Products, processes, and resources. In J. Carson & I. Leki (Eds.), *Reading in the composition classroom* (pp. 274–85). Boston: Heinle & Heinle.

Johns, A. (1997). *Text, role and context: Developing academic literacies.* New York: Cambridge University Press.

Johns, A. (2002). Genre and ESL/EFL composition instruction. In B. Kroll (Ed.), *Exploring the dynamics of second language writing* (pp. 195–217). Cambridge: Cambridge University Press.

Johns, A., & Mayes, P. (1990). An analysis of summary protocols of university ESL students. *Applied Linguistics, 11*, 253–71.

Johns, J. L. (2009). Contextualizing reading courses within political and policy realities: A challenge to teacher educators. In F. Falk-Ross, S. Szabo, M. B. Sampson, & M. M. Foote (Eds.), *Literacy issues during changing times: A call to action* (pp. 63–65). Texas A&M University-Commerce: The College Reading Association.

Johns, J. L., & Lenski, S. D. (1997). *Improving reading: A handbook of strategies* (2nd ed.). Dubuque, IA: Kendall/Hunt.

Johnson, S. (2008, Feb. 7). Dawn of the digital natives. *The Guardian*. Retrieved from http://www.guardian.co.uk/technology/2008/feb/07/internet.literacy.

Jolliffe, D. A. (2003). Who is teaching composition students to read and how are they doing it? *Composition Studies, 21*, 127–42.

Jolliffe, D. A. (2007). Learning to read as continuing education. *College Composition and Communication, 58*, 470–94.

Jolliffe, D. A. (Ed.). (2008). *Reading and writing analytically*. New York: The College Board.

Jolliffe, D. A., & Harl, A. (2008). Texts of our institutional lives: Studying the "reading transition" from high school to college: What are our students reading and why? *College English, 70*(6), 599–617.

Kalantzis, M., Cope, B., & Cloonan, A. (2010). A multiliteracies perspective on the New Literacies. In E. A. Baker (Ed.), *The New Literacies: Multiple perspectives on theory and practice* (pp. 61–87). New York, NY: The Guilford Press.

Kaplan, R. B. (1966). Cultural thought patterns in inter-cultural education. *Language Learning 16*, 1–20.

Kaplan, R. B. (2005). Contrastive rhetoric. In E. Hinkel (Ed.), *Handbook of applied linguistics* (pp. 375–91). Mahwah, NJ: Erlbaum.

Katz, I. R. (2007a). ETS research finds college students fall short in demonstrating ICT literacy. *College & Research Libraries News, 68*(1), 35–37.

Katz, I. R. (2007b). Testing information literacy in digital environments: ETS's iSkills assessment. *Information Technology and Libraries, 26*(3), 3–12.

Keck, C. (2006). The use of paraphrase in summary writing: a comparison of L1 and L2 writers. *Journal of Second Language Writing, 15*, 261–78.

Keene, E. O., & Zimmerman, S. (1997). *Mosaic of thought: Teaching comprehension in a reader's workshop*. Portsmouth, NH: Heinemann.

Kelly, K. (2006, May 14). Scan this book. *New York Times Magazine*, pp. 42–49, 64, 71.

Kennedy, M. L. (1985). The composing processes of college students' writing from sources. *Written Communication, 2*(4), 434–56.

Kenny, C. (2011). *Getting better: Why global development is succeeding—and how we can improve the world even more.* New York: Basic Books.

Kent, T. (1999). *Post-process theory: Beyond the writing-process paradigm.* Carbondale, IL: Southern Illinois University Press.

Kim, S. (2001). Characteristics of EFL readers' summary writing: A study with Korean university students. *Foreign Language Annals, 34,* 569–81.

Kim, C. (2009). *Improvements in L2 writers' paraphrasing skills for academic summary writing.* Paper presented at the Symposium on Second Language Writing. Tempe, AZ: Arizona State University.

Kirk, T. G. (1995). Foreword. In J. Sheridan (Ed.), *Writing-across-the-curriculum and the academic library: A guide for librarians, instructors, and writing program directors* (pp. ix-xi). Westport, CT: Greenwood Press.

Kirsch, I. S., Jungeblut, A., Jenkins, L. & Kolstad, A. (1993). *Adult literacy in America.* Washington, DC: Government Printing Office.

Kirszner, L. G., & Mandell, S. R. (2012). *Patterns for college writing: A rhetorical reader and guide* (12th ed.). Boston, MA: Bedford/St. Martin's.

Kovačević, M. (2005, January). Prikaz knjige (book review): Petera S. Gardnera: New directions: An integrated approach to reading, writing, and critical thinking. [Review of the book *New directions: An integrated approach to reading, writing and critical thinking,* by P.S. Gardner]. *Strani Jezici, 34,* 269–71.

Krashen, S. D. (1983). The din in the head, input, and the language acquisition device. In J.W. Oller, Jr. & P.A. Richard-Amato (Eds.), *Methods that work: A smorgasbord of ideas for language teachers* (pp. 295–301). Cambridge, MA: Newbury House.

Kress, G. (2003). *Literacy in the new media age.* London: Routledge.

Krikelas, J. (1983). Information seeking behavior: patterns and concepts. *Drexel Library Quarterly, 19*(2), 5–20.

Kucer, S. B. (2009). *Dimensions of literacy: A conceptual base for teaching reading and writing in school settings.* New York, NY: Routledge.

Kucer, S. L. (1985). The making of meaning: Reading and writing as parallel processes. *Written Communication, 2*(3), 317–36.

Kuh, G. D., Kinzie, J., Schuh, J. H. & Whitt, E. J. (2005). *Student success in college: Creating conditions that matter.* San Francisco, CA: Wiley/American Association for Higher Education.

Kuhlthau, C. C. (1985). A process approach to library skills instruction. *School Library Media Quarterly, 13*(1), 35–40.

Kuhlthau, C. C. (1991). Inside the search process: Information seeking from the user's perspective. *Journal of the American Society for Information Science (JASIS), 42*(5), 61–371.

Kuhlthau, C.C. (1994). *Teaching the library research process*. Metuchen, NJ: Scarecrow Press.

Kuhlthau, C. C. (2004). *Seeking meaning: A process approach to library and information services* (2nd ed.). Westport, CT: Libraries Unlimited.

Kuhlthau, C. C., Turock, B. J., George, M. W., & Belvin, R. J. (1990). Validating a model of the search process: A comparison of academic, public and school library users. *Library and Information Science Research, 12*(1), 5–32.

Labaree, D. F. (2008). An uneasy relationship: The history of teacher education in the university. In M. Cochran-Smith, S. Feiman-Nemiser, J.D. McIntyre, & K.E. Demers (Eds.), *Handbook of research on teacher education: Enduring questions in changing contexts* (3rd ed.) (pp. 290–306). New York: Routledge.

LaBaugh, R. (1995). Talking the discourse: Composition theory. In J. Sheridan (Ed.), *Writing-across-the-curriculum and the academic library: A guide for librarians, instructors, and writing program directors* (pp. 23–31). Westport, CT: Greenwood Press.

Lamb, A. (2001). *Information and communication literacy model comparison*. Retrieved from http://virtualinquiry.com/inquiry/topic71model.pdf.

Langer, J., & Flihan, S. (2000). Writing and reading relationships: Constructive tasks. In R. Indrisano & J. Squire (Eds.), *Perspectives on writing: Research, theory, and practice* (pp 112139). Newark, DE: International Reading Association.

Larson, R.L. (1982). The "research paper" in the writing course: A non-form of writing. *College English, 44*(8), 811–16.

Laskin, M. & Diaz, J. (2009). Literary research in a bilingual environment: Information literacy as a language-learning tool. In K.A. Johnson & S.R. Harris (Eds.), *Teaching literary research: Challenges in a changing environment*. (pp. 109–28). Chicago: Association of College and Research Libraries.

Leadley, S., & Rosenberg, B. R. (2005). Yours, mine and ours: Collaboration among faculty, library, and writing center. In J. K. Elmborg & S. Hook (Eds.), *Centers for learning: Writing centers and libraries in collaboration*. (pp. 61–77). Chicago: Association of College and Research Libraries.

Learning a living: First results of the Adult Literacy and Life Skills Survey. (2005). Ottawa, Canada and Paris, France: Statistics Canada and the Organisation for Economic Co-operation and Development. Retrieved from http://www.oecd.org/dataoecd/44/7/34867438.pdf.

Leckie, G.J. (1996). Desperately seeking citations: Uncovering faculty assumptions about undergraduate research. *Journal of Academic Librarianship, 22*(3), 201–08.

Lee, S. (2005). Facilitating and inhibiting factors in English as a Foreign Language writing performance: A model testing with Structural Equation Modeling. *Language Learning, 55,* 335–74.

Leki, I. (1992). Building expertise through sequenced writing assignments. *TESOL Journal, 1,* 19–23.

Leki, I. (2007). *Undergraduates in a second language.* Mahwah, NJ: Erlbaum.

Leki, I., & Carson, J. (1994). Students' perceptions of EAP writing instruction and writing needs across the disciplines. *TESOL Quarterly, 28,* 81–101.

Leki, I., & Carson, J. (1997). "Completely different worlds": EAP and the writing experiences of ESL students in university courses. *TESOL Quarterly, 31,* 39–69.

Leu, D. J., Kinzer, C. K., Coiro, J. L., & Cammack, D. W. (2004). Toward a theory of new literacies emerging from the Internet and other information and communication technologies. In R. B. Ruddell & N. J. Unrau (Eds.), *Theoretical models and processes of reading* (5th ed.) (pp. 1570–1613). Newark, DE: International Reading Association.

Leu, D. J., O'Byrne, W. I., Zawilinski, L., McVerry, G., & Everett-Cacopardo, H. (2009.) Comments on Greenhow, Robelia, and Hughes: Expanding the New Literacies conversation. *Educational Researcher, 38*(4), 264–69.

Lewin, T. (2010, July 21). Many states adopt national standards for their schools. *New York Times,* p. A1.

Lewis, C., & Fabos, B. (2005). Instant messaging, literacies, and social identities. *Reading Research Quarterly, 40* (4), 470–501.

Liu, Z. (2005). Reading behavior in the digital environment: changes in reading behavior over the past ten years. *Journal of Documentation, 61*(6), 700–12.

Loban, W. (1963). *The language of elementary school children.* Urbana, IL: National Council of Teachers of English.

Loban, W. (1964). *Language ability: Grades seven, eight, and nine.* Berkeley: University of California. (ERIC Document Reproduction Service No. ED001275)

Losey, K. (2009). Written codeswitching in the classroom: Can research resolve the tensions? *International Journal of Bilingual Education and Bilingualism, 12,* 203–10.

Luke, A. (2000) Critical literacy in Australia: A matter of context and standpoint. *Journal of Adolescent & Adult Literacy, 43*(5), 448–61.

Lunsford, A. A. (2011). *The St. Martin's handbook* (7th ed.). Boston, MA: Bedford/St. Martin's.

Lunsford, A. A., & Ruszkiewicz, J. J. (2010). *Everything's an argument* (5th ed.). Boston, MA: Bedford/St. Martin's.

Lunsford, A. A., Ruszkiewicz, J. J., & Walters, K. (2010). *Everything's an argument with readings* (5th ed.). Boston, MA: Bedford/St. Martin's.

Lutzker, M. (1995). What writing-across-the-curriculum instructors can learn from librarians. In J. Sheridan (Ed.), *Writing-across-the-curriculum and the academic library: A guide for librarians, instructors, and writing program directors.* (pp. 105–12). Westport, CT: Greenwood Press.

Lyotard, J. (1984). *The Post-Modern condition: A report on knowledge.* Minneapolis, MN: University of Minnesota Press.

Mackey, T. P., & Jacobson, T. E. (2010). *Collaborative information literacy assessments: Strategies for evaluating teaching and learning.* New York: Neal-Shuman Publishers, Inc.

Mackey, T. P., & Jacobson, T. E. (2011). Reframing information literacy as a metaliteracy. *College and Research Libraries, 72*(1), 62–78.

Macklin, A.S. (2007). *iSkills and ICT literacy assessment: Building a case for collaboration between school and academic librarians.* Retrieved from http://www.ala.org/ala/mgrps/divs/aasl/aaslpubsandjournals/knowledge-quest/kqwebarchives/v35/355/355macklin.cfm.

Mallozzi, C. A., & Malloy, J. A. (2007). International reports on literacy research: Reading and writing connections. *Reading Research Quarterly, 42*(1), 161–66.

Manning, C., Sisserson, K. Jolliffe, D. A., Buenrostro, P., & Jackson, W. (2008). Program evaluation as professional development: Building capacity for authentic intellectual achievement in Chicago small schools. *Education and Urban Society, 40*, 715–29.

Marzano, R. J. (2004). *Building background knowledge for academic achievement.* Washington, DC: American Society for Curriculum Development.

Mateos, S. M. (2001). *Metacognición y educación.* Buenos Aires, Argentina: Aique.

McCarthey, S. & Raphael, T. (1992). Alternative research perspectives. In J. Irwin & M.A. Doyle (Eds.), *Reading/writing connections: Learning from research* (pp. 2–30). Newark, DE: International Reading Association.

McCormick, K. (2003). Closer than close reading: Historical analysis, cultural analysis, and symptomatic reading in the undergraduate classroom. In M. Helmers (Ed.), *Intertexts: Reading pedagogy in college writing classrooms* (pp. 27–49). Mahwah, NJ: Erlbaum.

McCuen-Metherell, J. R., & Winkler, A. C. (2010). *Readings for writers* (13th ed.). Boston, MA: Wadsworth Cengage Learning.

McGuinness, C. (2007). Exploring strategies for integrated information literacy: From "academic champions" to institution-wide change. *Communications in Information Literacy, 1*(1), 26–38.

McQuade, D., & McQuade, C. (2010). *Seeing and Writing* (4th ed.). Boston, MA: Bedford/St. Martin's.

Medina, J. (2008). *Brain rules: 12 principles for surviving and thriving at work, home and school.* Seattle, WA: Pear Press.

Miller, R. E., & Spellmeyer, K. (2009). *The New Humanities Reader.* Boston, MA: Houghton Mifflin Harcourt Publishing Company.

Miller, S. (1997). Technologies of self-formation. *Journal of Advanced Communication 17,* 497–500.

Miller, T. (2006). What should college English be . . . doing? *College English 69*(2), 150–156.

Millet, M. S., Jeremy, D., & Wilson, D. W. (2009). Information literacy across the curriculum: Expanding horizons. *College & Undergraduate Libraries, 16*(2/3), 180–93.

Morrow, N. (1997). The role of reading in the composition classroom. *JAC: A Journal of Composition Theory, 17*(3), 453–72.

Muller, A., & Murtagh, T. (Eds.). (2002). Literacy—The 877 million left behind. *Education Today, 2,* 4–7. (ERIC Document Reproduction Service No. ED 468232)

Moje, E., Stockdill, D., Kim, K., & Kim, H. (2010). The role of text in disciplinary learning. In M. Kamil, P. D. Pearson, E. Moje, & P. Afflerbach (Eds.), *Handbook of reading research* (Vol. 4, pp. 453–86). New York: Routledge.

Murray, T. S., Kirsch, I. S. & Jenkins, L. B. (1998). *Adult literacy in OECD countries: Technical report on the first International Adult Literacy Survey.* Washington, DC: Government Printing Office. Retrieved from http://nces.ed.gov/pubsearch/pubsinfo.asp?pubid=98053.

Nathan, R. (2005). *My freshman year: What a professor learned by becoming a student.* Ithaca, NY: Cornell University Press.

National Council of Teachers of English. (2006). Commission on Reading. Retrieved from http://www.ncte.org/about/gov/commissions/106919.htm.

National Council of Teachers of English. (2007). 21st century literacies: A policy research brief. Retrieved from http://www.ncte.org/library/NCTEFiles/Resources/Positions/Chron1107ResearchBrief.pdf.

National Council of Teachers of English. (2009). *Standards for the assessment of reading and writing: Introduction.* Retrieved from http://www.ncte.org/standards/assessmentstandards/introduction.

National Council of Teachers of English. (2011). Reading and writing across the curriculum. *Council Chronicle 20*(3), 15–18.

Nelson, N. (1998). Reading and writing contextualized. In N. Nelson & R. Calfee (Eds.), *The reading-writing connection: Ninety-seventh yearbook of the National Society for the Study of Education* (Part II) (pp. 266–85). Chicago: University of Chicago Press.

Nelson, N., & Calfee, R. (1998). The reading-writing connection viewed historically. In N. Nelson & R. Calfee (Eds.), *The reading-writing connec-*

tion: Ninety-seventh yearbook of the National Society for the Study of Education (pp. 1–52). Chicago: University of Chicago Press.

New London Group. (1996). A pedagogy of multiliteracies: Designing social futures. *Harvard Educational Review, 66*(1), 60–93.

Nicholas, D., Huntington, P., Jamali, H. R., Rowlands, I., Dobrowolski, T., & Tenopir, C. (2008). Viewing and reading behavior in a virtual environment: The full-text download and what can be read into it. *Aslib Proceedings: New Information Perspectives, 60*(3), 185–98.

Nilson, L. B. (2010). *Teaching at its best: A research-based resource for college teachers* (3rd ed.). San Francisco: Jossey-Bass/Wiley.

Norgaard, R. (2003). Writing information literacy: Contributions to a concept. *References & User Services Quarterly, 43*(2), 124–30.

Norgaard, R. (2004). Writing information literacy in the classroom: Pedagogical enactments and implications. *References & User Services Quarterly, 43*(3), 220–26.

O'Brien, H. L., & Symons, S. (2007). The information behaviors and preferences of undergraduate students. *Research Strategies, 20*(4), 409–23.

Odell, L. & Katz, S. M. (2004). *Writing in a visual age*. Boston: Bedford/St. Martin's.

Olsen, P. R. (2011, December 18). Journey of a bookworm. *New York Times*, p. 9.

Organisation for Economic Co-operation and Development. (2010). *PISA 2009 Results: Executive Summary*. Retrieved from http://www.oecd.org/pisa/pisaproducts/46619703.pdf.

Paltridge, B., & Starfield, S. (2007). *Thesis and dissertation writing in a second language*. Ann Arbor, MI: University of Michigan Press.

Parker, W. R. (1967). Where do English departments come from? *ADE Bulletin 11*, 8–18.

Parodi, G. (2006). Reading-writing connections: Discourse-oriented research. *Reading and Writing, 20*(3), 225–50. doi: 10.1007/s11145–006–9029–7

Pearson, P. D. (2007). An endangered species act for literacy education. *Journal of Literacy Research, 39*(20), 145–62.

Pecorari, D. (2003). Good and original: Plagiarism and patchwriting in academic second-language writing. *Journal of Second Language Writing, 12*, 317–45.

Pennycook, A. (1996). Borrowing others' words: Text, ownership, memory, and plagiarism. *TESOL Quarterly, 30*, 210–30.

Penrose, A. M., & Geisler, C. (1994). Reading and writing without authority. *College Composition and Communication, 45*(4), 505–20.

Perfetti, C. (2010). Decoding, vocabulary, and comprehension: The golden triangle of reading skill. In M. McKeown & L. Kucan (Eds.), *Bringing reading research to life* (pp. 291–303). New York: Guilford Press.

Petrosky, A. (1982). From story to essay: Reading and writing. *College Composition and Communication, 33*(1), 19–35.

Pew Charitable Trusts. (2006). *The literacy of America's college students.* Retrieved from http://www.air.org/files/The20Literacy20of20Americas-20College20Students_final20report.pdf.

Pinker, S. (1994). *The language instinct.* New York: Harper Collins.

Plakans, L. (2008). Comparing composing processes in writing-only and reading-to-write test tasks. *Assessing Writing, 13,* 111–29.

Plakans, L. (2009a). The role of reading strategies in integrated L2 writing tasks. *Journal of English for Academic Purposes, 8,* 252–66.

Plakans, L. (2009b). Discourse synthesis in integrated second language writing assessment. *Language Testing, 26,* 561–87.

Prabha, C., Connaway, L. S., Olszewski, L., & Jenkins, L. R. (2007). What is enough? Satisficing information needs. *Journal of Documentation, 63*(1), 74–89.

Project SAILS (Standardized Assessment of Information Literacy Skills), Kent State University. (2010). Retrieved from https://www.projectsails.org.

Prose, F. (2006). *Reading like a writer.* New York: Harper Collins.

Pugh, S. L., Pawan, F., & Antommarchi, C. (2000). Academic literacy and the new college learner. In R. F. Flippo and D. C. Caverly (Eds.), *Handbook of college reading and study strategy research* (pp. 25–42). New York: Routledge.

Qin, J. (2009). *The analysis of Toulmin elements and use of sources in Chinese university EFL argumentative writing.* (Doctoral dissertation). Retrieved from ProQuest Dissertation and Thesis database. (AAT 3370640)

Ramage, J. D., Bean, J. C., & Johnson, J. (2007). *Writing arguments: A rhetoric with readings* (7th ed.). New York, NY: Pearson Longman.

Ramage, J. D., Bean, J. C., & Johnson, J. (2009). *The Allyn & Bacon guide to writing* (5th ed.). New York, NY: Pearson/Longman.

Ramey, J. (2004). The visual verbal rhetoric of a web site: MarineLINK as imagetext delivery system. In B. Huot , B. Stroble, & C. Bazerman (Eds.), *Multiple literacies in the 21st century* (pp. 209–26). Cresskill, NJ: Hampton Press.

Rand, L. (2003). Reading as a site of spiritual struggle. In M. Helmers (Ed.), *Intertexts: Reading pedagogy in college writing classrooms* (pp. 51–68). Mahwah, NJ: Erlbaum.

Raphael, T. E., Kirschner, B. W., & Englert, C. S. (1988). Expository writing programs: Making connections between reading and writing. *Reading Teacher, 41*(8), 790–95.

Rasinski, T. (2009). The lost art of teaching reading. In F. Falk-Ross, S. Szabo, M. B. Sampson, & M. M. Foote (Eds.) *Literacy issues during changing times: A call to action* (pp. 66–73). Texas A&M University-Commerce: The College Reading Association.

Raspa, R., & Ward, D. (2000). *The collaborative imperative: Librarians and faculty working together in the information universe.* Chicago: American Library Association, Association of College & Research Libraries.

Ravitch, D. (2010). *The death and life of the great American school system: How testing and choice are undermining education.* New York: Basic Books.

Reid, R. F. (1990). The Boylston professorship of rhetoric and oratory, 1806–1904: A case study of changing concepts of rhetoric and pedagogy. In E. P. J. Corbett (Ed.), *Essays on the rhetoric of the Western World* (pp. 261–82). Dubuque, IA: Kendall/Hunt.

Rideout, V. J., Foehr, U. G., & Roberts, D. F. (2010, January). *Generation M2: Media in the lives of 8- to 18-year-olds.* A Kaiser Family Foundation Study. Retrieved from http://www.kff.org/entmedia/8010.cfm.

Risemberg, R. (1996). Reading to write: Self-regulated learning strategies when writing essays from sources. *Reading Research and Instruction, 35*(4), 365–83.

Rockman, I. F., & Associates. (2004). *Integrating information literacy into the higher education curriculum: Practical models for transformation.* San Francisco: Jossey-Bass.

Roen, D., Glau, G. R., & Maid, B. M. (2009). *The McGraw-Hill guide: Writing for college, writing for life.* New York, NY: McGraw-Hill Higher Education.

Ronald, K. (1986). The self and other in the process of composing: Implications for integrating the acts of reading and writing. In B. Peteren (Ed.), *Convergences: Transactions in reading and writing* (pp. 231–46). Urbana, IL: National Council of Teachers of English.

Rosenblatt, L. (1978). *The world, the text, and the poem: The transactional theory of the literary work.* Carbondale, IL: Southern Illinois University Press.

Rosenfeld, M., Leung, S., & Oltman, P. (2001). *The reading, writing, speaking, and listening tasks important for academic success at the undergraduate and graduate levels.* [TOEFL Monograph Series MS-21.] Princeton, NJ: Educational Testing Service.

Rosenwasser, D., & Stephen, J. (2008). *Writing analytically with readings.* Boston, MA: Thomson Wadsworth.

Rosenwasser, D., & Stephen, J. (2009). *Writing analytically* (5th). Boston, MA: Thomson Wadsworth.

Rubin, D. (1984). Social cognition and written communication. *Written Communication, 1*(2), 211–46.

Russell, D. (2002). *Writing in the academic disciplines: A curricular history* (2nd ed.). Carbondale: Southern Illinois University Press.

Ruszkiewicz, J. E., Anderson, D., & Christy, F. (2009). *Beyond words: Reading and writing in a visual age* (2nd ed.). New York: Pearson Longman.

Ruszkiewicz, J. J., & Dolmage, J. (2010). *How to write anything: A guide and reference with readings*. Boston, MA: Bedford/St. Martin's.

Salvatori, M. (2003). Reading matters for writing. In Helmers, M. (Ed.) *Intertexts: Reading pedagogy in college writing classrooms* (pp. 195–218). Mahwah, NJ: Erlbaum.

Schlib, J. (2008). From the editor. *College English, 70*(6), 549–50.

Scholes, R. (1998). *The rise and fall of English: Reconstructing English as a discipline*. New Haven, CT: Yale University Press.

Scollon, R. (1997). Contrastive rhetoric, contrastive poetics, or perhaps something else? *TESOL Quarterly, 31*, 352–58.

Selfe, C., & Hilligoss, S. (1994). *Literacy and computers: The complications of teaching and learning with technology*. New York: Modern Language Association.

Shanahan, C. (2009). Disciplinary comprehension. In S. Israel & G. Duffy (Eds.), *Handbook of research on reading comprehension* (pp. 240–60). New York: Routledge.

Shanahan, T. (1984). Nature of the reading and writing relation: An exploratory multivariate analysis. *Journal of Educational Psychology, 76*, 466–77.

Shanahan, T., & Lomax, R. (1986). An analysis and comparison of theoretical models of the reading-writing relationship. *Journal of Educational Psychology, 78*, 116–23.

Shanahan, T., & Lomax, R. (1988). A developmental comparison of three theoretical models of the reading-writing relationship. *Research in the Teaching of English, 22*(2), 196–212.

Shanahan, T., & Shanahan, C. (2008). Teaching disciplinary literacy to adults. *Harvard Educational Review, 78*, 39–59.

Shaughnessy, M. (1977). *Errors and expectations*. New York: Oxford University Press.

Sheridan, J. (1995). An overview and some observations. In J. Sheridan (Ed.), *Writing-across-the-curriculum and the academic library: A guide for librarians, instructors, and writing program directors* (pp. 3–22). Westport, CT, Greenwood Press.

Sheridan, J. (Ed.). (1995). *Writing-across-the-curriculum and the academic library: A guide for librarians, instructors, and writing program directors*. Westport, CT: Greenwood Press.

Shi, L. (2004). Textual borrowing in second-language writing. *Written Communication, 21*, 171–200.

Shi, L. (2006). Cultural backgrounds and textual appropriation. *Language Awareness, 15*, 264–82.

Silva, T. (1993). Toward an understanding of the distinct nature of L2 writing: The ESL research and its implications. *TESOL Quarterly, 27*, 657–77.

Silva, T., Leki, I., & Carson, J. (1997). Broadening the perspective of mainstream composition studies: Some thoughts from the disciplinary margins. *Written Communication, 14*, 398–428.

Sisserson, K., Manning, C., Knepler, A., & Jolliffe, D. A. (2002). Authentic intellectual achievement in writing. *English Journal, 91*(6), 63–69.

Smagorinsky, P. (1992). How reading model essays affects writers. In J. W. Irwin & M. Doyle (Eds.), *Reading/writing connections: Learning from research* (pp. 160–76). Newark, DE: International Reading Association.

Smith, F. (2004). *Understanding reading: A psycholinguistic analysis of reading and learning to read* (6th ed.). Hillsdale, NJ: Erlbaum.

Sole, I. (2001). *Estrategias de Lectura (Materials para la Innovación Educativa)*[Lecture Strategies (Materials for education innovation)]. Barcelona: GRAO.

Spack, R. (1997). The acquisition of academic literacy in a second language: A longitudinal case study. *Written Communication, 14*, 3–62.

Spack, R. (2004). The acquisition of academic literacy in a second language: A longitudinal case study. In V. Zamel & R. Spack (Eds.), *Crossing the curriculum: Multilingual learners in college classrooms* (pp. 19–46). Mahwah, NJ: Lawrence Erlbaum.

Spencer, H. (1955). A behavioral model of rational choice. *Quarterly Journal of Economics, 69*(1), 99–118.

Spivey, N. N. (1991). *Transforming texts: Constructive processes in reading and writing.* Technical Report No. 47.

Spivey, N. N. (1997). *The constructivist metaphor: Reading, writing, and the making of meaning.* New York: Academic Press.

Spivey, N. N., & King, J. (1989). Readers as writers composing from sources. *Reading Research Quarterly, 24*(1), 7–26.

Squire, R. J. (1984). Composing and comprehending: Two sides of the same basic processes. In J. M. Jensen (Ed.), *Composing and comprehending* (pp. 23–31). Urbana, IL: National Council of Teachers of English.

Stahl, S., & Nagy, W. (2006). *Teaching word meanings.* Mahwah, NJ: L. Erlbaum.

Statistics Canada & the Organization for Economic Co-operation and Development. (2005). *Learning a living: First results of the Adult Literacy and Life Skills Survey.* Ottawa, Canada: OECD Publishing and Statistics Canada.

Sternglass, M. (1997). *Time to know them: A longitudinal study of writing and learning at the college level.* Mahwah, New Jersey: Erlbaum.

Stevenson, N. (2003). *Cultural citizenship.* Berkshire, England: Open University.

Stotsky, S. (1983). Research on reading/writing relationships: A synthesis and suggested directions. *Language Arts, 60*, 627–42.

Stotsky, S. (2010). Literary study in grades 9, 10, and 11: A national survey. *Forum: A Publication of the Association of Literary Scholars, Critics, and Writers, 4*, 1–75.

Street, B. V. (Ed.). (2001). *Literacy and development: Ethnographic perspectives*. London: Routledge.

Tan, L. H. (2005). Reading depends on writing, in Chinese. *PNAS, 102*(24), 8781–8785. doi:10.1073/pnas.0503523102

Tardy, C. (2005). "It's like a story": Rhetorical knowledge development in advanced academic literacy. *Journal of English for Academic Purposes, 4*, 325–38.

Tardy, C. (2009). *Building genre knowledge*. West Lafayette, Indiana: Parlor Press.

Thaiss, C. & Zawacki, T. (2006). *Engaged writers and dynamic disciplines: Research on the academic writing life*. Portsmouth, NH: Boynton/Cook Heinemann.

Tierney, R.J. (1992). Ongoing research and new directions. In J.W. Irwin & M.A. Doyle (Eds.), *Reading/writing connections: Learning from research* (pp. 246–59). Newark, DE: International Reading Association.

Tierney, R., & Leys, M. (1986). What is the value of connecting reading and writing? In B. Petersen (Ed.), *Convergences: Transactions in reading and writing* (pp. 15–29). Urbana, IL: NCTE.

Tierney, R. J., & and Pearson, P. D. (1983). Toward a composing model of reading. *Language Arts, 60*, 568–580.

Tierney, R. J. & Shanahan, J. (1991). Research on the reading-writing relationship: Interactions, transactions and outcomes. In R. Barr, M. Kamil, P. Mosenthal, & P. D. Pearson (Eds.), *Handbook of reading research* (Vol. 2, pp. 609–40). Hillsdale, NJ: Erlbaum.

Tierney, R J., Soter, A., O'Flahavan, J. O. & McGinley, W. (1984). The effects of reading and writing upon thinking critically. *Reading Research Quarterly, 24*, 134–73.

Townsend, M. (2008). Writing across the curriculum. In I. Ward & W. J. Carpenter (Eds.), *The Longman sourcebook for writing program administrators* (pp. 264–74). New York: Pearson Longman.

Truss, L. (2003). *Eats, shoots & leaves: The zero tolerance approach to punctuation*. New York: Gotham/Penguin Books.

Twinton, A. (2007). *Common reading programs in higher education*. Retrieved from http://gustavus.edu/library/Pubs/Lindell20007.html.

U.S. Department of Education. (2005). National Center for Education Statistics. *Integrated Postsecondary Education Data System*. Retrieved from http://nces.ed.gov/pubs2006/2006155.pdf.

U.S. Department of Education. (2006). *National assessment of adult literacy: A first look at the literacy of America's adults in the 21st century*. National Center for Education Statistics. Retrieved from http://nces.ed.gov/NAAL/PDF/2006470_1.PDF.

U.S. Department of Education. (2006). *A test of leadership: Charting the future of U.S. higher education.* Retrieved from http://www.ed.gov/about/bdscomm/list/hiedfuture/reports/final-report.pdf.

U.S. National Endowment for the Arts. (2004). *Reading at risk: A survey of literary reading in America.* Retrieved from http://www.nea.gov/pub/ReadingAtRisk.pdf.

U.S. National Endowment for the Arts. (2007). *To read or not to read: A question of national consequence.* Washington, DC: National Endowment for the Arts.

U.S. National Endowment for the Arts. (2009). *Reading on the rise: A new chapter in American literacy.* Washington, DC: National Endowment for the Arts.

U.S. National Endowment for the Arts. (2011). *The Big Read.* Retrieved from http://www.neabigread.org/.

Valentine, K. (2006). Plagiarism as literacy practice: Recognizing and rethinking ethical binaries. *College Composition and Communication, 58,* 89–109.

Valeri-Gold, M., & Deming, M. (2000). Reading, writing, and the college developmental student. In R. F. Flippo and D. C. Caverly (Eds.), *Handbook of college reading and study strategy research* (pp. 149–74). Mahwah, NJ: Erlbaum.

Vaughan, M. W., & Dillon, A. (2006). Why structure and genre matter for users of digital information: a longitudinal experiment with readers of a web-based newspaper. *International Journal of Human-Computer Studies, 64*(6), 502–526.

Vincent, D. (2000). *The rise of mass literacy: Reading and writing in modern Europe.* London: Polity Press.

Vygotsky, L. S. (1978). *Mind in society: The development of higher psychological processes.* (M. Cole, V. John-Steiner, S. Scribner & E. Souberman Eds. & Trans.). Cambridge, MA: Harvard University Press. (Original work published 1934).

Vygotsky, L. S. (1986). *Thought and language.* (A. Kozalin, Trans.) Cambridge, MA: The MIT Press. (Original work published 1962).

Wagner, D. A., Venezky, R. L., & Street, B. V. (Eds.). (1999). *Literacy: An international handbook.* Boulder, CO: Westview Press.

Wallace, D. (2006). Transcending normativity: Difference issues in college English. *College English, 68*(5), 502–30.

Wardle, E., & Downs, D. (2011). *Writing about Writing: A College Reader.* Boston, MA: Bedford/St. Martin's.

Way, D. (2010). The impact of Web-scale discovery on the use of a library collection. *Serials Review, 36*(4), 214–20.

Weiler, A. (2005). Information-seeking behavior in Generation Y students: motivation, critical thinking, and learning theory. *Journal of Academic Librarianship, 31*(1), 46–53.

Wengelin, A., Leitjten, M. & Van Wase, L. (2009). Studying reading during writing: New perspectives in research. *Reading and Writing, 23*(7), 735–742. doi:10.1007/s11145–009–9187–5

Wheeler, G. (2009). Plagiarism in the Japanese university: Truly a cultural matter? *Journal of Second Language Writing, 18*, 17–29.

Whitmire, E. (2002). Disciplinary differences and undergraduates' information-seeking behavior. *Journal of the American Society for Information Science and Technology, 53*(8), 631–38.

Wittrock, M. C. (1984). Writing and the teaching of reading. In Jensen, J.M. (Ed.), *Composing and comprehending* (pp. 77–83). Urbana, IL: National Council of Teachers of English.

Woodin, T. (2008). "A beginner reader is not a beginner thinker": Student publishing in Britain since the 1970s. *Paedogogica Historica: International Journal of the History of Education, 44*(1–2), 219–32.

Wysocki, A. F. (2004). The multiple media of texts: How onscreen and paper texts incorporate words, images, and other media. In C. Bazerman & P. A. Prior (Eds.), *What writing does and how it does it: An introduction to analysis of text and textual practices* (pp. 123–63). Mahwah, NJ: Lawrence Erlbaum and Associates.

Yancey, K. B. (2004a). Made not only in words: Composition in a new key. *College Composition and Communication, 56*(2), 297–28.

Yancey, K. B. (2004b). *Teaching literature as a reflective practice*. Ubrana, IL: National Council of Teachers of English.

Yang, L., & Shi, B. (2003). Exploring six MBA students' summary writing by introspection. *Journal of English for Academic Purposes, 2*, 165–92.

Yood, J. (2003). Writing the discipline: A generic history of English studies. *College English, 65*(5), 526–40.

Yu, G. (2008). Reading to summarize in English and Chinese: A tale of two languages? *Language Testing, 25*, 521–51.

Zemliansky, P. & Bishop, W. (2004). *Research writing revisited*. Portsmouth, NH: Heinemann.

Zhu, W. (2004). Faculty views on the importance of writing, the nature of academic writing, and teaching and responding to writing in the disciplines. *Journal of Second Language Writing, 13*, 29–48.

Zhu, W. (2005). Source articles as scaffolds in reading to write. *Journal of Asian Pacific Communication, 15*, 129–52.

Contributors

Jennifer Coon is a special lecturer in the Department of Writing and Rhetoric at Oakland University. She makes her publishing debut with her contribution to this volume.

Erik D. Drake is Coordinator of Cooperative Acquisitions at Regional Educational Media Center (REMC) Association of Michigan. His articles appear in *Media Spectrum* and *MACUL Journal*.

Jimmy Fleming is English Marketing Specialist at Bedford/St. Martin's Press. His chapter in this volume marks his first publishing contribution as an author.

William Grabe is Regents' Professor of English at Northern Arizona University. His own monographs include *Teaching and Researching Reading* [with Fredericka Stoller] (2002, 2011) and *Reading in a Second Language: Moving from Theory to Practice* (2008). He has previously contributed chapters to *Second Language Reading: Research and Instruction* (2009), *Teaching Reading* (2009), *Handbook of Second and Foreign Language Teaching* (2009), and the *Handbook of Applied Linguistics* (2009). His articles appear in *Modern Language Journal, Reading in a Foreign Language,* and *JACET Journal*.

Cynthia R. Haller is an associate professor in the Department of English, York College, City University of New York. She has contributed chapters previously to the books *Writing Spaces: Readings on Writing, Vol. 2* (2011) and *Essays in the Study of Scientific Discourse: Methods, Practice, and Pedagogy* (1998). Her articles appear in *Written Communication, WPA: Writing Program Administration, Technical Communication Quarterly,* and *Journal of Engineering Education*.

Allison L. Harl is an assistant professor of English at Ferrum College. She has contributed book chapters to *Teaching Developmental Writing:*

Background Readings (4th ed., 2012) and *Real Texts: Reading and Writing Across the Disciplines* (2nd ed., 2011). She has also published articles in the journals *College English, Mythlore: A Journal of J.R.R. Tolkien, C.S. Lewis, Charles Williams, and Mythopoeic Literature*, and *Discoveries in Renaissance Culture*.

David A. Joliffe is Professor of English and Curriculum and Instruction at the University of Arkansas, where he holds the Brown Chair in English Literacy. Most recently, he is the co-author, with Hephzibah Roskelly, of *Writing America: Language and Composition in Context*. His articles have appeared in *College English, College Composition and Communication*, and *Composition Studies*.

Kathleen Skomski is a special lecturer in the Department of Writing and Rhetoric at Oakland University. This is her first research publication.

Cui Zhang is an assistant professor in the Department of English and Theater at Eastern Kentucky University. Her chapter in this volume, co-authored with William Grabe, is her first publication.

About the Editors

Alice S. Horning is Professor of Writing & Rhetoric and Linguistics at Oakland University. Her previous books are *Reading, Writing and Digitizing: Understanding Literacy in the Electronic Age* (2012); *Untenured Faculty as Writing Program Administrators* (co-edited with Debra F. Dew) (2008); *Revision: History, Theory and Practice* (2006), and *Revision Revisited* (2004). Her articles appear in such publications as *Reading Matrix, ATD: Across the Disciplines*, and *Community Literacy Journal*.

Elizabeth W. Kraemer is Associate Professor and Coordinator of Instruction at Oakland University's Kresge Library. She has contributed chapters to the books *Computer-Mediated Communication: Issues and Approaches in Education* (2012) and *Outreach Services in Academic and Special Libraries* (2004). Her articles have appeared in *The Journal of Academic Librarianship, College & Research Libraries, The Reference Librarian, College and Undergraduate Libraries, Information Technology and Libraries*, and *College and Research Libraries News*.

Index

CPSIA information can be obtained at www.ICGtesting.com
Printed in the USA
LVOW08s2113130314

377325LV00002B/15/P